COLONIAL ULSTER

The Settlement of East Ulster
1600–1641

The monument to Sir Arthur Chichester in St Nicholas' Church, Carrickfergus
(Lawrence Collection, L_CAB_05945).
Image courtesy of the National Library of Ireland

COLONIAL ULSTER

The Settlement of East Ulster 1600–1641

1600–1641

Raymond Gillespie

ULSTER HISTORICAL FOUNDATION

For my family

'Sedula curavi, humanas actiones non ridere,
non lugere, neque destestare sed intelligere.'

—Spinoza

First published in 1985 by Cork University Press

This edition published 2021
by Ulster Historical Foundation
www.ancestryireland.com
www.booksireland.org.uk

© Raymond Gillespie, Cork University Press
and The Irish Committee of Historical Sciences

Ulster Historical Foundation would like to acknowledge Cork University Press and The Irish Committee of Historical Sciences for permission to republish the original work in facsimile.

ISBN 2021 edition: 978-1-909556-93-5
ISBN 1985 edition: 978-0-902561-31-1

Layout by J.P. Morrison
Printed by Gutenberg Press Ltd

CONTENTS

Contents

LIST OF MAPS

PATRONS, DONORS AND SUBSCRIBERS

Mary Jane Kuffner Hirt, PhD

PATRONS
Fionntán Adams
Sir Denis Desmond
John G. Gordon
Neil Mackie
Eleanor Macpherson
David O'Dwyer
Sir Andrew Parmley, Governor, The Honourable The Irish Society
Mary Schranz
Chris Traynor

DONORS
W.B. Bowden
Ann Buchanan
Gregory Dunstan
Terry Eakin
Terence Gordon
Colin D. Gowdy
Francis Higgins
Andrew Kane
Jeanette Lindsay *in memory of* James Ian Lindsay
Anne Odling-Smee CBE
W.N.B. Richardson
Jeremy Simons

SUBSCRIBERS

Genevieve Ahearne
Frances Bach
The Worshipful Company of Barbers
Geoff Barker
Margaret Barnes
D.I. Bartlett
Richard Alexander Barton
Colin Bendall
Mary Bergin
Caragh Briggs

David Brown
Rodney Brown
Sharon Brown
Frances van Bruggen
David Byers
Gerard Byrne
Marc Caball
Dr G. Johnston Calvert
Joyce Campbell
James Cannon

vii

Alan Clarke
Patrick Clarke
Diana Claussen
Mark Cornwall
Nicola Cousen
Gerard Crawford
Desmond Crilly
Megan Crook
Fr Colin Crossey
Tony Crowe
Professor James Stevens Curl
Chris Dart
Edward Davis
Ronald Dayman
Margaret Doherty
Mr Robert Epperson
Robert Ewing
Geraldine Faries
David R.H. and Pamela J. Fayle
Sheila Fields
Rosaleen Fisher
Ian Forsythe
Christa Freer
Stephen Glass
James Gregory
David Guthrie
Brett Hannam
Geoffrey Harbinson
Brooke Harlowe
Paul Harris
Tracey Hughes
William Hurford
Ann Igoe
John Johnston
Colin Jones
Donna Jones
Alan Keys
Kenneth King
Sherry King
Richard Lansdall-Welfare
Helen Livingston
Gordon Lucy
Dr Alec Lyons
Howard Mathieson
Richard Matthews
Arthur McCaughan
Richard Melville McClure
Robert David McClure
Denis McCoy
Ken McCracken

Moira McCracken
Pamela McCrory
Steve McDermott
Matthew McIlvenna
Margaret McInall
Michael McMillen
Richard McMurray
Douglas McTavish
William Mitchell
Edward Montgomery MBE, DL
Adrian Mooney
Brendan Mooney
David Moore
James Moore
P.L.T. Morrow
Robert Morrow
Gareth Neighbour
John T. Nichols
Irving Nixon
Patrick Norrington
North of Ireland Family History Society
Jack O'Hare
David R. Orr
Gail Orr
Cliff Radcliffe
Bayard Rea
Austin Reid
Don Revels
Mark Richardson
Elizabeth Richmond
Mervyn Rolls
William J. Roulston
Brendan Scott
Stephen Sheppard
James Simon
Edward Stewart
Christel Sudway
Ruth Sullivan
Brian Symonds
Edwin Tomlinson
Brian S. Turner
Dr Brendan Twomey
Mary Margaret Van Damme
Janet Wahlberg
Gerard White
Janice Wilson
John A. Wilson
Susan Wilson
Gerard Woods
Daniel Yarrow

INTRODUCTION TO 2021 REPRINT

ALL HISTORICAL WRITING is a product of its own time. This book had its origin in a PhD thesis written between 1978 and 1982 in Trinity College, Dublin. It is difficult to imagine that historiographical landscape. Describing the structures of past societies, especially the economic structures, was the cutting edge of the historical discipline. Culture as an analytical tool was still some years away though the English translation of Emmanuel Le Roy Ladurie's *Montaillou* created a brief frisson of excitement among undergraduates in Belfast when it appeared in 1978 and Carlo Ginzburg's *The cheese and the worms* had a similar impact when it followed two years later. *Colonial Ulster* was thus conceived as a study in social and economic history. Its method was to reduce the scale of the study to capture the realities of everyday social and economic life and as such was located within the school of local history as developed by H.P.R. Finberg, W.G. Hoskins and others in the Department of English Local History in the University of Leicester and ably promoted by Bill Crawford of the Public Record Office of Northern Ireland. It was not intended to be a 'case study' that would capture general features of early seventeenth-century Ireland but rather was to be taken on its own terms as representative of nothing but itself.

Seventeenth-century Ireland could hardly have been regarded as a historiographical 'hot spot' in 1978. In the previous decade, according to the bibliographic database Irish History Online, the decade 1968 to 1978 produced only one new book on plantation (and a reprint of an older work by George Hill) and thirteen articles. The only sure local study of the plantation process remained T.W. Moody's *The Londonderry plantation*, a product of forty years earlier in a different historiographical world. The understanding of the sixteenth century was in the process of reconstruction by Nicholas Canny, Brendan Bradshaw, Karl Bottigheimer and others, but it seemed that the final word on the early seventeenth century had been pronounced by Aidan Clarke in his magisterial chapters in the third volume of the *New History of Ireland,* edited by T.W. Moody, F.X. Martin and F.J. Byrne, that had appeared from Oxford University Press in 1976. Of particular interest here was the inclusion of a chapter on the early seventeenth-century Irish economy, an area that had last attracted the historian's pen in 1919 when George O'Brien published a monograph on the subject. In short it seemed that the history of plantation and colonisation in Ulster had been 'done' and it seemed a simple story of conquest and expropriation.

There were, however, hints that this was not the whole story. What drew me to the subject as an undergraduate was Michael Perceval-Maxwell's *Scottish migration to Ulster in the reign of James I*, published in 1973 as part of the Ulster-Scots Historical Foundation (as it was then) monograph series. This adopted a rather different approach from the 'top down' view of most of those who had written about the plantation. Rather it tried to reconstruct the world of the Scottish settler in Ulster, to define his hopes and fears, shaped by his motives for leaving Scotland, and to assess the extent to which his goals (rather than those of the government) were met. This shifted my perspective. As I later discovered, Bob Hunter in the University of Ulster was engaged on a similar exercise for the English settlers but the results of his patient combing of the archives remained mostly unpublished until after his death in 2007. His work has now seen the light of day thanks to the publishing endeavours of the Ulster Historical Foundation.

My choice of Antrim and Down as the place to explore this creation of a new society was an obvious one. The region was not part of the plantation scheme and hence developed its own personality. Whereas Ulster west of the Bann became a world of small, regular estates, the eastern part of the province was characterised by the massive estates of James Hamilton, Hugh Montgomery, Arthur Chichester and Randall MacDonnell. West of the Bann, landlord leasing policies were circumscribed by the 'Orders and conditions' of the plantation, while in Antrim and Down estates were shaped by negotiations between landlord and tenant and expectations were rather different there. In short, it was colonial world as opposed to a plantation one – hence the title of the book which expressed social relationships rather than political ones. It captured the Irish dilemma of a set of local colonial social and economic arrangements embedded in the constitution of a kingdom. There were obvious sacrifices to be made by studying Antrim and Down. The government plantation surveys of 1611, 1613, 1619 and 1622, which formed the spine of much of Bob Hunter's work, did not exist for those counties, but in compensation there were fine sets of estate papers (most particularly from the earl of Antrim's estate) that had no equivalents for the formally planted area. Other sets of estate papers from east Ulster had made their way back to Scotland (such as those of Edmonston of Dunreath and Agnew of Lochnaw) and these opened up the backgrounds and some of the dynamics of the Scottish settlement. The English settlers, by contrast, were more poorly documented, but the correspondence of George Rawdon at Lisburn survived in the hands of Lord Conway. Since he had been one of the secretaries of state in England the correspondence was preserved among the State Papers in The National Archives at Kew. This is still a much underused collection of correspondence, surviving as it does into the 1680s and providing a unique perspective on an east Ulster estate.

These circumstances serve to explain some of the shortcomings of the study, ably pointed out by reviewers. There is, for instance, nothing on the church or religion as a separate subject. It was not the case that the book rejected religion as important because of the contemporary circumstances then prevailing in Northern Ireland, but rather because the work was conceived as an analysis of the social and economic factors that shaped a colonial society rather than an institutional study of religion or the structures of belief. In this respect it may be that the models of English local history unduly influenced my approach here. I hope that I have compensated for it in more recent works. Secondly, there is little on the origins or progress of the 1641 rising. Again I would plead that this is a separate subject and the rich evidence for other parts of Ulster on this subject in the depositions taken after the outbreak of the rising are almost non-existent for east Ulster. Again I have turned to this subject in other publications. No doubt there are other sins of omission (as well as commission) but these can only provide opportunities for others.

In the course of writing the PhD thesis and the subsequent book it became clear that I was not a lone scholar. A remarkable generation of early modern Irish historians were also at work and some of that has manifested itself in later work that deals with east Ulster. Philip Robinson, a geographer, provided a rather different perspective on the plantation from mine by taking a model that he had developed in his PhD thesis on Tyrone and developing it to cover the whole of Ulster. *The Plantation of Ulster* (Dublin, 1984) provided a spatial perspective on the settlement, mapping almost everything that moved. A similar perspective has been provided for the east Ulster towns of the seventeenth century by the Irish Historic Towns Atlas project that has produced fascicles for Downpatrick, Carrickfergus and Belfast in a format that facilitates comparison between these different settlement types.

Impatient to see what this might produce, I have tried my hand at it in 'Colonial towns: 1500–1700: Carrickfergus, Downpatrick and Belfast' in H.B. Clarke and Sarah Gearty (eds), *More maps and texts* (Dublin, 2018), pp 182–98. For a different perspective, Rowan McLaughlin and James Lyttleton's *An archaeology of Northern Ireland, 1600–1650* (Belfast, 2017) devotes almost half its space to the archaeology of the settlement in Antrim and Down and opens up new perspectives that have barely begun to be explored. From a more traditional historian's perspective there have been a number of monographs that have cast considerable light on particular families in early seventeenth-century Antrim and Down. Harold O'Sullivan's 1985 MLitt thesis in Trinity College, Dublin, 'The Trevors of Rosetrevor: a British colonial family in seventeenth-century Ireland', opened up a perspective on the Welsh contribution to the settlement of Down and Rhys Morgan's *The Welsh and the shaping of early modern Ireland, 1558–1641* (Woodbridge, 2014) contains a section that analyses in forensic detail the Welsh settlement at Newry under the Bagenal family. More intriguing are the enigmatic Catholic earls of Antrim who settled in Antrim from the Scottish islands and became the largest landowners in east Ulster. Jane Ohlmeyer's *Civil war and restoration in the three Stuart kingdoms: the career of Randall MacDonnell, marquis of Antrim, 1609–1683* (Cambridge, 1993) reveals many of the contradictions of this family who flitted on and off the national stage.

Antrim and Down remain fascinating counties with a distinctive personality – industrial and urban as opposed to rural west Ulster. In the seventeenth century they were demographically part of the plantation arrangements but socially very different from the main scheme. Their seventeenth-century history will bear a great deal more retelling than that set out here. The story of the society created in the first thirty years or so of the early seventeenth century remains to be followed through into the later part of that century. At the beginning of the eighteenth century William Montgomery of Rosemount, when writing the history of the Montgomery family in north Down, proudly boasted that they had built towns 'with other great works done' and they had made a 'golden peaceable age'. Whether or not he was right remains to be decided.

Raymond Gillespie

PREFACE

THE RECONSTRUCTION OF the workings of society in early modern Ireland is a complex task. There are considerable methodological problems in dealing with the social revolution which occurred in Ireland but had no parallel in the contemporary European context. These difficulties are compounded by problems with sources. Much of the material so fruitfully used by social historians in England and elsewhere, parish registers, probate records, and the records of the courts of law, either never existed in Ireland or were destroyed during the fires of 1711 and 1922 in the record offices. Despite this enough has survived to give a series of glimpses of early modern Irish society although most of them are not as well focused or of as wide a vision as we would like. This book is an attempt to use these glimpses to reconstruct the society of one part of early seventeenth-century Ireland – the counties of Antrim and Down in Ulster.

A work embracing areas of politics, economics, law and society must draw heavily on the works of others and my footnotes demonstrate my debts to those who have shaped the history of early modern Ireland. I would like to express my thanks to the doyen of early modern Ulster historians, Robert Hunter, and to Mary O'Dowd, Michael P. Maxwell, Ciaran Brady, Nicholas Canny, Michael McCarthy Morrogh and Peter Roebuck, all of whom asked awkward questions or made perceptive comments. The work of an Irish historian would be impossible without the co-operation of a very wide range of archivists and librarians, and I am pleased to record my indebtedness to the staffs of the Bodleian, the British Library, Cambridge University Library, Dublin Diocesan Library, Edinburgh University Library, Leeds City Library the National Libraries of Ireland, Scotland and Wales, Sheffield City Library, and the Library of Trinity College, Dublin. The County Record Offices of Devon and East Suffolk, as well as the Public Record Office, London, the Public Record Office, Ireland, and the Scottish Record Office were all generous with assistance. I must make special mention of the Public Record Office of Northern Ireland which acts not only as a record repository but as an institute of historical research for all historians of Ulster. To it and its staff I owe a deep debt of gratitude. Where I have quoted from primary sources I am grateful for the permission of the relevant authority. Even with the willing co-operation of all these people the production of this volume would have been impossible without financial help from the Irish Committee of Historical Sciences and the Belfast Natural History and Philosophical Society and the enthusiasm of Cork University Press.

This book originated as a doctoral thesis in Trinity College, Dublin during the years 1978–82, and I would like to thank my supervisor, Professor Aidan Clarke, who was all that a good supervisor should be. To those who kept me sane throughout the vigil of those years, Bill Vaughan, Sarah Ward-Perkins, Virginia Davis, John McLoughlin, Ethmay Dunlop, Christine Kinealy, John McHugh, Gerry Moran, and Brian Mac Cuarta I am humbly grateful.

Invidious as the task is I should like to convey my special thanks to a number of people. First to Bernadette Cunningham whose scholarship, typing ability and catering skills are all embodied in this work. Secondly to my parents who never doubted the usefulness of what I was doing and have always supported my endeavours even though the logic behind them seemed vague. Thirdly, and most importantly to Dr W.H. Crawford without whose help, encouragement and insistence this work would never have been started let alone finished.

EDITORIAL NOTE

A GOOD BOOK needs no introduction, least of all from an editor, and the purpose of tis note is to draw attention to the fact that this is the first volume of a new series of *Studies in Irish History* which is being sponsored by the Irish Committee of Historical Sciences. Two series were previously published; the first by Faber & Faber which included seven volumes and the second by Routledge & Keegan Paul which extended to eleven volumes. These earlier series included some of the most original work published on Irish history during the past thirty years and provided a first publication forum for such noted historians of Ireland as R.B. McDowell, J.C. Beckett. E.R.R. Green, J.G. Simms, Kevin B. Nowlan and James Donnelly Jr. But while of the highest academic calibre, the books published in the early series were also produced to the highest standards on high quality paper, with notes at the foot of the page and a comprehensive bibliography and index to each volume. Rising production costs and slow returns on sales explain why commercial publishers retreated from those earlier ventures, and the Irish Committee of Historical Sciences is now reviving the series so that scholars of the rising generation who devote themselves to Irish history will have the same publication opportunities as their predecessors enjoyed.

The editorial board, appointed by ICHS to organize the new series, hope to maintain the high academic and production standards that characterized the earlier series. We hope that each contribution will, like the eighteen volumes that preceded it, add significantly to the corpus of detailed studies that are essential to the understanding both of Ireland's social, economic, and political problems and of Anglo-Irish relations. All the work involved in the preparation of manuscripts for the press is being offered on a voluntary basis, and the editorial board hopes that all who submit manuscripts for consideration will benefit from a critical appraisal of the text even when we cannot proceed to publish the manuscript as a book.

Because the new series is dependent on voluntary labour and because production costs remain extremely high we shall limit our output to one volume a year. Only manuscripts by younger scholars who have not previously published a book will be considered for publication, and then only when they are recommended by reputable academics. This series will also differ from its predecessors in that we hope to confine all manuscripts to a word-limit of 100,000 words and we expect authors to reduce appendices and supporting data to the absolute minimum. These restrictions should not deter younger scholars whose existing works do not meet these specifications from submitting them for our consideration, because we may be able to offer advice on how the manuscript should be re-cast to meet our requirements.

Even with voluntary labour and rigid word-limits we could not have hoped to re-launch the series without substantial external support. We are particularly indebted to Cork University Press for an advance of the venture capital that makes the production of this first volume possible. Our own organization, the Irish Committee of Historical Sciences, advanced a grant in aid of production from its slim resources, and a special grant was also made by the Belfast Natural History and Philosophical Society to help keep the purchase price of this particular volume within the reach of the book-reading public. In offering thanks for this generous support we hope that our success in producing this one volume will persuade generous donors or philanthropic bodies to come to our support so that a work well-begun can continue on a regular basis in the years ahead.

Professor Nicholas Canny
Series Editor
University College, Galway

Dr R.H. Buchanan, Queen's University Belfast
Dr Art Cosgrove, University College, Dublin
Dr Vincent Comerford, St Patrick's College, Maynooth
Dr Tom Dunne, University College, Cork

– Members of the Editorial Board

ABBREVIATIONS

A note on dating
All dates have been given old style except the year has been taken as beginning on 1 January. Dates on Scottish documents have been adjusted accordingly.

A note on references
References have usually been given in their most accessible form. In the case of state papers, where the calendar entry is sufficient to illustrate the point it has been given, but where it is necessary to consult the original document this has been cited instead of the calendar entry. Collections of documents have not usually been described in detail in the footnotes as full references will be found in the bibliography.

The abbreviations in T.W. Moody, F.X. Martin, F.J. Byrne, *A new history of Ireland*, iii (Oxford, 1976), pp xxvi–xxxvii, have been used throughout with the following additions:

B.L.	British Library (formerly British Museum).
Benn, *History*	G. Benn, *A history of the town of Belfast* (Belfast, 1877).
Blair, *Autobiography*	T. McCrie (ed.), *The life of Mr Robert Blair* (Edinburgh, 1848).
Brereton, *Travels*	E. Hawkins (ed.), Sir W. Brereton, *Travels in Holland and the United Provinces, England, Scotland and Ireland* (London: Chetham Society, 1844).
Erck.	J.C. Erck (ed.), *A repertory of the inrollments of the patent rolls ... Ireland*, i (Dublin, 1846, 1856).
Ham. MSS	T.K. Lowry (ed.), *Hamilton Manuscripts* (Belfast, 1873).
Hill, *Macdonnells*	G. Hill, *An historical account of the Macdonnells of Antrim* (Belfast, 1873).
Inq. Ult.	*Inquisitionum in officio rotulorum cancellariae Hiberniae Asservatarum*, ii (Dublin, 1829).

Ir. ec. and social hist.	*Irish economic and social history.*
Laud, *Works*	J. Bliss, W. Scott (eds), *The works of the most reverend father in God William Laud*, 7 vols (Oxford 1846–60).
Mont. MSS	G Hill (ed.), W. Montgomery, *Montgomery manuscripts* (Belfast, 1869).
O'Laverty, *Down and Connor*	J. O'Laverty, *An historical account of the diocese of Down and Connor, ancient and modern*, 4 vols (Dublin, 1878–87).
Perceval Maxwell, *Scottish Migration*	M. Perceval Maxwell, *The Scottish migration to Ulster in the reign of James I* (London, 1973).
Stone, *Crisis*	L. Stone, *The crisis of the aristocracy* (Oxford, 1965).
S.H.R.	*Scottish Historical Review*
SL	Sheffield City Library, Wentworth House Muniments, Strafford Letters.
SP 63	Public Record Office [now The National Archives, Kew], London, State Papers Ireland, Elizabeth-George II.
S.R.O.	Scottish Record Office [now the National Records of Scotland], Register House, Edinburgh.

INTRODUCTION

IN WRITING THE history of early modern Ireland historians have tended to approach problems of economic and social change, law and order, and sovereignty, from the perspective of the Dublin administration. Ireland, however, even after the completion of the military conquest in 1603, was not a uniform country in which government control or economic or social development spread evenly. It was, rather, a patchwork of regions, each with its own social, economic, and political structures bound together by ties of religion, of economic interdependence, and the imposition of a legal and governmental framework drawn up by the Dublin administration. The distinctiveness of each of these regions and the balance of the various forces within them has been little studied in Ireland and this work is an attempt to examine such themes for one area — east Ulster.

Throughout the medieval period, Ulster as a whole had been distinct from other areas in Ireland. This distinctiveness was highlighted in the sixteenth century as the control of the Dublin administration spread unevenly over the country. The establishment of provincial presidencies in Connacht and Munster in the 1570s and the plantation of the latter after the Desmond rebellion in 1579 enhanced royal control of these areas by limiting the powers of the principal native Irish and anglo-Irish lords. Only in Ulster were the powers of the traditional elite relatively undisturbed.

This is not to argue that royal authority had not attempted to penetrate into Ulster in the sixteenth century. The principal Gaelic family of Ulster, the O'Neills of Tyrone, had taken part in the surrender and regrant arrangements of 1541, and later, as part of the act of attainder following the rebellion of Shane O'Neill in 1567, the crown had declared in no uncertain terms its title to the whole of Ulster. However, while *de jure* the royal title may have been secure, *de facto* the land was held by the main Gaelic families of the O'Neills of Tyrone, the O'Donnells of

Donegal, and the Maguires of Fermanagh, and the royal writ rarely ran
in Ulster.

Attempts to expand the control of the central administration in Ulster
by military expeditions had only succeeded in provoking revolts which
were costly and difficult to subdue. Thus from the 1570s a new policy
began, haltingly, to evolve. Rather than engage in frequent open conflict with O'Neill and O'Donnell, successive lords deputy sought instead
to limit the sphere of influence of O'Neill and O'Donnell in Ulster by
establishing greater crown control in the borderlands of Ulster. The
main Gaelic families of the peripheral counties of Cavan, Monaghan,
Antrim and Down were often allied to O'Neill or O'Donnell by kinship
or marriage but were rarely under their direct control, principally
because they lay too far from the power base of these great lords. In
these borderland areas there was no one powerful overlord but rather a
number of less influential families often owing just a nominal allegiance
to O'Neill. As one sixteenth-century commentator, Fr. Wolfe, S.J.,
noted, Antrim and Down were ruled 'by diverse nobles (without the title
lord)' in contrast to the western parts of Ulster which were ruled by
Tyrone and Tyrconnell as overlords.[1]

In these parts of Ulster outside the direct sphere of influence of
O'Neill and O'Donnell the Dublin administration intervened in the late
sixteenth century to reorganise the traditional family spheres of influence by creating large numbers of freeholders who would hold their
land directly from the Queen, as in Cavan and Monaghan in the 1580s
and 1590s.[2] This created a system of checks and balances ensuring that
no one lord would become overpowerful and threaten the local influence of the central government. In a similar way successions to native
Irish lordships were manipulated to the advantage of the central administration.

In Antrim and Down a similar policy was pursued. The Tudor administration had established a foothold there in 1548 when Nicholas
Bagnall, a Warwickshire man, later Marshall of the army, was planted
at Newry, county Down as part of an attempt to secure the pale against
attack from the native Irish.[3] This small beginning however, had

---

[1] *Cal. S.P. Rome, 1572-8*, p. 152.

[2] P.J. Duffy, 'Patterns of landownership in Gaelic Monaghan in the late sixteenth century' in *Clogher Record*, x (1981), pp 304-22.

[3] P.H. Bagenal, *Vicissitudes of an Anglo-Irish family, 1530-1800* (London, 1925),
gives a full history of this family.

significant longer term consequences for the development of crown influence in east Ulster. By the late sixteenth century, Bagnall had extended his influence from the garrison at Newry into south Down and reached an accommodation with the main Gaelic lord there, Magennis, bringing him, as was later claimed by Sir Nicholas's son, Sir Henry, to civility. The policy of placing checks on the power of Magennis by creating freeholders had begun as early as 1576, and in consequence, by the end of the century, the political situation in south Down had been stabilized.

Still an unknown quantity politically was the area held by the O'Neills of Clandeboy, in north and east county Down and south county Antrim. Some initiatives had been made, as for instance by Sir Henry Sidney who proposed a plantation at Carrickfergus during his time as lord deputy. As with many projects of the sixteenth century administrators, the execution of policy was farmed out to private enterprise. Two plans were proposed. The first, in 1571, was a project for a settlement of the Ards peninsula by Sir Thomas Smith, a Tudor courtier and classical scholar, and the second in 1572 for a settlement of the southern part of county Antrim by Walter Devereux, earl of Essex. Both men attempted to establish settlements in east Ulster but, due to native resistance and conflict between colonists and the administration, neither succeeded.[4] Yet the experiment was not totally futile for it was clearly demonstrated that in such a peripheral situation the Tyrone O'Neills were unable to interfere decisively because the land involved was too far removed from their power base. However, it was Lord Deputy Perrot who effectively clipped the wings of the Clandeboy O'Neills when he seized the opportunity of a succession dispute between the three main native claimants for the lordship of Clandeboy to split the lordship between them in such a way that no one of them could prove a threat to the influence of the Dublin government.[5]

A further destabilizing force in east Ulster politics was the influence of the Macdonnell family, catholic Scots whose tenuous claim to land in north Antrim dated back to the fifteenth century and was periodically asserted in the late sixteenth century by a younger son of the main branch of the family, Sorley Boy. The land claimed by Macdonnell was actually held by the north Antrim family of MacQuillan who acted as an

[4] N.P. Canny, *The Elizabethan conquest of Ireland* (Harvester, 1976), pp 72-3, 85-92.
[5] Perrot, *Chron Ire., 1584-1608*, p. 36.

important buffer against O'Neill and O'Donnell on the north west border of Antrim. Since the Macdonnells lacked a stable power base in Ireland and had no predictable pattern of political allegiance, methods used successfully by Perrot in other parts of the Ulster borderlands could not be used in dealing with them. A combination of truces and hard hitting military expeditions were used in an attempt to control the growth of Macdonnell power. Nevertheless the Macdonnells, through a combination of political manoeuvres and military force, established themselves as one of the more important east Ulster families by the end of the sixteenth century.

As the Elizabethan era drew to a close, crown control was expanding in east Ulster, as in the Ulster borderlands generally, and the sphere of influence of the traditionally dominant earls of Tyrone and Tyrconnell was being more perceptibly restricted. Yet the Dublin administration's circle of influence in the borderland counties of Ulster was by no means as solid as it appeared. It had been created piecemeal and many of the details of the reorganization of the Gaelic lands in areas such as Cavan, Monaghan, and Antrim, in the 1580s and 1590s were as yet unresolved.

At the same time, collateral septs of the O'Neills were less than happy with the attempts by Hugh O'Neill, earl of Tyrone, who had recently become the chief of the lordship, to expand his influence within the lordship at their expense.[6] This internal discontent served to increase further the threat to the traditional power of the earls in Ulster. If an attempt was to be made by the earls of Tyrone and Tyrconnell and Maguire to secure their position in Ulster, it had to be made sooner rather than later. Early rumblings came from Fermanagh as early as 1593 as Maguire expelled English officials from his lands, a move which was replied to by sending an army to Fermanagh which took and garrisoned the castle of Enniskillen. Technically, the Nine Years War, the final attempt of the western earls to establish their dominance in Ulster, was under way, although it was only in 1595 that the military struggle began in earnest.[7] At first, O'Neill's power expanded as many of the border chiefs followed him, but after the decisive defeat by the English forces at the battle of Kinsale in December 1601 the influence of the Ulster lords was on

---

[6] N.P. Canny, 'Hugh O'Neill and the changing face of Gaelic Ulster' in *Studia Hib.*, x (1970), pp 23-32.

[7] For a narrative of the war, Cyril Falls, *Elizabeth's Irish wars* (London, 1950), pp 168-334.

the wane, and in March 1603 O'Neill submitted to the lord deputy at Mellifont.

In reality, the conclusion of the Nine Years War resolved little. The Dublin administration continued to use the techniques of their sixteenth century predecessors in an attempt to strengthen royal control in Ulster. Landholding was reorganised in both Monaghan and Cavan, to reflect the new political realities, and in Fermanagh freeholders were established to balance the power of Maguire. The powers of the earls were further undermined by the approach of Sir John Davies, the solicitor general, who encouraged the followers of O'Neill, especially the O'Cahans of Derry, to question his jurisdiction over them since English common law, rather than traditional Gaelic custom, now prevailed.

In east Ulster an important new dimension was added to this process. A number of native Irish landholders, their chief being Con O'Neill of Upper Clandeboy, found themselves in severe financial trouble as a result of the war and other more deep rooted economic forces, and were forced to sell a substantial part of their lands to English and Scots who looked to Ulster for investment opportunities and profit through the acquisition of landed estates. In this way, a colonization of east Ulster began. This informal colonization process was paralleled by a more formal plantation scheme in the western parts of Ulster as a result of the flight of the earls in September 1607.[8] Religious, political, and economic pressures from the central administration, intent on reducing the power of the lords, had all pressed hard on the main western earls, O'Neill, O'Donnell, and Maguire and their followers and so, convinced they had no future in Ireland, they fled to the continent. Their lands, the six counties of Cavan, Armagh, Fermanagh, Donegal, Londonderry, and Tyrone were confiscated and after some debate, a formal scheme, the *Orders and Conditions*, was drawn up in 1609 to regulate the progress of the settlement. The two eastern counties, Antrim and Down, where the western earls had had no claim to land and hence were not escheated, were left free from these formal regulations, and were left to evolve as a more informal settlement.

The social consequences of both the informal colonization of east Ulster, and the more formal plantation of the escheated counties of

---

[8] N.P. Canny, 'The Flight of the earls' in *I.H.S.*, xvii (1970-71), pp 380-99.

Ulster were far-reaching. It was noted at the Synod of Drogheda, convened in 1614 to promulgate the counter reformation decrees in the diocese of Armagh, that

> now a fearful change has taken place in this province . . . especially since the arrival of new Scotch and English settlers, who profess a different religion from the native Irish, we are now called upon to consider what is more expedient amidst this variety of customs and tribes.[9]

The detail of these social changes resulting from the settlement of Ulster in the early seventeenth century have been little studied, and such studies as do exist have concentrated on the evolution of the formal plantation scheme. This book is an attempt to add to that scant corpus an examination of east Ulster — the two non-escheated counties of Antrim and Down — which formed a distinct region within Ulster, a distinctiveness reinforced by its omission from the official scheme for the Ulster plantation. The analysis concerns itself principally with the strivings of both settlers and natives to establish a *modus vivendi* in the new political, social, and economic climate of the early seventeenth century.

Given the state of the social history of early seventeenth-century Ireland, many of the conclusions of this work must remain tentative. I can claim no more for it than was claimed by that eminent late seventeenth century biographer, antiquarian, and gossip, John Aubrey, for his work on Stonehenge, that 'although I have not brought it into a clear light yet I can affirm that I have brought it from utter darkness to a thin mist'.

---

[9] G.F. Renehan, *Collections on Irish church history*, i (Dublin, 1861), p. 435.

I

THE PHYSICAL WORLD

THE PHYSICAL ENVIRONMENT was in many ways one of the most important factors which shaped the settlement of east Ulster, especially since the state of agricultural technology was such that the natural landscape was virtually unchangeable. It was possible to modify the terrain slightly by clearing woodland or reclaiming marginal land but the limited size of the labour force available and the lack of effective artificial drainage considerably restricted the scale of these activities. The landscape affected a wide range of activities; influencing warfare, controlling the types of farming practised and affecting communications. During the early years of the upheaval of the 1640s, for example, the landscape slowed the progress of Robert Munroe, the commander of the Scots forces in Ulster, through county Down because of the number of fortified islands which he had to take.[1] The influence of the landscape was also reflected in local choices of building material. Where wood was available, as, for example, in the Lagan valley, timber framed buildings were common, while stone predominated as a building material in other areas.[2] The hilly nature of the county Down landscape also helped the survival of the tower house there, at a time when its popularity was waning in other areas.[3]

---

[1] Gilbert, *Contemp. hist., 1641-52*, i, p. 420; O'Laverty, *Down and Connor*, iii, pp 392-3.

[2] P. Robinson, 'Vernacular housing in Ulster in the seventeenth century' in *Ulster Folklife*, xxv (1979), p. 15.

[3] H.G. Leask, *Irish castles* (Dundalk, 1973), p. 125; W.D. Simpson, *Scottish castles* (H.M.S.O., 1959), pp 21-2. For castles in Down, see E.M. Jope (ed.), *An archaeological survey of county Down* (H.M.S.O., 1966), pp 123-4, 227, 233, 236; *Cal. S.P. Ire., 1601-3*, p. 152.

As well as the physical landscape, climatic and seasonal fluctuations also had a significant impact on the Antrim and Down settlement. The weather was the main factor in determining the success or failure of the harvest which was vital both as the main source of food and of cash to pay rent when the surplus was marketed. Excessive rain or drought could cause a failure of the harvest with resulting severe economic dislocation. The effect was cumulative since a poor supply of grain in any one year meant that part of the next year's seed crop was consumed, thus diminishing the possibility of a good harvest the following year. Very dry weather could also diminish the capacity of the rivers to supply power to mills in east Ulster, and hence bring milling to a halt. The result was a shortage of flour and hence bread. Heavy rain on the other hand could bring equally severe economic dislocation by destroying mills and roads. One such incident was recorded by Gerald Boate in 1652 when 'a great and lasting rain' destroyed the bridge at Dromore in west Down.[4] Transport and communications were also severely affected by the elements. For example, Henry Leslie, the dean of Down, failed to reach the Down assizes in 1631 because of 'contrary winds' and in April 1601, Sir Arthur Chichester, the governor of Carrickfergus, and later lord deputy, explained to Robert Cecil, the queen's principal secretary of state, that he had not written recently because 'the season of the year has seldom afforded us means to convey our letter'.[5] Even within the confines of east Ulster the weather hampered communications, as for example during the Nine Years War when supplies being transferred from the garrison at Carrickfergus to the outlying forces at Belfast, Inishloughlin, Toome, and Masserine were frequently lost because the roads were bad 'by reason of wet and foul weather'.[6]

The environment was, therefore, one of the principal factors shaping the settlement of east Ulster but before the colonization of Antrim and Down in the early seventeenth century the English and Scottish governments knew little of this environment. The earliest maps of east Ulster, such as that of 1558 were scanty. South-east Down was the best known area topographically because of the early sixteenth-century settlement at Newry by Nicholas Bagnall, a Warwickshire man, who later became

---

[4] G. Boate, *Ireland's natural history* (London, 1652), p. 59.

[5] P.R.O.I., Ferguson MSS, ix, p. 25; *Cal. S.P. Ire., 1625-32*, p. 629; *Cal. S.P. Ire., 1600-01*, pp 268, 275.

[6] P.R.O.I., M2441, ff 22, 23, 43-4, 52, 62; *Cal. S.P. Ire., 1600-01*, p. 334.

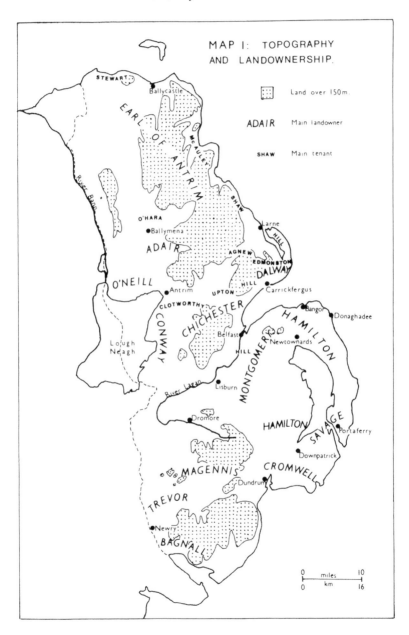

MAP I: TOPOGRAPHY
AND LANDOWNERSHIP.

Land over 150m.

ADAIR   Main landowner

SHAW   Main tenant

Marshall of the army in Ireland. One consequence of this settlement was that a number of surveys were made of the area, as for example that of Robert Lythe, one of the principal Tudor mapmakers, in 1568. The area around Belfast was also well charted because of the strategic significance of the castle there.[7] Geographical knowledge was increased in the 1560s when the threat of an invasion from Scotland resulted in a spurt of map-making in the coastal regions of east Ulster to assist an enlarged coastal garrison, but knowledge of the geography of the inland areas remained vague.[8] The settlements of Sir Thomas Smith in east Down and of the earl of Essex in Antrim in the 1570s further speeded up the acquisition of geographical knowledge as both men tried to ascertain the extent of their newly acquired lands. In the early stages of his settlement, Essex's only knowledge of his lands of lower Clandeboy was that they could feed 100,000 cattle, an estimate probably drawn from native sources.[9] As the attempted settlement progressed, attempts were made to quantify the acreage of the Ards, and Smith commissioned a special map of the area which was referred to as 'the plot annexed' in his tract advocating the settlement. The presence of an army with Essex in Ulster also resulted in a growth of geographical knowledge as route books were constructed to help mobility.[10] Topographical information for the army became one of the main reasons for the exploration of the east Ulster environment in the latter half of the sixteenth century. As the renewed threat of a Scottish invasion grew in the late sixteenth century more maps were made of the coastline to help the garrisons.[11] A good example of these is the series of maps made of Clandeboy in 1593, when a Scottish attack was felt to be imminent.[12] Other areas received less attention until the Nine Years War forced the government to construct maps of the strategic inland areas of east Ulster; the Glens of Antrim, Lough Neagh, Coleraine and the Lagan valley.[13] Towards the end of the sixteenth century the central government came to realise the significance of

---

[7] P.R.O., MPF 92; B.L., Cotton Aug. 1, vol. 2, f. 21; J.H. Andrews, 'Robert Lythe's petition, 1571' in *Anal. Hib.*, xxiv (1967), p. 235; SP63/31/36.

[8] P.R.O., MPF 77, MPF 98.

[9] SP63/45/37, 67 i.

[10] *Ulster maps c. 1600*, p. 31; B.L., Harley 5938, no. 129; Hill, *Macdonnells*, p. 408; B.L., Add. 48017 'A route of the several principal seats'.

[11] P.R.O., MPF 86, 87, 88, 89, 93.

[12] SP63/170/4iv, 47, 58.

[13] P.R.O., MPF 312, 133; *Ulster maps c. 1600*, p. 12.

detailed maps of the counties. It was the opinion both of Sir Robert Gardiner, the chief justice of the queen's bench, and Sir Henry Wallop, the lord treasurer, that the only way to bring east Ulster under control was to map the country and then impose sheriffs. In 1609 Sir John Davies, the solicitor general, was also enthusiastic about mapping for it would, he argued, limit 'ignorance of their [the natives'] places of retreat and fastnesses [which] made them confident in their rebellion'.[14] As a result of these developments officials had, by 1610, come to know the outline geography of east Ulster and they possessed a detailed appreciation of the disposition of woodlands and the location of the principal castles, abbeys and towns.[15]

The picture which emerged from this growing body of geographical knowledge was a favourable one for the settlers for east Ulster appeared as a rich area well endowed with good agricultural land as well as other exploitable resources such as woodland and fisheries. Two assessments made in 1627, probably for the support of the army, ranked Antrim and Down among the wealthiest counties in Ireland and the subsidy of 1634 again showed them to have a high proportion of wealth per acre. The ecclesiastical picture was little different as can be seen from the royal commission of 1615 which rated Down and Connor as the seventh bishopric in Ireland in terms of wealth and the diocese of Dromore the sixth. Dromore deanery was regarded as the third wealthiest in Ireland and that of Connor seventh. The picture of the Roman Catholic church was similar and their surveys rated Down and Connor among the five most wealthy Irish dioceses.[16]

Contemporaries were lavish in their praise of the agricultural land in county Antrim. Barnaby Rich, an Elizabethan soldier, described the Route in north Antrim as the best corn land in Ireland and the Jesuit missionary, Fr. Wolfe, thought that Clandeboy was among the best land in Ulster.[17] The Route was described as 'pleasant and fertile',

[14] P.R.O.N.I., T695/1, f.7; H.M.C. *Salisbury*, xxi, p. 121; Davies, *Discovery*, p. 270-1.

[15] P.R.O., MPF, 35, 67.

[16] *Acts privy council, Sept. 1627-June 1628*, p. 400; *Cal. S.P. Ire., 1625-32*, pp 250-55. An army assessment of the 1630s presents a similar picture, SL, 1, f 32; *Commons jn. Ire.,* i, p. 106; *Cal. S.P. Ire., 1625-32*, p. 48. The figures for Dromore were high because there were few impropriations there. Brereton, *Travels*, p. 129; H.M.C., *Franciscan*, p. 84.

[17] B. Rich, *A new description of Ireland* (London, 1610). Introduction; *Cal. S.P. Rome, 1572-8*, p. 152.

Lecale in east Down was 'champion country' as was Island Magee and Clandeboy was ranked among 'the best soil in Ireland having many good commodities'.[18] Only one area was despaired of by contemporaries — the Glens of Antrim which were heavily wooded, boggy and backed by steep cliffs.[19] However, most of these early writers saw only the accessible coastal margins, which also comprised the best land. Inland, the quality of the land degenerated considerably. The Civil Survey recorded of north-east Antrim that 'the soil toward the sea coast is indifferent good . . . [but] towards the south-east is utterly barren and mountainous'.[20] In the core of both counties lay boggy mountainous masses which were unsuited to tillage. Sir William Brereton, who travelled east Ulster in 1636, described this type of land around Dromore, in west Down, as 'the worst part of this kingdom and the poorest land and ground'.[21] Between the poor inland uplands and the usually fertile coastal lowlands lay land of mixed quality. Other areas such as Kilwarlin, on the south-east corner of Lough Neagh, and the Dufferin in east Down were wooded and boggy and, despite some clearance, remained so until 1641.[22] The land on the east coast of Lough Neagh was rather better, Brereton commenting that it 'may be made good with labour and charge' but being furthest away from the coast this land was settled late and so little effort was put into its development before the outbreak of rebellion in 1641.[23] The land between Lough Neagh and Belfast was regarded as clear and fertile as was the land on the north-east corner of Lough Neagh.[24] Antrim and Down were both punctuated by river valleys, the Six Mile Water, the Bann and the Lagan valleys for example, which provided not only stretches of good arable

[18] T.C.D., MS 743, ff 59, 61; J. Dymmok, 'A treatise of Ireland' in R. Butler (ed.), *Tracts relating to Ireland*, ii (Irish Archaeological Society, Dublin, 1842) p. 21; *Civil Survey*, x, p. 63; SP63/146/47; W. Camden, *Britannia* (London, 1637), p. 160.

[19] E. Hogan (ed.), *A description of Ireland c. 1598* (Dublin, 1878), p. 15.

[20] *Civil Survey*, x, p. 56.

[21] Brereton, *Travels*, p. 129.

[22] *Cal. Carew, 1589-1600*, p. 298; W. Camden, *Britannia*, p. 101; R. Pike, *A true relation of the proceedings of the Scots and English in the north of Ireland* (London, 1642), pp 1 2; *Ulster maps c. 1600*, p. 30.

[23] Brereton, *Travels*, p. 129; W. Basil, *Two letters of William Basil* (London, 1649), pp 3, 6.

[24] Cambridge U.L., KK1.15 f 281ᵛ; *Civil Survey*, x, pp 57, 58.

land but also important inland communications routes.[25]

This impressionistic picture of the landscape of east Ulster is partly confirmed by an assessment made for the county cess of Antrim in mid-1656.[26] The wealthiest part of the county lay in the south around the coastal towns of Belfast and Carrickfergus but this was followed closely by an assessment of 0·2 pence per acre in the northern coastal baronies of Dunluce, Carey and the lowlying inland baronies of Massarine and Toome. A third, lower, rate was imposed on the barony of Glenarme in eastern county Antrim where the Antrim glens were still wooded, and on the wooded barony of Antrim. The poor land in the core of the county, the barony of Kilconway, was assessed at a still lower level.

The wealth of the agricultural land was considerably supplemented by other natural resources, the fishing and the woods. The significance of the fishing was stressed by at least one tract of the early seventeenth century which highlighted the economic significance of the salmon of the Bann and claimed that there was cod and ling in Lough Neagh.[27] The Bann salmon fishings had been recognised from at least the fifteenth century when Bann salmon were exported to Bristol[28] and during the sixteenth century there had been attempts to exploit the fishing rights of the river by leasing them to farmers. The first of these grants was made to John Travers in 1536 but because of his failure to pay the crown rent the fishing rights were granted in 1571 to Henry Piers of Carrickfergus. Since the Bann itself was *de facto* in the hands of the O'Neill family for most of the sixteenth century it was difficult to make any real attempt to exploit the fisheries and lessees were reluctant to pay rent for only sporadic control of them.[29] In the early seventeenth century convey-ancing problems with the Bann fishing rights drew attention to the economic importance of the royal claim to the fishings which resulted in a series of inquisitions in 1619 into royal fishing rights in east Ulster and

[25] *Civil Survey*, x, pp 57-8.

[26] S.R.O., GD54/518.

[27] B.L., Royal MSS, 18 A L111 f. 12.

[28] E. Power, M.M. Postan, *Studies in English trade in the fifteenth century* (London, 1933), p. 198.

[29] *Cal. pat. rolls Ire., Hen VIII-Eliz.*, p. 12; SP63/11/71; SP63/21/10; *Cal. pat. rolls Ire., Eliz.*, p. 562; T.M. Healy, *Stolen waters* (London, 1913), p. 192. *Cal. Carew, 1575-88*; p. 431; *Cal. S.P. Ire., 1586-8*, p. 505.

the important salmon rights of north Antrim and Belfast were granted
to the earl of Antrim, the main landholder in north Antrim, and Sir
Arthur Chichester.[30]

A second important natural resource in east Ulster was timber, which
was already in short supply in England and was an important economic
incentive to colonization. Woodland could be easily converted into
building timber, fuel for iron works, or pipe staves for export. Contemporaries were well aware of this asset and in 1591, Charles Egerton, the
governor of Carrickfergus, argued that a plantation in the northern part
of Clandeboy would not only reform the natives but also provide an opportunity to exploit both the fishings and the woodland.[31] Most of the
early seventeenth century settlers made extensive use of the woodland of
east Ulster for their own ends and in the development of the settlement.
Sir Edward Conway, for instance, proposed in 1635 to remove timber
from his Irish estates on the east shore of Lough Neagh to repair his
Welsh residence at Conway, but the plan proved abortive.[32] There was
also a project to set up a ship building industry at Belfast based on the
crooked timber in the Lagan valley.[33] Such was the clearance of
woodland in east Ulster as a result of colonization that by the 1640s there
may have been a shortage of good building timber in the area and when
the castle at Larne was repaired in 1640 timber had to be brought from
Londonderry.[34] The Dufferin, in south Down, for example, one of the
most economically important wooded areas in the sixteenth century,
had been cleared by 1640 leaving only scrub of little value.[35] By 1640 the
only area where any timber of real value remained was on the east shore
of Lough Neagh, an area which was settled late and never fully
developed before the outbreak of war in 1641.[36]

Thus by the early years of the seventeenth century the central administration were aware of the outlines of the physical and economic
geography of east Ulster but they were slow to appreciate its detail and

---

[30] P.R.O.I., RC9/1 James I no. 5.

[31] SP63/160/24.

[32] *Cal. S.P. dom., 1635,* pp 469, 509; Royal commission on ancient monuments
(Wales), *An inventory of ancient monuments in Caernarvonshire,* i, (H.M.S.O.), 1956, p.
47.

[33] *Cal. Carew, 1575-88,* p. 37; *Cal. S.P. Ire., 1608-10,* p. 89.

[34] Bodl., Carte 1, f 230.

[35] SP63/16/45; SP63/20/11, 11i; SP63/31/31; *Civil Survey,* x, p. 64.

[36] *Civil Survey,* x, p. 59.

problems. There was still considerable uncertainty in the minds of government officials on important problems such as the geography of ownership and lay out of administrative units. In the sixteenth century the Dublin administration had relied for geographical information on the knowledge of local officials. Thus in 1598, Nicholas Dawtry, a former governor of Carrickfergus, stressed his local knowedge as a prime reason for his promotion to the governorship of Clandeboy.[37] These rough geographical methods of the sixteenth century were insufficient to deal with the seventeenth-century problems of the construction of detailed land grants or the establishment of an administrative framework for the new local government officials. Many of the local sixteenth-century records of land title or administrative divisions, if they ever existed, were lost during the Nine Years War and ecclesiastical records had fared no better, although in Connor diocese the bishop's registrar provided a human link with the past.[38] In an attempt to understand the administrative geography of east Ulster various sources were searched by the Dublin officials for material; Giraldus Cambrensis's *Topographia* was used as was a sixth century life of St. Columba and the medieval *Chronicle of Man and the Isles*.[39] The central government also began to create a new body of information about the geography of east Ulster. In this attempt the main instrument was the inquisition, a sworn statement from local inhabitants on placenames and landholding, but the inquisition was not without its problems and there were a number of allegations of inaccuracy.[40] Gaps in the information from this source soon appeared because although inquisitions were, in law, necessary before any new patent could be issued to a settler (18 Henry VI, c. 6) they were often avoided by the insertion of a clause in the land grant dispensing with the inquisition. In the short term the administration, which was anxious to pass new land grants to settlers as rapidly as possible to ensure stability, approved of this practice but it had serious long term repercussions as the central administration, already bedevilled by poor record keeping in Dublin, began to lose track of what had been granted and what remained. Two case studies will illustrate this process clearly.

On 2 March 1605 a patent was granted to John Wakeman of the

[37] H.M.C., *Salisbury*, viii, p. 267.

[38] O'Laverty, *Down and Connor*, iv, p. 367.

[39] *Cal. Carew, 1603-24*, pp 351-3, 356, 374; *Cal. S.P. Ire., 1615-25*, p. 215.

[40] SL, 24/25, no. 295; *Mont. MSS*, p. 36.

fishing rights of the river Bann from the salmon leap at Coleraine to the sea without an inquisition being held.[41] Almost a year later, on 14 February 1606, the rest of the river was granted on similar terms to James Hamilton, a major north Down landowner, again without inquisition. Part of these rights, however, had already been granted in 1603, and confirmed in 1604, to Sir Randal Macdonnell, the main landowner in north Antrim, through whose lands the river ran.[42] Wakeman's grant was subsequently transferred to Hamilton and Sir Randal found himself 'dispossed' of his portion of the fishery. The situation was aggravated by the support for Hamilton given by the farmer of Sir Randal's part of the fishery, Captain Thomas Phillips, who had had a number of disputes with Sir Randal previously. The crown sequestered Macdonnell's fishings until the matter was brought to law in April 1610.[43] In the interim the confusion was increased by a grant of 1608 to Sir Arthur Basset, in trust for his uncle, Sir Arthur Chichester, the lord deputy, of part of the fishings which Hamilton had sold to Chichester.[44] The case was heard at king's bench in Michaelmas term 1610 and the judgement found that the portion of the Bann granted to Wakeman and Macdonnell without inquisition was tidal, and therefore the property of the king, and should not have been granted at all. Sir Randal's grant was annulled and Wakeman's grant, by this time in the hands of Chichester, was surrendered.[45]

A similar problem arose when old claims to land were not fully examined by inquisition before new grants were made. One such case was the claim of the descendants of Sir Thomas Smith, the sixteenth century colonizer of the Ards. The grant to Smith of the Ards, made in November 1571, had been conditional on a settlement being established by March 1579, and failing this the land would revert to the crown. The expedition to establish the colony proved a disaster and the land remained *de facto* in the hands of the Clandeboy O'Neills.[46] While the

---

[41] Erck., pp 28, 189. It was sold to James Hamilton on 3 Mar., Erck., p. 281.

[42] Erck., pp 8, 58, 137, 217. Hamilton later conveyed his interest to Sir Arthur Chichester.

[43] *Cal. S.P. Ire., 1603-6*, p. 518; *Cal. S.P. Ire., 1606-8*, pp 252, 566; *Cal. S.P. Ire., 1608-10*, p. 21; Healy, *Stolen waters*, p. 126. The sequestration was temporarily lifted in 1607.

[44] P.R.O.N.I., D389/1.

[45] Bodl., Carte 61, f 85; Healy, *Stolen waters*, pp 167-8, 180-85.

[46] *Cal. pat. rolls Eliz.*, v (1569-72), p. 281.

land title thus reverted to the crown it showed no desire to enforce its claim in the late sixteenth century for as Patrick Plunkett, Lord Dunsany, a member of one of the most influential pale families and an M.P. in 1585, advised Secretary Cecil 'if Sir Thomas Smith's patent be brought into question or the heirs thereof be put in authority there it will breed rebellion'.[47] The possibility of a claim to the lands by the Smith family was raised in 1605 but Sir Arthur Chichester dismissed this idea. The Smith family did not share his view and in 1608 Sir Thomas's nephew, Sir William Smith, challenged the rights of two of the new grantees in Down, Sir James Hamilton and Chichester, both of whose patents had been granted without inquisition. The claim of Sir William Smith was dismissed on the grounds that his uncle had forfeited all right to the land by failing to fulfil the terms of his grant of Clandeboy by not introducing the required number of settlers.[48]

These two examples demonstrate the results of relying almost entirely on inquisitions but nevertheless they remained the main source of information for the Dublin administration on the political and landholding divisions in east Ulster. The reliance on inquisitions, taken mainly from native Irish inhabitants, for information about the geography of east Ulster meant that new settler units were mainly adaptations of older native ones.[49] What were to become the county boundaries for the new settlers were already well established boundaries for the native inhabitants. The river Bann, which formed the western boundary of county Antrim in the seventeenth century, had been an important physical and mental barrier in the sixteenth century. As a tract of *c.* 1590 explained, one way of terrorising unruly children in west Ulster was to threaten to 'send them over the Bann . . . where you never hear a word of Irish' and in 1587 an attempt to establish the extent of the lands of Turlough O'Neill, of Tyrone, deemed them to be bounded 'on the east by the Bann and on the west by the country of Maguire'.[50] The

[47] *Cal. S.P. Ire., 1600-01*, p. 44.

[48] *Cal. S.P. Ire., 1603-6*, p. 295; J. Strype, *The life of the learned Thomas Smith* (London, 1689), p. 192; *Cal. S.P. Ire., 1606-8*, pp 383, 398, 436; *Cal. S.P. Ire., 1608-10*, p. 168; G. Benn, *A history of the town of Belfast* (Belfast, 1877), app. 2; this decision was confirmed by an inquisition of 1625 *Cal. pat. rolls Ire., Chas I*, pp 231, 318.

[49] Other schemes of new geometrical units were proposed (B.L., Lansdowne 156, f 267, for example) and were used by the earl of Essex (*Cal. S.P. Ire., 1509-73*, p. 522), but proved unworkable on a large scale.

[50] P.R.O.N.I., T1180/4, f 1; *Cal. S.P. Ire., 1586-8*, pp 334-5, 376.

Armagh/Down border was more difficult to fix since it lacked a distinctive physical feature such as a river, and the heavy woodland of Kilwarlin also caused problems of boundary definition. Tradition had however defined this boundary well, apart from a minor controversy involving six townlands.[51] The Dublin administration rarely interfered much with these traditional boundaries and only two significant changes in the sixteenth century 'county' boundaries were made. The boundary of Antrim and Londonderry was altered so that nine townlands between the rivers Bush and Bann could be transferred to the new settlement of county Londonderry to provide the town of Coleraine with land. Again in 1605 the size of county Down was reduced by transferring the large, mainly wooded, area of Killultagh to Antrim in order to make Down more manageable for the sheriff.[52]

This policy of reliance on traditional units is even more clearly shown in the case of smaller areas such as estates and baronies. In the early stages of the settlement no detailed English style administrative units existed in east Ulster and so land grants were made in native Irish land units. The 1603 patent to Sir Randal Macdonnell, for example, granted him lands 'in which country of the Route are contained nine territories, otherwise called toughes, and seven in the Glenns' and similarly, Sir Arthur Chichester was granted lands in the tuatha of Falls and Malone in south Antrim.[53] Other Irish ways of naming land, such as referring to whoever exercised lordship over it were also used in making grants. Thus John Hibbots and John King, both Dublin speculators, were granted lands in north Down 'being in or near the country of Con Neal McBrian Fertagh' and Sir Edward Cromwell's lands in Lecale were 'the entire moiety of the territory . . . called Killenarten, commonly called McCarten's country'.[54] Even older units, such as the tricha cét, an early medieval unit of landholding, survived into the seventeenth century in Lecale and lower Iveagh.[55]

[51] T.W. Moody (ed.), 'Ulster plantation papers' in *Anal. Hib.*, viii (1938), pp 266-9, 272.

[52] Moody, 'Plantation papers', pp 256-8; P.R.O.N.I., D265/1; *Cal. S.P. Ire., 1603-6*, pp 321, 323.

[53] *Cal. pat. rolls Ire., Jas I*, pp 3, 48-9, 58, 76, 89.

[54] Ibid., pp 38, 74.

[55] J. Hogan, 'The tricha cét and related land measures' in *R.I.A. Proc.*, xxxviii, sect. C (1929), pp 186-7, 209-10.

The use of traditional units had the advantage of simplicity and the boundaries were established by tradition as well as by law but these traditional units also had their problems. In many cases, such as that of the lordship, they were not fixed by written document but fluctuated according to the amount of support a lord could command or coerce at any one time. Boundaries were usually preserved by tradition and had to be discovered orally by the new administrators using the inquisition — 'by the oaths of good and lawful men of the county of Down', as one inquisitor put it.[56] The Dublin officials however found the native Irish system of land units a strange one, one administrator complaining that the 'tuath' of the Glens of Antrim 'designated no shire, county or place of one jurisdiction but hills with valleys between them bounded by woods'.[57] In order to bring this system more into line with English ideas and to produce a neat patchwork of stable administrative units, administrators 'froze' the old fluctuating boundaries of lordships. In many cases the new barony became coterminous with the old tuath or lordship, whichever was the more convenient, so that in 1612 a grant could be made to the archbishop of Armagh, Henry Ussher, of land in the barony of 'Iveagh otherwise Magennis's country'.[58]

Similar forces were also working at a lower level to preserve smaller units such as the townland. In the sixteenth century townlands were economic units and hence their size and disposition fluctuated over time because of changing population distribution.[59] In parts of east Ulster, such as Lecale and the Greencastle area, where occupation had been continuous over long periods, the townland had become a stable unit, but in other areas, such as Iveagh, where there was high population mobility the townland boundaries fluctuated considerably.[60] Dublin administrators wanted not an economic unit but a standard one to make it useful for property grants and so attempted to devise the 'standard townland'. In the 1570s Sir Thomas Smith saw 220 Irish acres as a convenient unit for all townlands, but by the early seventeenth century 120

[56] *Inq. Ult.*, pp xli-xliv.

[57] *Cal. Carew, 1603-25*, p. 360.

[58] *Cal. pat. rolls Ire., Jas I*, pp 197, 278.

[59] P. Robinson, 'Irish settlement in Tyrone before the Ulster plantation' in *Ulster Folklife*, xxii (1976), pp 59-69.

[60] T.E. McNeill, *Anglo-Norman Ulster* (Edinburgh, 1980), pp 89-90; E.E. Evans, *Mourne country* (Dundalk, 1967), 2nd edn, pp 111-14.

acres was seen as an optimum unit and in the 1630s, during a dispute between the earl of Antrim and one of his tenants, an 'honest sworn
surveyor' was instructed to regard 60 acres as a townland.[61] In reality
such a move towards standardization was impossible given its variance
with the already established system and the wide variations in land
quality over east Ulster, but despite this the townland remained the basic
unit in land grants.

The usefulness of the townland to the landlord in the administration
of his estate was an important factor in its preservation. Newly
established landlords required a unit which could be used for leasing
purposes and the townland fulfilled all their requirements, being convenient for both new and native Irish tenants. In the early stages of the
settlement many landowners insisted that their tenants enclose the
boundaries of their lands with hedges and began to make surveys of
their lands delineating townland boundaries.[62] Sir James Hamilton had
his lands surveyed in 1625 by Thomas Raven, who had been surveyor for
the Irish Society in Londonderry, and by 1630 Archibald Edmonston, a
cousin of Hamilton's, was considering a survey of his mid-Antrim
lands.[63] The making of written leases and their registration in manor
courts also helped stabilise boundaries as the details of the boundary
were documented and so could be checked later.[64] This process of defining boundaries was helped by the growth of population, especially in the
coastal areas, which meant that the property rights of individuals had to
be more clearly delineated as pressure on land, and hence its value,
increased.[65]

This clarification of the geography of land ownership was of fundamental importance to the success of the settlement in east Ulster, since
tenants could only be attracted to an estate if the title to that land was
secure. One grant to Sir Arthur Chichester underlined this by explaining

[61] H.M.C., *L'Isle and Dudley*, ii, p. 15; *Cal. S.P. Ire., 1603-6*, p. 321; *Cal. pat. rolls Ire., Chas I*, p. 505.

[62] SP63/255/62; Tenants were not legally bound to enclose their lands until 1721 (8 Geo. I c.5 (Ir.)).

[63] P.R.O.N.I., T811; R. Gillespie, 'Thomas Raven and the mapping of the Clandeboy estate, 1625' in *Bangor Historical Soc. Jn.*, 1 (1980), pp 1-5; R. Gillespie, *Ulster planta-tion maps: a guide for teachers* (Q.U.B., 1977), passim; H.M.C. *Various v.*, p. 136.

[64] For example, N.L.W., Cross of Shaw Hill MSS, Deeds, no. 174.

[65] R.A. Dodgshon, 'Landholding foundations of the open field system' in *Past and Present*, lxvii (1975), pp 28-9.

that it was 'as well in regard of his services as also that his tenants in said lands may be the better encouraged to plant and manure the same when they may have from him certain estates therein'.[66] The incorporation of the older forms of geographical organization in these new grants helped to minimise disputes by providing a degree of continuity. Some disputes involving estate boundaries, which were usually also townland boundaries, did occur, the most notable being that between two of the most important Down landowners, Sir James Hamilton and Sir Hugh Montgomery. Such disputes were both disruptive and expensive. The total cost of the action between Hamilton and Montgomery came to more than £1400, and during one phase of the disagreement alone Montgomery claimed that he spent £300.[67] In the case of a claim made against Sir Randal Macdonnell by Sir Awla McAwley, a Dumbartonshire man, over the lands of the Glens, Chichester claimed 'but if Sir Randal should be called over there [England] for every occasion of complaint framed as he now is . . . he may spend more in one year than his lands will yield again in three or four'.[68] Prolonged disputes were, however, uncommon.

By the 1620s therefore, geographical and administrative units had been stabilized successfully and the work of map makers had given a broad view of the political and economic geography of east Ulster. But a major geographical problem remained to be surmounted in the development of an infrastructure for the settlement, particularly a communications network. The maintenance of roads was the responsibility of the parish through which they ran, the parish organising six days labour per annum to repair roads with stones and gravel.[69] There is no evidence as to how effectively this was carried out, but one suspects it had limited success since the quality of the roads remained poor and there was even difficulty in knowing where they were. Sir Josias Bodley, travelling from Newry to Downpatrick in 1603, lost the road shortly after leaving Newry, and Sir William Brereton, travelling between Dromore and

---

[66] Erck, p. 23.

[67] This dispute has been examined in Perceval Maxwell, *Scottish migration*, pp 234-42; N.L.S., Denmilne MSS, vi, no. 8; J. Maidment (ed.), *Letters and state papers during the reign of James VI* (Abbotsfort Club, Edinburgh, 1836), pp 230-33.

[68] SP63/229/93.

[69] 11, 12, 13 Jas I, c.8 (Ir.); R. Bolton, *A justice of the peace for Ireland* (Dublin, 1637), bk 1, pp 51-5.

Newry, over thirty years later in 1636 found the road 'a most difficult way for a stranger to find out', and eventually he had to hire a local guide as Bodley had done.[70] By 1641 the situation was little improved since before the army could march into Antrim it was necessary to issue writs to the sheriff to have the roads repaired.[71]

The quality of roads depended in large measure on the terrain through which they ran. In the wooded area of Killultagh roads were 'straight having moss and bogs on every side' while in the coastal area of Carrickfergus the road was 'a most base way, deep in winter though now [July 1636] it is hard and dry' with grass and shrubs at the side.[72] Natural ridges in the landscape and the flanks of valleys were frequently used for roads since they were dry. It was ordered, for example, in connection with the Londonderry settlement that 'there be highways made, as well through the country as along the [river] Bann side; and that every man, by water or land, may have free passage with his goods'.[73] This adaptation of the roads to the surrounding environment meant that the network of roads established in the sixteenth century could be developed in the seventeenth century as the clearing of woodland and the establishment of law and order helped make travel less hazardous.[74] Thus the Newry to Hilltown road in south Down, developed because more effective law enforcement made travel safer in the early seventeenth century, eclipsed the old longer coastal route from Newry to Downpatrick via Dundrum and Narrow Water. In many areas woodland was cleared to make travel safer so that by 1640 even the notorious refuge for outlaws, Kilwarlin, had a road through it.[75] Urban development also encouraged the growth of a more complex road system in the early seventeenth

[70] 'Sir Bodley's visit to Lecale' in *U.J.A.*, 1st ser, ii (1854), p. 76; Brereton, *Travels*, p. 132.

[71] Bodl., Carte 1, f 179; this was not done and considerable difficulty ensued. Gilbert, *Contemp. hist., 1641-52*, i, p. 241; R.M. Young, *Historical notices of old Belfast* (Belfast, 1896), p. 50.

[72] Brereton, *Travels*, p. 128; *Cal. S.P. Ire., 1596-7*, p. 465.

[73] *Cal. S.P. Ire., 1611-14*, p. 41.

[74] SP63/13/48; J.H. Andrews, 'Road planning before the railway age' in *Ir. Geography*, v (1964-8), pp 17-41; for roads from woodland, *Cal. S.P. Ire., 1625-32*, p. 217; H.M.C., *Salisbury*, xviii, p. 303.

[75] *Acts privy council, June 1623 - March 1625*, p. 328; *Acts privy council, March 1625 - May 1626*, p. 159; B.L., Add. 39853, f 8.

century since towns needed links between them, and thus the road between Belfast and Downpatrick grew up mainly because of the development of Belfast. Similarly the road through the Dundonald gap, between Belfast and Newtownards, to Donaghadee and Comber was a result of the growth of these new centres.[76]

One problem in the development of the road network was the absence of bridges. A bridge across the Bann had been advocated as early as 1592 because of its strategic importance, but none was built by 1640 when the crossings were still provided by four fords and a ferry.[77] After 1603 however, bridges began to feature in the landscape; across the Lagan at Lisburn by 1611, across the Quoile at Downpatrick by 1640, at Newcastle by 1640, over the Lagan at Dromore by 1652 and because of its strategic significance, at Newry by 1640.[78] Yet by 1640 bridges were still confined to major communications routes and the normal means of crossing water was by ford or ferry. Part of the explanation for this situation lies in the high cost of bridge building incurred because of the engineering problems involved in their erection.[79]

Ferries, in contrast, concentrated mainly on passage over large bodies of water, such as between Strangford and Portaferry or across Carlingford Lough between Narrow Water and Omeath, county Louth. Belfast Lough was also served by a ferry between Bangor and Carrickfergus.[80] Ferries were important economic assets for their operators as Sir Thomas Phillips, who controlled the ferry at Toome showed. At this strategic crossing point of the river Bann, he could charge a halfpenny per passenger, one penny for each cow or horse and fares in proportion for smaller animals.[81] Indeed when Lord Cromwell petitioned the Dublin parliament in 1640 for a grant towards the

[76] J.T. Fulton, 'The roads of county Down, 1600-1900' (Ph.D. thesis, Q.U.B., 1972), pp 104-6; R. Pike, *A true relation*, pp 1-2.

[77] SP63/164/47; *Civil Survey*, x, p. 56; Cambridge U.L., Add. 4352, f 66^v; bridges were the responsibility of Grand Juries, (10 Chas I, s.2, c.26 (Ir.)).

[78] Fulton, 'Roads', pp 134-5, 261, 265; *Commons jn. Ire.*, i, pp 370-71; Gilbert, *Contemp. hist., 1641-52*, i, p. 240; P.R.O.N.I., D671/M8/1, T811/3.

[79] The cost of one bridge in county Cork was estimated at £500, excluding materials, in the 1620s, *Lismore papers*, 1st ser. ii. p. 218.

[80] P.R.O.N.I., D552/B/1/1/12-13; *Cal. S.P. Ire., 1608-10*, p. 506; Blair, *Autobiography*, p. 70; Fulton, 'Roads', pp 134-5, 261, 265; *Cal. pat. rolls Ire., Jas I*, p. 83.

[81] *Cal. S.P. Ire., 1601-3*, p. 454; *Cal. pat. rolls Ire., Jas I*, p. 83.

erection of a bridge on his lands over the river Quoile at Downpatrick he claimed that he had 'lost the great advantage of a beneficial ferry'.[82] Ferry travel, like road travel had its dangers. Supplies brought from Carlingford to Newry by ferry in the early years of the seventeenth century were frequently lost during storms and even if the ferry was not sunk salt water could cause considerable damage to the cargoes.[83]

Rivers were one of the most effective means of communication within Antrim and Down. The Bann, for example, was frequently used to bring goods from the town of Antrim to the coast.[84] With the development of markets the demand for river transport became so great that a number of proposals were made for artificial waterways. In the early stages of the settlement of Antrim there were plans to make the river Lagan navigable as far as Lough Neagh to ship timber out of Killultagh but nothing came of the plan.[85] A similar scheme to straighten and deepen the Lagan was suggested in 1637 by George Rawdon, the agent on the Conway estate to the east of Lough Neagh, who estimated that it would cost £3,000 but that it would add £10,000 per annum to Conway's revenue by improving the marketing of the tenants' produce. Again nothing was done because of fears that the cutting would drain Lough Neagh and the Bann.[86]

If communications within east Ulster were poor, attempts to make contact with the wider world were even more fraught with difficulty. Traditionally Antrim and Down had looked not west for markets and social contacts but south, to the pale. In the 1570s Sir Henry Sidney, a former lord deputy, noted that much of Carrickfergus's trade was southward and lawyers, merchants, and ecclesiastics from the pale all frequented the town. There were also strong landholding connections between the Anglo Irish of the pale and those of Lecale in Down and in 1611 Thomas Barnwall of Sheepland in the barony of Lecale was fined for not attending a jury in Meath where he also had land.[87] In this

[82] *Commons jn. Ire.,* i, pp 370-71.

[83] P.R.O.I., M2441 ff, 6, 18, 37-8.

[84] B.L., Add. 4756, f 121ᵛ; SP63/170/44; *Cal. S.P. Ire., 1600-01,* p. 334; *Cal. pat. rolls Ire., Jas. I,* p. 83.

[85] *Cal. S.P. Ire., 1608-10,* p. 89.

[86] SP63/256/59, 89.

[87] 'Sir Henry Sidney's memoir of his government of Ireland' in *U.J.A.,* 1st ser., iii (1855), p. 96; P.R.O.I., Ferguson MSS IX, p. 24; connections are also shown in C. McNeill, A.J. Otway Ruthven (eds), *Dowdall Deeds* (I.M.C., 1960), nos 240, 499, 607; J.W.H., 'The Anglo-Norman families of Lecale' in *U.J.A.,* 1st ser., i (1853), pp 94-7.

context coastal shipping had considerable importance. During the later stages of the Nine Years War supplies had been shipped along the coast to Newry from Dundalk and Dublin and by the 1620s a flourishing coastal trade had developed between Dublin and east Ulster in grain and other commodities.[88] After 1603 there was increasing communication with west Ulster, especially after boats had been established on Lough Neagh, and by 1611 Sir Thomas Phillips considered it feasible to ship goods from county Londonderry across the lough and then move them to Newry from where they could be exported.[89]

Communications with England and Scotland were more difficult and even a short journey, such as that between east Ulster and Scotland, was frought with problems. The North Channel was frequently rough and crossing it in a small, open boat was uncomfortable as Sir William Brereton discovered when he crossed in 1636 and was violently seasick, and on the Irish coast the ship could not land because of rough weather and the passengers had to swim ashore.[90] Passages were slow, taking up to twelve hours, and ships had to wait for favourable conditions before sailing. Physical hazards were not the only problem as much of the North Channel was pirate infested. Between August and October 1633 the port of Carrickfergus was closed because it was blockaded by pirates from the Isle of Man, and in 1639 the boats of some of the earl of Antrim's tenants attempting to cross from Scotland to Ireland were seized by pirates.[91] The chief problem with communications between east Ulster and England or Scotland was cost. Brereton for instance paid £1 for a boat to carry five men and their horses and a further two shillings was extracted from him illegally on a pretext of customs dues.[92] As movement of settlers from Scotland to Ulster increased, the demand for shipping forced up the rates of carriage so that by 1612 a number of

[88] P.R.O.I., M2441, ff 15, 24, 34; *Cal. S.P. Ire., 1600*, p. 172; P.R.O.N.I., D1071B/B/1, pp 24, 29; D.R. Hainsworth (ed.), *Commercial papers of Sir Christopher Lowther* (Surtees Society, Newcastle-upon-Tyne, 1977), pp 34, 39, 81.

[89] *Cal. S.P. Ire., 1611-14*, p. 227.

[90] G. Boate, *Ireland's natural history* (London, 1652), pp 13, 45-6, 48-51; Bodl., Carte 44, f 343 described the passage as 'broken and dangerous'; Brereton, *Travels*, pp 125-6; he was not alone in this experience, Blair, *Autobiography*, p. 53; SP63/208/5.

[91] Strafford, *Letters*, i, pp 106, 127; ii, p. 340; SP63/229/108; *Cal. S.P. Ire., 1603-6*, p. 295; J. Patterson, *A history of the counties of Ayr and Wigton* (Edinburgh, 1863), p. 71.

[92] Brereton, *Travels*, pp 123-4.

Scots settlers in Ireland, including two from east Ulster, complained to the Scottish Privy Council that the charges for shipping 'are risen to such an extraordinary height as no man shall be able to travel between the said countries'. The problem of the control of charges was referred to J.P.s on the Scottish coast but any action which they took had little effect, and new rates for shipping and machinery for their enforcement had to be devised within four years.[93] So expensive was the move from Scotland to Down that in 1612 James I granted to James Dundas, the newly appointed bishop of Down and Connor, the rents from his churchlands for the year previous to his appointment 'in regard of the great charge he must sustain in transporting himself'.[94] The problem was compounded by the small size of ships that had to be used in the hazardous North Channel, under ten tons in most cases, as Francis Jobson's map of the Ulster coast, drawn in 1598, illustrates.[95] Thus a large number of journeys were necessary to transport any substantial quantity of goods at rates which were very high.

Problems of transport meant that information and news was slow to reach east Ulster. In the case of letters, expense made it necessary to accumulate sufficient letters to merit sending a messenger to Ireland with them. One messenger carrying estate correspondence to George Rawdon, the agent on the Conway estate, waited at a London inn for a week until he considered he had enough letters for Rawdon.[96] Even within Ireland letters took a considerable amount of time by English standards. From Dublin to east Ulster a letter could take between four and twelve days, the average being seven, although one proclamation sent from Dublin on 5 May 1640 had not yet reached Carrickfergus by 18 May.[97] Poor communications meant that merchants had difficulty in circulating information and bills of exchange which discouraged them from settling permanently in east Ulster and hence no substantial merchant community had developed there by 1640. More important was the

---

[93] *Reg.P.C. Scot., 1610-13*, pp 478-9; Bodl., Carte 62, f 384.

[94] *Cal. S.P. Ire., 1611-14*, p. 248.

[95] P.R.O., MPF 312/ 2; Bodl., Carte 62, f 384.

[96] *Cal. S.P. dom., 1631-3*, p. 387.

[97] SL, 19, nos 44, 67, 70, 71, 74, 77, 80, 92, 94, 95; Bodl., Carte 1, f 218; Steele, *Tudor & Stuart proclam.*, ii, no. 335. For comparable English figures, J. Crofts, *Packhourse, wagon and post* (London, 1967), pp 86-8; H. Kamen, *The iron century* (London, 1976), pp 7-9 which suggest four days for a comparable distance.

effect on the settlers who developed a sense of isolation from authority. Sir Edward Cromwell, based at Downpatrick, felt this acutely when faced with the problems of 'how to keep that rebellious nation [the Irish] quiet without means of authority . . . being far from my lord deputy and all civil administration'.[98] This feeling of remoteness from central administration coupled with the desire of many of the new landlords to exploit their holdings in their own interests was to be fundamental in the shaping of the east Ulster settlement. The physical, economic, and political geography set the limits for what the ambitious new settlers could effectively achieve.

---

[98] H.M.C., *Salisbury*, xviii, pp 97, 155.

II

THE HUMAN BACKGROUND

DESPITE PROBLEMS OF geography and communications east Ulster was an attractive area for settlers in the early seventeenth century. It had the advantage of being a wealthy region and the acquisition of wealth was one of the main concerns of the early promoters of colonization. Antrim and Down had a number of other features attractive to potential settlers. The Anglo-Norman lordship, which was established in east Ulster during the thirteenth century, marked it off from the rest of Ulster, and the medieval settlement had established an administrative structure which had survived, at least in name, into the seventeenth century. The Anglo-Norman lordship also gave the crown a claim to title of most of Antrim and Down, a necessary prerequisite of any settlement.[1] Antrim also had the additional advantage of being close to a source of potential colonists, Scotland.

There had been a number of sixteenth-century schemes to colonise east Ulster, the most notable being those of two royal favourites, Sir Thomas Smith and Walter Devereaux, earl of Essex, but none had succeeded to any great extent.[2] As the Nine Years War drew to a close, many men, such as the future lord deputy Sir Arthur Chichester, began to see east Ulster as a suitable outlet for surplus capital and population from England and Scotland and they devised plans for new settlements in county Down.[3] Attempts to attract people to east Ulster were matched by circumstances in England and Scotland which induced certain

[1] See pp 85-6 below.
[2] SP63/23/20,48; SP63/164/47; SP63/21/56; *Sidney S.P.*, no. 42; R. Dunlop, 'Sixteenth century schemes for the plantation of Ulster' in *S.H.R.*, xxii (1924), pp 51-60, 115-26, 199-212.
[3] *Cal. S.P. Ire., 1600,* pp 417-18, 484; *Cal. S.P. Ire., 1601-3*, pp 63-5.

groups in the population to migrate. These groups were well defined; the ambitious, younger sons, and those who wanted an opportunity to reverse declining fortunes. Many of these migrants saw in Antrim and Down the prospect of wealth and the creation of new dynasties which would perpetuate their own names and these views were encouraged by the polemicists of colonisation. The aspirations of these groups did not however have free rein. The native Irish inhabitants also had expectations, shaped by their sixteenth century experience, of how east Ulster should develop and they strove as best they could in the seventeenth century to realise these expectations.

I

Those settlers who moved to Antrim and Down in the early seventeenth century were socially a very diverse group. At the upper end of the scale there were small landowners such as Sir Hugh Montgomery of Braidstane, Ayrshire. Born in 1561, the eldest son of Adam Montgomery, he studied at Glasgow University and soldiered in France and Holland before inheriting the family estate in 1587. By 1600 he had already begun to expand his patrimony both by purchase and by inheritance from other branches of the family.[4] There were also those who enjoyed a high social status but lacked an economic foundation for this. Sir Edward Cromwell of Okeham in county Rutland, for example, wrote to Lord Cecil in 1598 asking for employment under the earl of Essex 'in order to readvance the estate of his decaying house'. His family had been in decline for some time and things had become so bad for Sir Edward that by 1600, he was forced to dispose of most of his English land to pay his debts.[5] Others belong in this group also and include younger sons of important English and Scottish families. Sir Fulke Conway, Sir Arthur Chichester and Sir Faithful Fortescue, all major Antrim landowners, are examples of younger sons who had little or no patrimony in England but saw prospects of advancement in the fluid Irish land market. Sir Fulke, for example even claimed that 'his father never gave him anything for his advantage' even though the family was

---

[4] *Mont. MSS*, p. 10; B.L., Add. 4820 ff 30-33.

[5] H.M.C., *Salisbury*, viii, p. 421; Stone, *Crisis*, pp 485, 778.

in a comfortable financial position in England.[6]

From a slightly lower level on the social scale small landowners and substantial tenants on estates in England and Scotland came to Ulster in the hope of advancement. Thomas Nevin, the brother of the laird of Monkredding, in Ayrshire, left a large holding in Scotland to settle on an even larger one at Ballycopeland under Sir Hugh Montgomery. He later returned to Scotland and died there in 1651, leaving his county Down land to his son.[7] A second example from this group of migrants is David Boyd, one of the five largest tenants on Sir Hugh Montgomery's estate and brother of Lord Boyd, a prominent Ayrshire landholder. David Boyd owned a small estate in Ayrshire which had been built up by his father in the late sixteenth century and added to by himself in the early seventeenth.[8] Similarly Patrick Montgomery of Blackhouse in the parish of Largs, Ayrshire, who also settled under Sir Hugh, was a small landowner in Scotland.[9] From England, George Carnock of Maldon in Essex who settled in north Antrim also belonged to this group.[10] By the 1630s the movement of the elite of Scottish tenants, the leaseholders, from Scotland to Ireland was so appreciable that the Scottish Privy Council, fearing that the supply of reliable tenants for Scottish landlords would dry up, ruled that no tenant was to move to Ulster without the permission of his landlord.[11]

The status of migrants below these two relatively high social groups is difficult to determine but it is clear there was a wide social spread. Large numbers of landless labourers moved to east Ulster as did persons fleeing from justice in Scotland and England. The proximity of east Ulster to Scotland and the lack of checks on migrants made it easy for criminals

[6] SL 24/25, no. 351; *Cal. S.P. dom., 1591-4*, p. 280. Victoria County History, *Warwickshire*, iii (London, 1945), pp 180, 279-80; Lord Clermont, *A history of the family of Forescue* (London, 1869), pp 75-6; Devon Record Office, 1262M/F83; *D.N.B.*, sub Sir Edward Conway, Sir Arthur Chichester.

[7] G.F. Savage-Armstrong, *A genealogical history of the Savage family in Ulster* (London, 1906), p. 201; J. Patterson, *A history of the county of Ayr*, ii (Ayr, 1847), p. 253.

[8] J. Fullerton (ed.), T. Pont, *Topographical account of the district of Cunningham* (Glasgow, 1858), p. 31; S.R.O., GD 90/1/207; GD86/554, GD8/388, 470, 500, 612, 620, 628, 682; *Inquisitionum ad capellam domini regis retornatarum quae in publicis archivis Scotiae*, i, Ayr, nos 18, 99, 102.

[9] *Inq. in publicis archivis Scot.*, i, Ayr, no. 258.

[10] F.O. Fisher, *Memoirs of the Camacs of county Down* (Norwich, 1887), pp 72, 75.

[11] *Reg. P.C. Scot., 1635-7*, p. 198.

and the profits of their crime, especially stolen horses, to pass with little hindrance to Ulster.[12] There were frequent complaints that criminals from Scotland were sheltered by east Ulster landlords because tenants were in short supply. John Bramhall, the bishop of Derry, alleged in 1634 that landlords sheltered 'dangerous' presbyterians because they 'merely wanted to plant their lands and cared for nothing else.'[13] Attempts were made by the Scottish administration to control this traffic, as in 1624 when an elaborate scheme was drawn up to impose restrictions on movement from Scotland to Ulster. The scheme required certificates to be issued by Scottish J.P.'s to all those intending to go to Ireland, and boatmen who transported persons without a certificate were liable for punishment.[14]

It is clear, therefore, that there was a wide social spread of migrants. The comments of some contemporaries who insisted that only the poor and criminal elements came to Ulster were often exaggerated for their own purposes. The Rev. Andrew Stewart, presbyterian minister of Donaghadee in the 1670s stated that

from Scotland came many, and from England not a few, yet all of them generally the scum of both nations, who, for debt or breaking and fleeing from justice, or seeking shelter, came thither . . . Going for Ireland was looked on as a miserable mark of a deplorable person.[15]

His motivation in so degrading the early settlers was to demonstrate how godly these 'rogues' had become by the 1670s as a result of the efforts of the presbyterian church. Earlier in the 1620s Robin Gordin of Lochinvar claimed the Irish migrants were 'the meaner sort, such as artisans, labourers of the ground who were known to have scarce competent means to defray their passage'. His aim was to emphasise how quickly the migrants rose to wealth as the result of the settlement thus providing a fine example for the settlement of Nova Scotia for which he was recruiting.[16]

---

[12] *Reg. P.C. Scot., 1610-13,* pp 320-21, 624-5; ibid., *1613-16,* pp 210, 519-20; ibid., *1622-5,* p. 20; ibid., *1627-8,* p. 445; ibid., *1632,* pp 175, 545-6, 553; ibid., *1633-5,* p. 449.

[13] *Cal. S.P. Ire., 1611-14,* pp 234, 241; Shirley, *Ch. of Ire., 1631-9,* p. 41.

[14] *Reg. P.C. Scot., 1625-7,* pp 605-6, 621-6, 681.

[15] W.D. Killen (ed.), P. Adair, *A true narrative of . . . the presbyterian church in Ireland* (Belfast, 1866), pp 313-15.

[16] D. Laing (ed.), *Royal letters, charters and tracts relating to the colonization of New Scotland* (Edinburgh, 1867), not paginated; Blair, *Autobiography,* p. 57.

MAP 2: ORIGINS OF SCOTTISH SETTLERS
BY SURNAME, c. 1630.

■   Principal settler

·   One settler

In contrast to their wide social spread, settlers were drawn from fairly restricted geographical areas in both England and Scotland. In the case of Scotland it is possible to deliniate these areas by using the surnames of migrants to east Ulster recorded on the muster roll of *c.* 1630.[17] This is possible because population mobility in late sixteenth and early seventeenth-century Scotland was low and hence surnames can be readily assigned to a particular locality.[18] Such an exercise is of dubious validity for England because of the high mobility of population in certain areas. Thus relatively little can be said with any degree of certainty about the English settlers in east Ulster. The evidence from the surnames of Scottish settlers in Antrim and Down is shown on map 2. The Scottish setlers came, predominantly, from the south west coast and the counties of Lanarkshire, Renfrewshire and Stirlingshire. There was also a substantial minority of east Ulster settlers from Argyllshire and the southernmost Isles, Bute and Arran. The southern uplands and the Borders, Kircudbrightshire and Dumfries, also produced a considerable number of settlers. Most of the English settlers in Antrim and Down appear to have been drawn from Devon, Cheshire and Lancashire.[19] Thus the migrants were socially diverse but geographically restricted in their origins. Yet this does not explain why they migrated nor why they settled in east Ulster rather than another colony nor what shaped their expectations of the settlement of Antrim and Down. The forces which influenced them may be classified into two groups: the push of Scotland or England and the pull of Antrim and Down.

The push factors which created migrants were complex and diverse. Political factors, for example, could force a man to leave his home and become a settler. The political situation in Scotland forced Sir Randal Macdonnell to settle in Antrim even though his main concern continued to be the Scottish branch of his family.[20] The rise of the Campbell family in sixteenth-century Scotland combined with an attack on the Macdonnell lordship of the Isles by the central government led to a collapse of Macdonnell power in Scotland. By 1595 the Macdonnells of

[17] B.L., Add. 4770.
[18] For continuity of tenants see S.R.O., GD 27/1/55, ff 1-2, 29-33; GD109/2957, 2977; G.F. Black, *The surnames of Scotland* (New York, 1946); on England, E. Rich 'The population of Elizabethan England' in *Econ. Hist. Rev.*, 2nd ser., ii (1950), pp 247-65.
[19] Brereton, *Travels*, p. 128; P.R.O.N.I., T811/3.
[20] On Macdonnell, see pp 144.

Kintyre, already in severe economic difficulty, had lost much of their land and influence to the earl of Argyll, Archibald Campbell, and the central administration. Sir Randal Macdonnell, who had been in Ireland since 1595, had no chance of returning to a family inheritance because the lands had been declared confiscate and the family had been discredited in Scotland.[21] Other Scottish settlers had also become discredited because of their political activity, as in the case of James Edmonston, the father of an Antrim settler, who had been involved in the Ruthven raid of 1582.[22] Many of the English and Welsh migrants to east Ulster, such as Sir Edward Cromwell and Sir Richard Trevor, both of whom settled in south Down, had been involved in the abortive conspiracy of the earl of Essex in 1601, and for this reason they also had become discredited at home.[23]

Political factors however affected only a small minority of settlers. The main reasons why men left England and Scotland were social and economic. English and Scottish population rose so rapidly in the late sixteenth and early seventeenth centuries that even contemporary commentators deemed this alone a sufficient reason for migration.[24] One English writer of 1619 advocated that the settlement of Ireland would be 'an easy course for the transport . . . of the superfluous multitudes of poor people which overspill the realm of England to the weal of both kingdoms' and an earlier suggestion had proposed the shipping to Ireland of all those dispossessed by clearances for sheep.[25] The reality was, however, more complex than this. It was the indirect effects of a rising population rather than simple overcrowding which promoted migration. Such effects can be shown most clearly at a regional level and so it is proposed to examine the social and economic structure of south-

---

[21] A. McKerrall, *Kintyre in the seventeenth century* (Edinburgh, 1948), ch. 2; *Reg. P.C. Scot., 1592-9*, p. 321; *Reg. P.C. Scot., 1604-7*, pp 749-50; S.R.O., RH9/4/8; E.J. Cowan, 'Clan, kinship and the Campbell acquisition of Islay' in *S.H.R.*, lviii (1979), pp 132-57.

[22] H.M.C., *Laing*, i, pp 38, 41, 46; H.M.C., *Mar and Kellie*, i, p. 46; W. Nimmo, *A history of Stirlingshire*, ii (Glasgow, 1881), pp 88-9; *Reg. P.C. Scot., 1578-85*, p. 722; *Reg. P.C. Scot., 1585-92*, pp 32-3.

[23] B.L., Sloane 1856, f 22ᵛ; Stone, *Crisis*, pp 231, 238; E.S. Jones, *The Trevors of Trevalyn and their descendants* (n.p., 1955), pp 30-33; A.H. Dodd, 'North Wales in the Essex revolt' in *E.H.R.*, lix (1944), pp 367-9.

[24] M.W. Flinn, *Scottish population history* (Cambridge, 1977), pp 107-32.

[25] B.L., Cotton Titus X B, ff 267-70; Royal 18 A LIII, ff 12ᵛ-13; H.M.C., *Salisbury*, xxi p. 281; *Cal. S.P. Ire., 1608-10*, p. 386; B.L., Add. 41613, f 35.

west Scotland, which was the main source area for the migrants to east Ulster in the early seventeenth century.

All the indicators point to a rapid rise in the population of south-west Scotland in the late sixteenth century. In the poorer areas of Ayrshire land was reclaimed 'through multitudes of houses and industry of the labourers [and] through liming and other husbandry' according to one account in 1627 and as population pressure mounted men moved off the land into nearby towns.[26] Another observer, Thomas Pont, observed as early as 1597 that in the barony of Cunningham, in western Ayrshire, 'the dwellings of the yeomanry are very thickly powdered over the face of this country . . . so that one may wonder how so small a bounds can contain so very many people.'[27] The church responded to this growth in its flock by creating new parishes, four in Ayrshire, two in Galloway, five in Wigton and three in Kircudbrightshire before 1660.[28] Such a growth of population inevitably placed considerable strain on fixed resources and food prices as well as rents, began to rise.[29]

In addition to rising prices and rents other burdens were also imposed on the landholders of south-west Scotland in the late sixteenth and early seventeenth centuries. The most important of these were the reorganisation of the system of tithe collection by the church and the new royal policy towards the Borders and the Isles. As a result of an overhaul in the system of tithe collection in 1617 collection was taken out of the hands of the secular landlord and given to the church and in some areas the tithes were also commuted from kind into cash. As a result collection became more efficient and letters of inhibition were issued against tenants who would not or could not pay. Thus those who had previously evaded payment of tithes were now forced to pay. Tithe was also increased in 1633 from one-tenth to one-eighth of a farmer's produce,

[26] *The state of parishes* (Maitland Club, Glasgow, 1936), p. 193; Flinn, *Scottish population history*, pp 116-32.

[27] Pont, *Topographical account*, p. 6; B.R.S. Megaw, 'The date of Pont's survey and its background' in *Scottish studies*, xiii (1969), pp 71-3.

[28] J. Strawhorne, 'Ayrshire's population' in *Ayrshire archaeological and nat. hist. collections*, 2nd ser., viii (1967-9), p. 12; M. Sanderson, 'Kilwinning at the time of the reformation' in *Ayrshire arch. and nat. hist. collection,* 2nd ser., x (1970-72), pp 122-3. In the Isles new settlements were also created and old ones split (R.A. Dodgshon, *Land and society in early Scotland* (Oxford, 1981) pp 191-2, 197).

[29] Dodgshon, *Land and society*, pp 134-8.

imposing yet a further burden upon him.[30] A second major factor affecting the social and economic climate of late sixteenth and early seventeenth-century south-west Scotland was the introduction of effective royal authority into the Borders and the Isles. This involved the clearance of potential rebels and the installation of loyal tenants in these areas.[31] Many inhabitants fled from the Borders to Ireland to escape execution, while in the Isles the new landowner, the Earl of Argyll, began to remove the tenants of the former landowners the Macdonnells from Argyll, Kintyre and the islands of Bute and Barra.[32] These factors explain why between 1596 and 1605, the amount of waste land in north Kintyre rose from 26 per cent to 41 per cent and from 22 per cent to 25 per cent in south Kintyre.[33] In addition to this the economic forces described above were also placing pressures on the inhabitants of these areas. In this situation migration to Ireland made good sense to many of the inhabitants of the Isles.

Against this picture of apparent decline must be set the considerable growth of the Scottish economy in the late sixteenth and early seventeenth centuries which also had a bearing on the Scots migrating to Ireland. Trade grew, agriculture improved considerably and the relative peace of the reign of James VI allowed considerable economic growth.[34] The ensuing prosperity meant that many landowners and merchants from south-west Scotland began actively to seek outlets for their accumulated capital. Some families extended their landed interests into

[30] A. Cormack, *Teinds and agriculture* (Oxford, 1930); W. Mackey, *The church of the Covenant, 1637-51* (Edinburgh, 1979), ch. I; S.R.O., GD 149/72, 97, 101, 112, 120, 138; GD8/576.

[31] For debts in the Isles, W. Lamont (ed.), *Inventory of Lamont papers* (Edinburgh, 1914), pp 20, 111-13, 125, 126, 170-71; F. Shaw, 'Landownership in the western Isles in the seventeenth century' in *S.H.R.*, lvi (1977), pp 43-5; R.A. Dodgshon, 'Agricultural change and its social consequences in the southern uplands, 1600-1780' in T.M. Devine, D. Dickson, (eds.), *Ireland and Scotland 1600-1850*, (Edinburgh, 1983) pp 48-53; Reg. P.C. Scot., 1635-7, p. 18.

[32] *Cal. S.P. Ire., 1606-8*, pp 193, 223; McKerral, *Kintyre*, p. 27; H.M.C., *6th Report*, pp 611-12; G. Hill, 'Gleanings in family history from the Antrim coast' in *U.J.A.*, 1st ser., viii (1860), pp 139-40, 200; on the Borders, B.S. Turner, 'An observation on settler names in Fermanagh' in *Clogher Record*, viii (1973-6), pp 285-9.

[33] J.R.S. McPhaill (ed.), *Highland papers*, iii (Scottish History Society, Edinburgh, 1920), pp 72, 79.

[34] T.M. Devine, S.G.E. Lythe, 'The economy of Scotland under James VI' in *S.H.R.*, l (1971), pp 93-5, 105.

the Isles during James's abortive plantation of the island of Lewis in 1597 and others (such as the three sons of James Boswell of Auchinleck who went to Sweden and the Kirkubrightshire landlord, Sir Robert Gordon, who settled in Nova Scotia) went further but the most usual destination for the adventurers was Ulster.[35]

It was from the products of this set of economic conditions that the east Ulster settlers were to be gathered and the way in which they had reacted to the Scottish economic situation was to determine their attitude to Ireland. Some Scottish landowners who moved to east Ulster, such as Archibald Edmonston of Stirlingshire, were in a poor financial condition. The Edmonstons had made the mistake of making long grants of land at fixed rents in the early sixteenth century so that by the end of a century which experienced rapid inflation their real income had been considerably eroded. Throughout the late sixteenth century the members of this family had mortgaged most of their lands and by 1606 they had begun to sell part of the estate in order to meet the mortgage repayments. Further mortgages were made between 1606 and 1610 but these did not improve the family's position and in 1609 letters of horning for debt were sued out against Archibald and finally, in 1614, the whole estate was mortgaged as a block to Sir William Graham of Braid in Stirlingshire. As a result of this background Edmonston's main aim in east Ulster was to make enough profit to redeem the mortgages on the family's Scottish property, a task which he had achieved by 1630.[36] Edmonston's career can be mirrored by that of his brother-in-law, William Adair, a settler in mid-Antrim. William's father, Ninian, had been mortgaging the family property in Wigtonshire since the 1590s but this had done little to alleviate his economic plight for he was horned for debt in 1608. His son inherited the lands the same year but the situation did not improve and by the 1630s he had sold most of the Scottish lands to Sir Hugh Montgomery, the north Down settler, and he had moved to north Antrim.[37]

[35] McKerrall, *Kintyre*, p. 93; Patterson, *History of Ayr*, i, p. 238; ii, pp 17, 190.

[36] *Reg. P.C. Scot., 1604-7*, pp 253, 281, 660; *Reg. P.C. Scot., 1607-10*, p. 264; S.R.O., GD97/1/161, 186, 192, 202, 274, 324, 386, 403; GD97/2/3/313, 333, 334; H.M.C., *Various*, v. pp 137-9.

[37] S.R.O., GD154/75, 80; E. Suffolk R.O. HA12/A2/1/37; *Reg. P.C. Scot., 1607-10*, pp 3, 14, 168; *Reg. P.C. Scot., 1619-22*, p. 374; J. Patterson, *A history of lands and their owners in Galloway and Wigtonshire*, i (Edinburgh, 1870), pp 84-6; S.R.O., GD 237/171.

Other landowners who moved to Ulster did so as part of the expansion generated by the economic environment of Scotland. The Scottish land market in the late sixteenth and early seventeenth centuries was sluggish, and little church land was available because most of it had been granted on feu charters in the early sixteenth century.[38] In desperation Sir Hugh Montgomery attempted in the early 1600s to expand his small Scottish estate by purchase and inheritance from adjoining landlords, but this method only allowed for limited expansion.[39] Therefore, even before the rebellion in 1601 of Conn O'Neill, the chief lord of north Down, Montgomery had decided that 'Ireland must be the stage to act upon' and from which he could expect rapid returns.[40] The Agnew family of Loughnaw in Galloway were also in a position to expand in the early seventeenth century. They purchased a considerable amount of land from improvident neighbours in Scotland and in the 1630s expanded into south Antrim by becoming substantial tenants of the earl of Antrim.[41]

A third reaction by Scottish landlords to the economic changes of the late sixteenth century, that of estate reorganisaton and rationalisation of tenures, also had a significant impact on the supply of settlers for east Ulster. In order to combat the economic problem of rising prices and static rents many landlords in south-west Scotland set about reorganizing their estates. First they recast the tenurial structure of their lands. This involved the removal of the 'kindly tenants' (tenants-at-will with no rights to their lands other than tradition) or the conversion of them into rentallers (leaseholders) at a greatly increased rent. The earl of Cassills removed a considerable number of kindly tenants from his estate in Dumfries and Galloway as did other landlords in Ayrshire.[42] Other disadvantageous tenures such as feuing (the granting of land to a tenant by a charter with a high entry fine (a grassum) and a relatively low

---

[38] M. Sanderson, 'The feuars of kirklands' in *S.H.R.*, lii (1973), pp 117-36.

[39] S.R.O., Acts and decrees of the Lords of Session, 194, f 324.

[40] *Mont. MSS*, pp 19-20; N.L.S., Denmilne MSS, 6 no. 53.

[41] S.R.O., GD 154.

[42] H. Maxwell, *A history of Dumfries and Galloway* (Dumfries, 1896), pp 228-9; Patterson, *History of Ayr*, ii, p. 48; R. Van Agnew (ed.), 'Letters by John, fifth earl of Cassills' in *Arch. coll. relating to Ayr and Galloway*, 1st ser., v (1885), pp 194-5; S.R.O., GD180/91; GD 219/6; GD 25/8/138A; GD25/9/78; I.D. Whyte, *Agriculture and society in seventeenth century Scotland* (Edinburgh, 1979), pp 30-32; Dodgshon, *Land and society*, pp 201, 269.

rent) were also attacked by landlords. Feuing was most common in north Ayrshire and south Renfrewshire and in these areas landlords began to raise the nominal rents on the land by augmentation and to force many small owners to leave their holdings. Many feuers tried to keep their heads above water but failed. Lawrence Young, who held lands near the town of Ayr in the late sixteenth century, mortgaged his lands twice to burgesses of Ayr before admitting defeat, then sold his land to the earl of Eglinton, the major landholder in the area, and finally, moved to Ireland. Robert Stewart of Gass, in south Ayrshire, also made several attempts to make his holding viable by mortgages before leaving Scotland for east Ulster.[43] It was at the expense of many of these feuers that most landlords in south-west Scotland expanded and consolidated their hold on their estates. The earl of Eglinton, for example, expanded his sizeable estate in west Ayrshire by absorbing a large number of surrounding small landowners.[44] A second element in the reorganisation of estates by Scottish landlords was the increasing of rents, in one case by up to 410 per cent, between 1620 and 1641. Some rents, formerly paid in kind, such as on the Bargany estate in south Ayrshire, were commuted to cash payments and the rent was increased in the process.[45] Such leases as were made were short, usually nineteen years, which enabled rent to be raised in line with inflation as the leases were renewed.[46] The fate of those who could not pay the increased rent was simple — eviction.[47]

Growing population, tenurial reorganisation and rent increases in early seventeenth-century south-west Scotland created a pool of people who had been deprived of land and had little prospect of obtaining new holdings. Nor had they much chance of moving into domestic industry for this sector of the economy was poorly developed in Scotland. Many of these men were looking for outlets for what little capital they had and an opportunity to reverse their ill fortune, and Ireland provided a rich

[43] S.R.O., GD180/367; GD25/8/95, 183; M. Sanderson, 'The social and economic implications of the feuing of ecclesiastical property in Scotland' (Ph.D. thesis, Edinburgh, 1972) pp 390-92.
[44] S.R.O., GD8/582, 617, 667; Sanderson, 'Implications of feuing', p. 394.
[45] S.R.O., GD25/9/475; GD26/9/48; GD27/1/55, ff 36-7, 47; RH15/39/2.
[46] I.D. Whyte, 'Written leases and their impact on Scottish agriculture' in *Ag. H.R.,* xxvii (1979), pp 2-8; S.R.O., 5/9/73-4; RH15/91/11/4.
[47] S.R.O., GD39/1/78; GD103/2/113; GD25/185a-b; GD86/386, 426; GD10/972, 976, 977, 978, 981, 982; Pont, *Topographical account*, pp 117-24.

field. William Brereton, travelling through south-west Scotland in the 1630s, judged that it was this state of affairs which contributed most to the decision of an individual to migrate to Ireland.[48] Similar economic profiles could probably be constructed for English areas from which, it appears, settlers moved to east Ulster. Devon, for example, had a rapidly growing population in the late sixteenth century but the economy, like that of south-west Scotland, was mainly pastoral and hence did not require intensive labour. Rents also rose as the increased population placed pressure on the limited resources of good land. Thus Devon was a fruitful source of colonists, not only for Ireland but also for America, in the early seventeenth century.[49]

The pull factors which brought these men, who were migrants by virtue of economic or political circumstances in Scotland and England, to east Ulster, were diverse. The economic attractions of cheap land with secure title, woodlands and fishings were powerful magnets. East Ulster was also widely known about in late sixteenth-century south-west Scotland because of trading contacts between Antrim and Ayrshire. Sir Hugh Montgomery, for example, was looking to east Ulster as a possible area of expansion before 1603.[50] Many future settlers were already in Ireland in the late sixteenth century. Discharged soldiers from the army which had come to Ulster during the Nine Years War were also an important recruiting ground for settlers. These men knew the country as a result of the military campaigns in which they had participated and often had little incentive to return to England. Sir Edward Trevor, of Brynkinalt in north Wales, who settled in south Down, and John Dalway who settled in south Antrim had both come to east Ulster as officers in the army of the earl of Essex in the late sixteenth century, as had Sir Arthur Chichester, the future lord deputy, who became governor of Carrickfergus in 1603 and subsequently settled there.[51] Others acquired

[48] Brereton, *Travels*, p. 119.

[49] E.A. Wrigley, 'Family limitation in pre-industrial England' in *Econ. Hist. Rev.*, 2nd ser., xix (1966), pp 84-6; W.J. Blake, 'Hooker's "Synopsis chorographical of Devonshire" ' in *Reports and Transactions of the Devonshire Assoc.*, xxxvii (1915), pp 343-7; W.G. Hoskins' 'The reclamation of waste in Devon' in *Econ. Hist. Rev.*, 1st ser., xiii (1943), pp 80-92; R.D. Brown, 'Devonians and the New England settlement' in *Rep. and Trans. of Devon Assoc.*, lxxxxv (1963), pp 221-2. I am indebted to Michael McCarthy Morrogh for a discussion on the role of Devon in the Munster settlement.

[50] *Mont. MSS*, pp 16, 20.

[51] A.T. Lee, 'Notes on bawnes' in *U.J.A.*, 1st ser, vi (1858), p. 128; A.H. Dodd, *Studies in Stuart Wales* (Cardiff, 1971), p. 83; other cases of this include Moses Hill,

land in Ulster for different reasons. Many clergy in east Ulster were able to accumulate enough capital from their own kinsmen and from their livings to purchase lands. Both Alexander Colville, the precentor of Connor, and Robert Echlin, bishop of Down from 1613 until 1635, built up considerable landed estates in east Ulster. Echlin's income of at least £550 per annum from his benefice enabled him to purchase lands from the Savage family in the Ards, to make loans to Lord Cromwell at Downpatrick and to build an imposing house at Ardquin near Portaferry in east Down.[52] Sir James Hamilton, who became one of the main landholders in north Down, had been in Dublin since 1588, firstly as a school master, then, in 1591, as one of the fellows of the infant Trinity College, and finally, since the position at the college was not lucrative enough, as an agent for James VI of Scotland at the English court. This latter position enabled him, after James's accession to the English throne, to acquire his north Down lands.[53]

When many of these late sixteenth-century settlers acquired their lands in the early seventeenth century they brought other men to join them. Hamilton, for example, brought his five brothers to Ireland and set them up in estates.[54] Sir Arthur Chichester also hoped to benefit his

Marmaduke Whitechurch and Humphrey Norton (*Cal. S.P. Ire., 1598-9*, pp 241, 244, 249; SP63/206/87). Soldiers often remained as tenants to their former officer such as Richard West who settled under his former commander, Lord Cromwell, in Lecale and John Lloyd of Basidris, north Wales, who settled under Trevor (*Cal. S.P. Ire., 1608-10*, p.79; *Cal. S.P. Ire., 1615-25*, p. 491; N.L.W., Cross of Shaw Hill MSS, Deeds, no. 174).

[52] For Echlin, P.R.O.N.I., LPC 13763; R.E. Parkinson, *The city of Down* (Belfast, 1928) pp 35-6; D.M. Waterman, 'A vanished Ulster house: Echlinville, county Down' in *U.J.A.*, 3rd ser. xxiii (1960) p. 124. For Colville, P.R.O.N.I., D671/D3/2/18; D671/D3/2/2; P.R.O.I., D15,239, D15240.

[53] J.T. Gilbert (ed.), *Calendar of the ancient records of Dublin,* ii (Dublin, 1891), p. 219; J.P. Mahaffy (ed.), *The particular book of Trinity College, Dublin* (London, 1904), pp 5, 66; H.M.C., *Salisbury,* x, pp 266, 291; H.M.C., *Salisbury,* xv, p. 380; H.M.C., *L'Isle and Dudley,* ii, p. 480; J. Cameron (ed.), *The letters of John Johnston and Robert Howie* (Edinburgh, 1963), p. 184; Hamilton came from an important Scottish landed family, the Hamiltons of Raplock, which had been in decline in 1571. His father was vicar of Dunlop in north Ayrshire; J.S. Dobie, 'The church of Dunlop' in *Arch. coll. relating to Ayrshire and Galloway*, 1st ser., iv (1884), p. 29; N.L.I., MS8792/2; M. Sanderson, 'Some aspects of the church and Scottish society in the era of the reformation' in *Records of the Scottish church history society*, xvii (1972), p. 45; Sanderson, 'Implications of feuing', p. 463.

[54] H.M.C. *Hastings,* iv, p. 164; *Ham. MSS*, p. 12; P.R.O.N.I., T808/2758.

family since in June 1605 he wrote to his brother-in-law, John Trevelyn: 'finding the uncertainty of our profession [the army] and means of raising my fortunes and others of my blood by the course we began in the wars, I have advised to settle them in part of the waste lands in the north within my government of Knockfergus, where they shall have some scope to work on'.[55] In the same year he attempted to obtain the castle of Toome for 'an honest kinsman of mine' but he failed. Chichester also introduced to east Ulster members of families with which he had been connected in Devon, including Sir Hugh Clotworthy, Sir Hercules Langford and Humphrey Norton, and when Sir Hugh Montgomery settled in north Down he brought with him a considerable number of his Scottish friends and relations.[56] Even small settlers, such as William Adair in mid-Antrim brought with them some of their Scottish tenants to settle on their east Ulster lands.[57] Many smaller tenants were recruited through similar networks of kinship or friendship since landlords wanted reliable tenants who could afford the rent and would not strip the assets from their holdings. Sir Hugh Montgomery, for instance, recruited tenants for his Down lands from among his followers on his Scottish estate, and Sir George Rawdon, agent on Lord Conway's estate in south-west Antrim, recruited most of the tenants from his master's Warwickshire lands.[58]

Thus, bonds of kinship, obligation, tenure or simply friendship drew together men who were the products of a particular set of economic and social circumstances in England and Scotland. Rising population placed increasing pressure on land and reduced the outlets for the ambitious and the younger sons at home. Under similar strains many men declined in fortune. Others left their holdings under pressure from landlords who were increasing rents and reorganising the letting of their lands. All

[55] T. Birch (ed.), *A collection of the state papers of John Thurloe*, v, pt 3 (London, 1742), p. 81.

[56] *Cal. S.P. Ire., 1603-6*, p. 341; *Cal. S.P. Ire., 1601-3*, p. 635; J.C. Roberts, 'The parliamentary representatives of Devon and Dorset, 1589-1601 (M.A., London, 1958), app. 1, 3; Perceval Maxwell, *Scottish migration*, p. 58. In addition to this, Edmonston had held lands from Montgomery at Braidstane since 1588 (*Reg. P.C. Scot., 1585-92*, p. 243). Links can also be established between the Adair, Montgomery and McClelland families who all settled in east Ulster. J. Patterson, *A history of the counties of Ayr and Wigtonshire*, ii (Ayr, 1964), p. 20.

[57] *Registrum magni sigilli regnum Scotorum, 1620-33*, no. 206.

[58] *Mont. MSS*, p. 43; *Cal. S.P. dom., 1635-6*, p. 450.

these men joined the pool of potential migrants and all had one ambition in common — to rise in the world. The availability of lands in east Ulster after 1603 offered the prospect of fulfilling that ambition.

II

Like the expectations of the settlers the expectations of the native Irish of east Ulster were shaped by their sixteenth-century experience. East Ulster in the late sixteenth century was a border area in which three groups sought influence: the English administration, the earl of Tyrone from the west and the Scottish Macdonnells from the north. The Macdonnells were a relatively minor force until the early years of the seventeenth century, the main contenders for influence in east Ulster being the Tyrone O'Neills and the Dublin administration. In this situation the reaction of the native Irish of east Ulster was to sway with the political wind and back the group whose influence prevailed at any time; an attitude of expediency. This ability of the native Irish to move with changing political realities was commented on by most of the sixteenth-century English writers on east Ulster and the possibility of winning over the natives of east Ulster became an important part of English policy in east Ulster during the late sixteenth century.

Sir Henry Bagnall emphasised how his father, Sir Nicholas, through his settlement at Newry had won over Sir Hugh Magennis, the chief gaelic lord of county Down, from allegiance to the O'Neills to hold his lands from the queen. Even the lord deputy in the 1580s, Sir John Perrott, believed that the Irish could be won over to hold their lands from the queen and he tried to implement policies reflecting such a view. An account of the state of the realm made by the lord deputy in 1594 went as far as to emphasise the loyalty of the Antrim and Down natives and to argue that they were only in rebellion because of pressure from Brian McArt O'Neill, the earl of Tyrone's nephew. Again in 1596 the governor of Carrickfergus, Charles Egerton, was so convinced of the loyalty of Neal McHugh O'Neill, the lord of Lower Clandeboy, that he put him in charge of Belfast Castle, a key strongpoint in the defence of the whole of east Ulster. The problem was how to win the potentially loyal natives away from the influence of the earl of Tyrone, a dilemma to which one of a series of questions propounded by the lords of the council in 1598 for the prosecution of the rebels in Ulster addressed itself.[59] This policy of winning the natives of Antrim and Down away from the O'Neills showed itself further in the 1598 grant of the castle of Belfast to Sir Ralph Lane, an inveterate coloniser and expert on military fortification, when he was instructed 'to take from the woodmen of these parts, such bonnaughts as they have answered to the earl of Tyrone or the Scots, if you can win the goodwill of the captains of those countries'. Tyrone, on the other hand, claimed authority over Antrim and Down and was prepared to exercise it.[60]

This analysis of 1598 was reasonable on the basis of the political geography of Ulster in the late sixteenth century. The earl of Tyrone's lines of communication were rarely strong enough for him to reach into Antrim and Down and so these two counties were regarded as separate from his main area of control. In 1573, for example, O'Cahan in north Derry had been 'wearied with Turlough Lenoghe's impositions and wanted to bring all his cattle over the Bann into Clandeboy' where he might hold his land at a fixed rent from the queen 'and be rid of Turlough and the Scots'.[61] The Bann was regarded as an important dividing line and the archbishop of Cashel argued that if it were fortified it would stop the Scots moving from Clandeboy to Tyrone.[62] Thus the political geography of Antrim and Down was dominated by whoever could command the most support at any one time. In late 1579 and early 1580 for instance Magennis resisted attempts by Turlough O'Neill to push him into rebellion because there was an English garrison on his doorstep at Newry. In August 1580 his refusal to defect resulted in a major raid on his lands by Turlough. When, on 29 August, he wrote to Lord Deputy Grey asking for aid none came and so by 4 September Magennis was forced into rebellion.[63] A similar pattern of events surrounds the involvement of Magennis in the Nine Years War. In the late 1580s Magennis had repeatedly complained to Dublin that O'Neill was raiding his lands and these complaints culminated in April 1593 when he warned Bagnall that Tyrone was planning a rebellion. Rebellion broke out in late 1593 and by August 1594 Antrim and Down had been invaded

---

[59] *Cal. Carew, 1575-88*, pp 436-7; *Cal. Carew, 1589-1600*, pp 28, 93, 288; Perrott, *Chron. Ire., 1584-1608*, pp 35-6; SP63/53/46-7; SP63/188/67v.

[60] *Fiants Eliz.*, no. 6235; Hayes-McCoy, *Scots mercenary forces*, p. 79.

[61] B.L., Add. 48015, ff 305-15; SP63/48/58.

[62] *Cal. S.P. Ire., 1588-92*, p. 492.

[63] *Cal. S.P. Ire., 1574-85*, pp 202, 204, 246; SP63/76/7; Bagwell, *Tudors*, iii, p. 64.

by Brian McArt O'Neill. Although Magennis had not yet gone into rebellion he was paying 'protection money' to the O'Neills and as one contemporary observed of the outbreak of the war 'those of Lecale and Little Ards be for the queen but overcome by Tyrone they were forced to give way to him'.[64]

In reality the main external influence on the gaelic Irish of east Ulster in the late sixteenth century was that of the Dublin administration. The main aim of the central administration was the limitation of the power of the greater gaelic lords which they tried to achieve in two ways. First the Dublin government became involved in local native Irish power struggles in an attempt to turn them to its advantage. The dispute over the Magennis succession in 1596 provides an example of government action in this way. Sir Hugh Magennis died on 12 January 1596 leaving his eldest son, Sir Arthur, appointed as a successor but Glasney McAwley Magennis of the Clanconnell branch of the family, backed by Tyrone, claimed succession by the traditional Irish right of tanistry. The government in Dublin backed Sir Arthur while still conciliating Glasney McAwley so that by 1599 not only was Sir Arthur holding his father's lands but Glasney had agreed to serve the queen.[65] Secondly, sixteenth-century English writers on Antrim and Down all agreed that the crucial relationship was that of master and man, a relationship they tried to control. In 1576, for example, the government's response to Magennis's petition to hold his lands from the queen was that he should hold his own lands from the queen and be made a baron but that he should create many freeholders in his country to hold lands directly from the queen in order to counterbalance his power. Later in the 1590s, the chief justice of common pleas, Sir William Weston, in his analysis of the methods for the reformation of Down concluded that the creation of freeholders was the best way to enforce law and order in the counties.[66] Large numbers of freeholders holding directly from the queen meant that the greater Gaelic lords could no longer command large hostings in the field since their number of dependants were greatly reduced and it also curbed their prestige which was measured by the numbers of their followers. As a

---

[64] *Cal. S.P. Ire., 1592-6*, pp 95, 149.

[65] *Cal. Carew, 1589-1600*, pp 136, 180-81; *Cal. S.P. Ire., 1592-6*, p. 457; *Cal. S.P. Ire., 1600*, p. 25; E.D. Atkinson, 'The Magennises of Clanconnell' in *U.J.A.*, 2nd ser., 1 (1895), p. 31; *Cal. S.P. Ire., 1598-9*, p. 168.

[66] SP63/171/21; *Cal. Carew, 1575-88*, p. 36.

result there were a number of attempted territorial redistributions in the sixteenth century which tried to create freeholders. In 1589 and 1592 for example there was a redistribution in Clandeboy when those gentlemen who were previously lords under Shane Oge Neale O'Neill were created freeholders who owed allegiance directly to the queen.[67]

The sixteenth century experience had established the ideas and aims of English policy among the native Irish inhabitants of east Ulster and gave them the basic skills for political — if not economic — survival under the new order. The expectations of the Gaelic Irish lords in the early seventeenth century were of continued survival and adaptation to the new order as had been the case in the late sixteenth century. The extent to which the aspirations of both settler and native, created by their sixteenth-century experience, were to be fulfilled, was determined by the evolving social and economic structure of east Ulster.

---

[67] SP63/140/61; SP63/167/366; Perrott, *Chron. Ire., 1584-1608*, p. 36; Healy, *Stolen waters*, pp 30-31.

III

THE DEMOGRAPHIC
STRUCTURE

ONE OF THE MAIN barriers to fulfilling the expectations of both settlers and natives in east Ulster was the level of population since this affected aspects of the settlement as diverse as economic growth and government administration. It is extremely difficult to quantify the population of east Ulster in the late sixteenth century but it is clear that it was low. In 1586, Sir John Perrott, the lord deputy, justified a grant of the Route, in north Antrim, to Sorley Boy Macdonnell on the basis that the existing owner, Rory McQuillan, did not have enough followers to occupy it. Later, in 1593, Sir William Weston, chief justice of common pleas, on assize in Antrim, commented that Antrim and Down were 'very slenderly inhabited, and a great part thereof, very good and fruitful land, do lie desolate'.[1] The already low population almost certainly fell in the 1590s as a result of the Nine Years War since both military casualties and migration out of east Ulster, forced by lord deputy Mountjoy's 'scorched earth' policy in the closing stage of the war, combined to reduce population levels.[2] The years immediately after the peace of 1603 were characterised by poor harvests and a severe outbreak of influenza which did little to improve the situation. It was clear that in the early seventeenth century the population would have to rise if the settlement was to

---

[1] *Cal. S.P. Ire., 1592-6*, p. 141; *Acts privy council, 1590*, pp 50-1; B.L., Cotton Titus B XII, ff 445, 448.

[2] After the nine years war there were a number of complaints of the low population of east Ulster. North Down was described as 'depopulated and wasted' and Sir Randal Macdonnell found his lands so underpopulated that he requested an abatement of rent for two years. P.R.O.I., Ferguson MSS ix, pp 84-5; *Cal. S.P. Ire., 1603-6*, p. 267; *Cal. S.P. Ire., 1606-8*, p. 403; P.R.O.N.I., T618/1; *Ham. MSS*, Appendix 1, p. i.

be put on a viable footing and the expectations of the settlers of east Ulster fulfilled. The whole settler system of local government, for example, depended on a pool of settlers who could be drawn on for juries, commissions and local offices since in the early stages of the settlement it was felt that the native Irish could not be relied on to operate the common law processes impartially. Moreover, one of the ways in which seventeenth-century commentators judged the health and prestige of any settlement was its level of population. As one political theorist observed 'one should never be afraid of having too many subjects . . . for the strength of the commonwealth is in men'.[3]

People were a vital economic asset in the settlement since labour was the most important factor of production in this, as in any pre-industrial economy. It appears that men providing specialised services, such as carpenters, masons, and traders for instance, were not numerous in the Irish economy in the sixteenth century, and so skilled labour had to be attracted to the east Ulster settlement. Even ordinary tenants were an important economic asset, since the bulk of a landowner's income came from his rents. In the sixteenth century the native lords had gone to such lengths to retain their followers, who were sources of prestige as well as cash and food, that the English observers branded them as despots.[4] A shortage of tenants had been felt by the few sixteenth-century settlers in east Ulster. The 1574 grant to the earl of Essex of lands in Antrim, for example, had specified that his lands should be bounded 'that we [the queen] may understand who shall be our tenants and who the earl's [of Tyrone]'.[5] This concern to establish and retain tenants carried on into the seventeenth century and on one occasion, in 1637, it was the tenants rather than the land which was the main attraction in the sale of part of one estate. The point was again underlined in 1641 when it was for the loss of an economic asset rather than for the act of murder that Gilduff O'Cahan cursed his eldest son who had murdered one of Gilduff's tenants during the Portnaw 'massacre'.[6] Thus, to meet immediate needs

[3] M. Campbell, 'Of people either too few or too many' in W.A. Aiken, B.D. Henning, *Conflict in Stuart England* (London, 1960), p. 177; D.C. Coleman, 'Labour in the English economy in the seventeenth century' in *Econ. Hist. Rev.*, 2nd ser., viii (1955-6), pp 280, 292-3.

[4] SP63/171/30; *Cal. pat. rolls Ire., Hen. VIII-Eliz.*, pp 228-9; K.W. Nicholls, *Land, law and society in sixteenth century Ireland* (National University of Ireland, 1976), p. 11.

[5] *Cal. S.P. Ire., 1601-3*, p. 589; B.L., Cotton Titus B X, f 204ᵛ.

[6] H.M.C., *Various*, v, pp 140-41; T.C.D., MS 838, ff 24-6ᵛ.

the low level of native population had to be increased by migration from Scotland and England to tenant the new settler estates and to provide the personnel to operate juries and the local administration. In the wider context of the Ulster plantation, Sir Arthur Chichester, the lord deputy, had argued that if sufficient numbers of people were not imported the main aim of the plantation would have failed and for this reason each undertaker in the plantation was required to import a specified number of settlers.[7] Similar considerations explain why the king's letter which granted the lands of north Down to James Hamilton in 1605 contained a clause that 'the aforesaid James Hamilton should promise to inhabit the said territory and lands with English and Scotchmen'.[8]

There had been some early migration to the coastal areas of Antrim and Down by Scottish islanders in the sixteenth century but the impact of this was limited. The movement into the Glens of Antrim by Scots was sporadic, even regarded by some commentators as seasonal, between May and the harvest. Since the leaders of these Scots all had political and economic interests in Scotland, these concerns took precedence over their Irish ventures. Only Sorley Boy, the younger son of Alexander Macdonnell, lord of Isla, Kintyre and the Glens, took any sustained interest in Ulster and even this was intermittent.[9] There was also some sixteenth-century Scottish migration to the wooded areas of east Down, the Dufferin. The landowners in this area, the White family, were frequently absent, so that by the 1550s the Scots had begun using it as a base in Down since they met little resistance there and by the 1570s they had penetrated into the adjoining baronies of Ards and Lecale.[10] The numbers involved in these movements were small, six or seven hundred estimated in the early part of 1567 and eight or nine hundred later that year and few families from this phase of the migration survived into the seventeenth century.[11]

---

[7] SP63/229/126; Hill, *Plantation*, p. 83; T.W. Moody, 'Ulster plantation papers' in *Anal. Hib.*, viii (1938), no. 4.

[8] *Ham. MSS*, Appendix p. 1; J. Maidment (ed.), 'Letters and papers relative to Irish matters from the Balfour MSS' in *Abbotsfort Club Miscellany* (Edinburgh, 1838), p. 271.

[9] SP63/72/53; SP63/102/21; G.A. Hayes-McCoy, *Scots mercenary forces in Ireland* (London, 1937), pp 12, 25-6.

[10] *Cal. S.P. Ire., 1509-73*, pp 111, 118, 245, 444; N. Canny, 'Rowland White's "Discours of Ireland" ' in *I.H.S.*, xx (1976-7), p. 440; 'Marshal Bagenal's description of Ulster' in *U.J.A.*, 1st ser., ii (1854), p. 153.

[11] For estimates of numbers, *Cal. S.P. Ire., 1509-73*, pp 261, 350; SP63/20/93; Bodl., Laud 612, f 41; *Cal. S.P. Ire., 1574-85*, p. 155; Hayes-McCoy, *Mercenary forces*, p. 35.

It was only in the early years of the seventeenth century that movement of settlers to east Ulster began in earnest. The chronology of the
movement can be roughly illustrated by the number of letters of denization sued out by settlers.[12] There are difficulties in interpreting these,
principally because of the time lag between settlement and the grant of
denization, but the letters represent a significant sample of migrants
who settled in east Ulster since failure to become a denizen of Ireland
meant that a settler could not carry out any legal transactions there.
Thus, David Boyd, for example, who acquired lands from Conn O'Neill
and Sir Hugh Montgomery in 1606-7, failed to become a denizen and on
his death in 1626 the lands were declared forfeit and his son was forced
to petition the English Privy Council for a regrant.[13] The pattern of
grants of denization suggests that the migration began slowly and speeded up during the second decade of the century but fell off thereafter
apart from a slight revival in the 1630s. This pattern is confirmed by
other more impressionistic evidence.

It is possible to detect some movement from lowland Scotland to
Ulster before 1605, such as that of Robert Hamilton, a tailor, who was
expelled from Ayr in 1604 because it was thought that he carried plague
from Ulster.[14] The sustained movement of population to east Ulster,
however, began only after the main landlords there had secured their
title to their new lands in 1605. The delivery of seisin of Sir Hugh
Montgomery's lands in north Down 'much encouraged the plantation'
according to the author of the *Montgomery Manuscripts*, and although
plans to bring over settlers were afoot before 1605 it was not possible to
implement these until landlords were securely in possession of their
lands and able to lease them to tenants.[15] After 1605, when
Montgomery, Hamilton, and Macdonnell had secured title to their
lands, the movement of people to Antrim and Down began in earnest.
As Sir Thomas Craig, one of the commissioners for the abortive Anglo-
Scottish union of 1604, commented in late 1605, 'every day sees a stream
of migrants thither [Ireland]' and by 1606 the movement was well under

---

[12] Appendix A, ii.

[13] *Mont. MSS*, pp 41, 53 n.26; *Acts privy council, June 1626-Dec. 1626*, p. 65; *Cal.
S.P. Ire., 1625-32*, pp 136, 139; *Cal. pat. rolls Ire., Chas I*, p. 156; automatic denization
was granted in 1635 by 10 Chas. I, s.2, c.7 (Ire.).

[14] J. Patterson, *A history of the county of Ayr*, i (Ayr, 1874), p. 214.

[15] P.R.O.I., Ferguson MSS, ix, pp 84-5; *Mont. MSS*, p. 42.

way.[16] In Antrim a large number of Scots arrived in 1607 as a result of Angus Macdonnell's rebellion in Kintyre and in July of that year a royal letter granting charters to Belfast, Coleraine and Bangor spoke of the 'new colonies of English and Scotch which do daily endeavour to make a civil plantation in the counties of Down and Antrim'.[17] Some of this initial migration was temporary, to view the lie of the land or to establish trading connections, but many of those who went to east Ulster on a temporary basis remained.[18] By 1610 the effects of five years of migration were beginning to be felt. Sir James Hamilton reported that his coastal lands in Down were much sought after and pressure was also being put on services connected with the migration such as shipping. Ships operating between Ulster and Scotland were in such short supply and demand so great that the resulting increase in fares compelled the Scottish Privy Council to intervene to control them.[19]

The settlement appears to have expanded at a greater rate in the second decade of the century. The gravestone inscription of John Gibson, the dean of Down, for instance, recorded that the number of communicants at Bangor increased by 1,160 between 1609 and 1623. Later in the decade, George Allayne, the muster master general, found Antrim and Down even better settled than some of the escheated counties.[20] Such a development is not surprising since east Ulster was closer to Scotland and northern England than the planted areas of Ulster and many settlers landed there first.[21] Indeed before the official plantation of Ulster was got under way in 1610, the eastern part of Ulster was the only part open to British settlers. All this supports the evidence of the denization lists which suggest an increased flow of settlers between *c.* 1610 and *c.* 1620, but from the 1620s the denization lists suggest a

[16] R.S. Terry (ed.), *Sir Thomas Craig's 'De unione de regnum Britannica tractus'* (Scottish History Society, Edinburgh, 1909), p. 446; Perceval Maxwell, *Scottish migration*, p. 56.

[17] *Cal. S.P. Ire., 1606-8*, pp 193, 223, 225; B.L., Cotton Titus B X, f 185; Bodl., Carte 62, f 177; E. Hogan (ed.), *A description of Ireland c. 1598* (Dublin, 1878), pp 16-17. On the dating of this, Perceval Maxwell, *Scottish migration*, p. 63 n. 47.

[18] *Mont. MSS,* p. 60.

[19] T.C.D., MUN P/24/4; P.R.O.I. Ferguson MSS, ix, p. 82; *Reg. P.C. Scot., 1610-13,* pp 478-9.

[20] *Memorials of the dead in Ireland,* ii (1892-4), p. 61; *Cal. S.P. Ire., 1615-25,* p. 228; Perceval Maxwell, *Scottish migration,* pp 243-4.

[21] For the importance of this, see P. Robinson, 'British settlement in County Tyrone, 1610-60' in *Ir. ec. and social hist.,* v (1978), pp 25-6.

slowing down of migration into east Ulster. In the early 1630s there was a brief revival of immigration from Scotland noted by Sir William Brereton during his travels in the west of Scotland.[22] On the earl of Antrim's estates a large number of new denizens appeared in the early 1630s but in order to obtain a holding many had to become sub-tenants of the native Irish who had already obtained tenancies there.[23]

After this short spurt of growth the population stabilized and subsequently fell. The decline was precipitated by a series of harvest failures and political crises in the late 1630s. New settlers were becoming more difficult to attract and government policy was beginning to turn away from encouraging migration as an escape valve for surplus people because by the 1630s it was felt that the drain on British resources was becoming excessive. In Scotland, as early as 1635 Brereton noted that emigration was 'much taken notice of and disliked' as many Scottish landowners felt that their lands would be waste because their tenants had gone to Ulster.[24] By the mid-1630s Lord Conway was attempting to recruit settlers from England for his lands at Lisburn but without success, and in Down Sir Hugh Montgomery was experiencing similar difficulties which he blamed partly on the dangerous state of the harbour at Portpatrick, the main point of embarkation on the Scottish side for migrants to county Down.[25]

By the late 1630s therefore, east Ulster population was falling — mainly because of migration back to Scotland and England. Although the Irish harvest failure of 1628-32 did not affect east Ulster seriously it did cause panic among those most at risk from failure, the poor and the farmer on marginal land, and these fled back to Scotland. The Scottish Privy Council attempted to stem this movement in September 1630 by ordering the deportation of these returned emigrants who were unwanted there because the Scots were also experiencing dearth.[26] However, migration to Scotland remained a feature of the 1630s and accelerated considerably in the later part of the decade. In July 1638, for instance, a number of persons from Ireland, probably tenants of the earl

[22] Brereton, *Travels*, pp 119-20.

[23] B.L., Harley 2138, ff 111-5ᵛ.

[24] Brereton, *Travels*, p. 119; *Reg. P.C. Scot., 1635-7*, p. 198; K.G. Davies, *The north Atlantic world in the seventeenth century* (Oxford, 1974), p. 60.

[25] Brereton, *Travels*, p. 129; S.R.O., GD237/177/1/4.

[26] *Reg. P.C. Scot., 1630-32*, pp 22-3.

of Antrim, arrived in Kintyre following the partial failure of the harvest and cattle disease in Antrim. The fall in population caused by this movement back to Scotland meant tenants were in even shorter supply than usual throughout east Ulster, and in south Antrim land values fell by 25 per cent as a consequence of the scarcity of tenants.[27] The events of 1639, a partial harvest failure and the imposition by the government of a compulsory oath of strict obedience to the king, the 'Black Oath', accelerated this movement back to Scotland. The oath, which was insisted upon by Lord Deputy Wentworth, required people in effect to deny the Covenant, and rather than do this many Scots in east Ulster fled home. Sir Edward Chichester, younger brother and heir to Sir Arthur, complained that settlers 'daily go away into Scotland by great numbers together and carry with them their horses, cows, sheep and leave what else they have'.[28] By 1640 some of these men had begun to drift back to east Ulster again after the fall of Wentworth, but the outbreak of rebellion in the following year stemmed this movement and created a new flow outwards.[29]

Migration, although important, was not the only factor affecting the demographic history of east Ulster in the early seventeenth century since natural increase also played a role. The almost total lack of parish registers for Antrim and Down makes it impossible to make firm statements about birth or death rates, but the age of marriage, one of the main determinants of the child-bearing period of women, and hence family size, appears to have been lower than in England.[30] Most men in the major landed families of east Ulster were married in their early twenties compared to the late twenties of their English counterparts, and this

---

[27] SL, 18, no. 89; SP63/256/89.

[28] SL, 19, nos 80, 92; SP63/257/26; P.R.O.N.I., D1071B/B/1, pp 39-40; Thomas Houston, (ed.), *A brief relation of the life of Mr John Livingston* (Edinburgh, 1848), pp 104, 108.

[29] For example, J. Hogan, *Letters and papers relating to the Irish rebellion of 1641* (I.M.C., 1936), pp 6-7; Hill, *Macdonnells,* p. 63; T.C.D., MS 838, ff 41^v, 63; Houston (ed), *Brief relation,* pp 109-10.

[30] One fragment of a register for the parish of Blaris, near Lisburn, 1639-41, survives, P.R.O.N.I., Mic 1/3. The birth/death ratio in these years for Blaris was about 1·4, indicating an annual rate of natural increase of between 0·8% and 1·4% which was high by English standards, E.A. Wrigley, R.S. Schofield, *The population history of England* (London, 1981), pp 180-3.

may have led to a higher birth rate.[31] Furthermore, the death rate was probably lower than in England or Scotland. Many contemporary writers commented on the absence of epidemics in Ireland and in east Ulster — only one epidemic, of smallpox, seems to have occurred in the early seventeenth century.[32] As well as a low frequency of epidemics the incidence of harvest failure was also low, ensuring a good food supply. The author of the *Montgomery Manuscripts* recorded good harvests in 1606 and 1607, stressing the lack of imports from Scotland, and the 1609 harvest was also good. The harvest of 1616 was so good that Sir James Hamilton had great difficulty in obtaining a good price for the surplus from his north Down lands. The continuing success of the Ulster harvests in the 1620s was reflected in increasing concern in Scotland about grain imported from Ulster and resulted in the imposition of a set of 'corn laws' intended to control imports from the province. The crisis of the early 1630s had little effect on Antrim and Down for although most of the major Irish towns sought permission from the English Privy Council to import grain, none from east Ulster did so. By the mid-1630s the balance of the harvest was more delicate. Between 1635 and 1637 there were partial failures each year but there was no serious failure until 1640 and again in 1641, both failures leading to disorder in county Down.[33] The problem was a cumulative one for the partial failure of one harvest meant a shortage of seed corn for the next year and hence a smaller subsequent harvest. These shortages do not appear to have been subsistence crises, and the food supply was apparently able to keep pace with the expanding population and nourish it sufficiently to permit apparently rapid natural increase.

While it is clear that population rose rapidly it is less easy to quantify this. It is almost impossible to determine the population of east Ulster *c.*

[31] Appendix Ai. In addition to this table nineteen men were stated to be over twenty-one of which seventeen were married. E.A. Wrigley, 'Family limitation in pre-industrial England' in *Econ. Hist. Rev.*, 2nd ser., xix (1966), pp 86-7.

[32] *Cal. S.P. dom., 1631-3*, pp 382. This also affected other places SP63/255/108; *A.L.C.*, ii, p. 519. Almost nothing is known of the state of medicine in east Ulster, although Thomas Arthur, the eminent seventeenth century physician, visited the area on three occasions. M. Lenihan, 'The fee book of a seventeenth century physician' in *R.S.A.I. Jn.*, viii (1867), pp 22, 27.

[33] *Mont. MSS*, p. 62; *Cal. Carew, 1603-25*, p. 152; P.R.O.N.I., D1071B/B/1, pp 24-5; Perceval Maxwell, *Scottish migration*, pp 304-10; SP63/256/89; SP63/258/92ii.

1600.[34] The pardon lists drawn up at the end of the Nine Years War record 1,217 adult male individuals in east Ulster and the impression of genealogies and the evidence of the chancery pleadings suggest about five males per family making a population of *c*. 243 families in about 1600. Nothing is known about total completed family size but even a figure as high as ten would give a relatively low population of 2,430 pesons in 1600. Thirty years later the male population, as recorded in the muster rolls, stood at 2,008 for Antrim and 3,668 for Down.[35] Using an estimate of 3·14 adult males per family, the 1630 figures would represent 639 families in Antrim and 1,168 families in Down.[36] The problem of completed family size is a more complex one for nothing is known of the sex ratio in east Ulster. The evidence from other contemporary colonial situations suggests that the population was predominantly male; by 1624-5 the ratio of men to women in Virginia was 4:1 and in Massachusetts the ratio was 3:2. Most of the male American migrants however were unmarried while many of those who moved to east Ulster already had wives and families. Alexander Macdonnell, who settled at Ardwhin in Lecale, for example, brought his whole family with him, while Sir Robert McClelland, a minor landholder in Down and later an important settler in Londonderry, was more circumspect, acquiring his lands at Drumbo and building a house before bringing over his family. This suggests that there was a higher sex ratio than in America, perhaps as high as 3:2, a conjecture supported by the low incidence of sexual misdemeanours.[37] Such a ratio would give a completed family size of 5·21 in east Ulster, similar to its English counterpart.[38] Calculations based on these figures would give a settler population of 3,329 persons for Antrim and 6,086 for Down, or a total of 9,415 persons by

---

[34] Other figures for family size suggest a higher figure, e.g. about seven at Ballydavy in north Down, but this includes daughters and servants, T.C.D. MS 837 ff 155, 185.

[35] B.L., Add. 4770.

[36] This figure is the average size of a family in the escheated counties as recorded in Pynner's survey. Hill, *Plantation*, pp 588-9. The spread is from 5·5 adult males per family in Tyrone to 1·84 males for Cavan.

[37] R. Thompson, *Women in Stuart England and America* (London, 1974), pp 23-7, 29; H. Holler, 'Sex composition and correlated culture patterns in colonial America' in *William and Mary Quarterly*, ii (1945), passim; *Reg. P.C. Scot., 1610-13*, p. 597; S.R.O. RH15/91/40/8; on sexual conduct see chapter 8.

[38] J. Kraus, 'The medieval household: large or small' in *Econ. Hist. Rev.*, 2nd ser., ix (1956-7), p. 432; P. Laslett, *Household and family in past time* (Cambridge, 1972), p. 138.

1630.[39] Total population for east Ulster by 1630 may have been in the region of 11,737 persons allowing for natural increase of the native Irish element since 1600.

Such estimates are obviously very tentative and are subject to wide error margins. The spread of family size in Pynnar's survey, for example, is an indication of how misleading mean family sizes can be. Despite the very provisional nature of these estimates, it is possible to draw two general conclusions. First, the population of east Ulster grew very rapidly in the early seventeenth century, mainly by immigration, and second, although there was a rapid increase in population by migration in the early seventeenth century, east Ulster was still a thinly populated area. In 1614 the earl of Abercorn estimated the Scots male population of north Down, an area of predominantly Scots settlement, at 2,000. Using the estimates above, the total settler population would have been more than 3,261 persons.[40] By 1630 the estates of Sir James Hamilton and Sir Hugh Montgomery in north Down could muster 2,718 males or a settler population of 4,509, an increase of almost forty per cent in only sixteen years, but this population was thinly spread.

While the size of the population is important, its age, sex and occupational structures were of considerable significance in the consolidation and development of the settlement. Some indication of the age structure of the settler population in 1641 is given through the ages of deponents in 1653 from which twelve years can be subtracted.[41] Such a sample is clearly biased against those who were very young or very old in 1641 but allowing for this it is clear that in 1641 about half the settlers were between thirty and fifty years of age. This had important repercussions for the labour supply and the economy of east Ulster generally.[42] A man's working life was short, and a population with its predominant age grouping at 30-50 meant fewer labouring years per individual and a consequent need for a large number of new labourers.[43] East Ulster did

---

[39] These figures compare well with Perceval Maxwell's estimates of 4-5,000 male Scots or 2,000 families, Perceval Maxwell, *Scottish migration,* p. 251.

[40] J. Maidment (ed.), *Letters and state papers during the reign of King James VI* (Abbotsfort Club, Edinburgh, 1838), p. 233.

[41] Appendix A, iii.

[42] Ages given in depositions must be regarded with a wide margin of error as there was a tendency to 'round up' or down. K. Thomas, 'Age and authority in early modern England' in *Brit. Acad. Procs.,* lxii (1976), pp 206-7.

[43] D.C. Coleman, 'Labour in the English economy in the seventeenth century' in *Econ. Hist. Rev.* 2nd ser., viii (1955-6), pp 284-8.

not have this large labour pool and to resolve this problem landlords were forced to include services in labour as part of the rent, especially in the early stages of the settlement. This delicately balanced labour situation collapsed as population began to fall in the late 1630s, particularly with the increased movement of people back to Scotland in 1639, and in that year the corn could not be harvested in many areas of Antrim and Down because of the shortage of labour.[44]

This problem of scarcity was not confined to labourers since the migrants to east Ulster were mainly aspiring tenants and unskilled labourers hoping for employment. In both England and Scotland craftsmen's wages were rising rapidly and thus there was no incentive to emigration. Yet skilled craftsmen were essential to the creation and development of a colonial economic infrastructure. Sir Arthur Chichester and Sir James Hamilton both stressed the need to import craftsmen into Ulster to develop the new settlement, but these were not forthcoming.[45] At Carrickfergus during the rebuilding of the town wall in 1610 masons and labourers had to be imported from the pale and Leinster and in 1639 the problem reappeared when the earl of Antrim wrote that his failure to prepare boats for an attack on the earl of Argyll in Kintyre was because 'carpenters, especially Scots, are very hard to be found and unless they are pressed they will not work for this occasion'.[46] The early seventeenth-century population of east Ulster, though increasing, was small, thinly scattered and because of the nature of the migration, its structure was unsuited to the heavy demand for labour in the new, rapidly developing, settlement. The development of the settlement was also governed by another demographic factor, the distribution of the population.

One of the significant contributions of the early seventeenth-century settlement to the demographic history of Antrim and Down was that it altered the distribution of the population. The disposition of the population *c.* 1600 can only be seen indirectly but the levies of men by the native lords for the campaigns of the Nine Years War give some indication of the numbers of men in the various regions of east

[44] S.R.O., GD180/194; P.R.O.N.I., D1071B/B/1, pp 39-40; SL, 19, nos 80, 92.

[45] T.C.D., MUN. P/24/4; T.W. Moody, 'Ulster plantation papers' in *Anal. Hib.*, viii (1938), p. 288.

[46] *Cal. pat. rolls Ire. Chas I*, p. 639; SL, 19, no. 22.

Ulster.[47] The greatest levies came from south Antrim and mid-Down as well as the sixteenth-century Scottish settlements of the Route and the Glynnes in north and east Antrim. The heavily wooded areas of Killultagh, in south west Antrim, and Kilwarlin in north west Down, produced relatively few soldiers. This pattern is confirmed by an analysis of pardons issued at the end of the war which reflects a much wider spectrum of people than just soldiers.[48] This pattern of population distribution was also recorded by Sir Henry Sidney who in 1575 found Magennis's country, the Ards and the Glynnes well inhabited while Clandeboy and McCartans country in north and east Down were little settled.[49]

By 1659 the distribution had changed. Clandeboy and west Down were densely settled and the central part of Antrim, previously little settled, now had large numbers of English and Scots. The river valleys, the Bann, Lagan, and Six Mile Water, were also heavily settled as were parts of the lowlands around Lough Neagh but the still wooded area of Kilwarlin remained thinly populated.[50] The immigration of Scots and English made a fundamental impact on the distribution of population in east Ulster since it exploited areas previously sparsely settled that had been laid open by the establishment of crown title and by subsequent grants to new landlords. The scale of the redistribution was demonstrated by the alterations made by Bishop Echlin in the parochial structure of Antrim and Down when he reorganised the medieval parishes to concentrate livings in south-east Antrim and north and east Down where there was greatest settler activity.[51]

The pre-existing distribution of the natives determined the areas available for settlers, and the points at which the new settlers entered, as well as the internal communications system all influenced the distribution of the settler population. Unlike the scheme for the escheated counties there was no intention to reorganise the distribution of the native

[47] Appendix A, iv; L. Price, 'Armed forces of the Irish chiefs in the early sixteenth century' in *R.S.A.I. Jn.*, lxii (1932), p. 205.

[48] Appendix A, v.

[49] B.L., Cotton Titus X B, ff 6-8ᵛ.

[50] This paragraph is based on *Census Ire., 1659.*

[51] S. Millsop, 'The state of the church in the diocese of Down and Connor during the episcopate of Robert Echlin, 1613-15' (M.A., Q.U.B., 1979), ch. 2.

Irish population to provide room for the settlers.[52] Thus in many areas the native population from the sixteenth century survived. The McAuleys continued to hold most of the land around Cushendall in north-east Antrim and the Magill family and an Irish branch of the Agnews also survived on the Hill estate in Down and on the earl of Antrim's estate in south Antrim.[53] Such survivals were not approved of by the central administration who forbade landowners to take native Irish as tenants. Most landowners passed on this injunction by forbidding lessees from taking Irish as sub-tenants, and Sir Hugh Montgomery, for instance, made forfeiture of the lease the penalty for breach of this.[54] In practice, these orders were widely ignored. A list of tenants on Henry Upton's lands at Templepatrick in 1626 for example shows twenty-seven out of thirty-nine were Irish despite a clause in his lease forbidding Irish tenants and again a petition from Margaret Gibbons, a tenant in Lecale, to Lord Deputy Wentworth in 1637 showed all her subtenants to be Irish or Old English.[55] The real factors determining the distribution of the native Irish element in the population were the availability of settlers and individual landlords' preferences. In areas where few settlers penetrated, such as mid-Down, most of the native population remained undisturbed, while in other areas, such as the Agnew estate in the Six Mile Water valley, most of the Irish were forced off the land by rising rents and the strong demand by settlers for land. Landlords' individual preferences also affected the distribution of native Irish. The antipathy of Sir John Clotworthy to the natives probably accounts for their scarcity on his lands in 1659 while the adjoining estate of Henry Upton had a large number of Irish since Upton had no such animosity and had even attempted to save some natives during the 1641 disturbances.[56] This ethnocentricity even extended to differences

---

[52] T.W. Moody, 'The treatment of the native population under the scheme for the plantation in Ulster' in *I.H.S.*, i (1938), pp 59-63.

[53] B. Turner, 'Distributional aspects of family name surveys illustrated in the Glens of Antrim' (Ph.D., Q.U.B., 1974), pp 91-3; S. O'Ceallaig, *Gleanings from Ulster history* (Cork, 1951), pp 97-100; P.R.O.N.I., D671/D8/1/67A-B.

[54] Erck., pp 201, 218, 245; P.R.O.N.I., T1030/41, D811/1, T956/21.

[55] P.R.O.N.I., T712/3; B.L., Harley 430, f 133.

[56] T.C.D., MS 838, ff 104ᵛ, 139, 181, 243; *D.N.B.*, sub. Clotworthy; W. Notestein (ed.), *The journal of Simon D'Ewes* (Yale, 1923), p. 13.

between English and Scottish settlers, for the only estates on which more than half of the tenantry were English in 1659 were those held by the English landlords Sir John Clotworthy and Sir Edward Conway.[57]

The distribution of the settler population was also controlled by other factors, principally communications since many of the east Ulster settlers were very mobile. In areas where population was low and land abundant there was considerable competition by landlords for tenants who could be induced to other estates by the attraction of a lower rent or a better holding. While this volatile situation persisted, and because of the need to raise the artificially low rents which had been used to attract settlers in the early stages of the settlement, many landlords were unwilling to give stable tenures. Thus on the Savage estate in south Ards, 44 per cent of the tenants held their lands only 'at pleasure', c. 1650.[58] This lack of secure tenure when added to the competition among landowners for existing tenants resulted in a high rate of geographic mobility among tenants in north-east Ulster. We learn, for example, that of those who held lands 'at pleasure' on the Savage estate c. 1650 only a third had been there five years previously whereas two thirds of the leaseholders remained constant.[59] In some cases landlords moved their own tenants around as is clear in the case of Sir James Hamilton who colonised some newly acquired lands in county Armagh with tenants from county Down, and when these same lands were subsequently sold he brought the tenants back 'from whence they came'.[60] Ultimately the mobility of settlers was controlled by the state of communications. The poor state of roads in east Ulster dictated that it was the coastal areas, where Irish settlement was weak, which would be settled first. It was the wish of the author of the *Montgomery Manuscripts* that 'the sea coast might be possessed by Scottish men who would be traders and prosper for

[57] Even the presbyterianism on Clotworthy's estate was English rather than Scottish inspired, W.S. Smith, *Historical gleanings in Antrim and neighbourhood* (Belfast, 1886), pp 36-7.

[58] P.R.O.N.I., D552/B/3/2/1. Comparable figures for other areas are 33 per cent on estates in Tyrone and 3 per cent in Donegal. V. Treadwell, 'The plantation of Donegal' in *Donegal Annual*, iii (1955-7), pp 41-6; ibid., 'The survey of Armagh and Tyrone in 1622' in *U.J.A.*, 3rd ser., xxiii (1960), pp 128-35, xxvii (1954), pp 140-54.

[59] P.R.O.N.I., D552/B/3/2/5; W. Macafee, V. Morgan, 'Population in Ulster 1660-1760' in P. Roebuck (ed.), *Plantation to partition* (Belfast, 1981) p. 47.

[60] R.J. Hunter, 'The Ulster plantation in the counties of Armagh and Cavan' (M. Litt., T.C.D., 1969), p. 220.

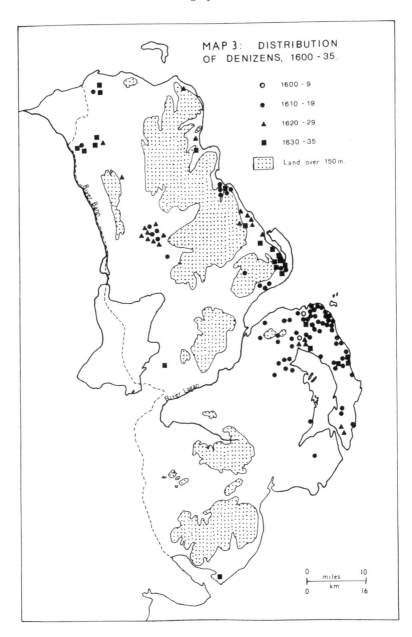

MAP 3: DISTRIBUTION
OF DENIZENS, 1600 - 35.

○	1600 - 9
●	1610 - 19
▲	1620 - 29
■	1630 - 35
⠿	Land over 150 m.

River Bann

River Lagan

0	miles	10
0	km	16

his Majesty's future advantage'.

By 1610 this was coming true and the coastal lands on Sir James Hamilton's estate were becoming much sought after.[61] As the coastal land was settled, later migrants began to move inland. The lowland around the shores of Lough Neagh, for example, began to be settled from the mid-1620s and consequently land values rose. Churches also began to be renovated and built in this area to accommodate new congregations at Glenavy and Crumlin. A new church was also built at Muckamore to accommodate part of the congregations of Umgall and Dundesert who had moved inland. The presbyterian church also recognised this trend as ministers such as James Glendinning and James Hamilton forsook their coastal charges and moved inland to set up congregations there.[62] In north and mid-Antrim a similar process was under way with the opening up of Sir William Adair's estate around Ballymena which previously was 'a most barbarous place and receptable of rebels' and on the earl of Antrim's estate, churches at Ballyrashane, Derrykeighan and Dunagh were all repaired to accommodate settlers from the coast moving inland.[63] In Down there was less room for manoeuvre since the native Irish were already well settled in mid-Down, restricting expansion inland. This pattern of a settlement moving inland can best be charted by using the denization lists as in map 3 although this probably underrepresents the strength of the inland movement since the acts of denization were sued out by new immigrants not internal migrants. Within this limitation the pattern of initial coastal settlement in the first two decades followed by a considerable movement inland in Antrim and a lesser movement in Down is clearly illustrated.

By 1641 the demographic structure which had evolved in east Ulster was imbalanced as the population had not grown to the level necessary to adequately develop the economy. As a result the labour force and the supply of tenants was small in number, unbalanced in age and occupational structure and uneven in its geographical distribution. This situation more than anything else was to retard the realization of the new landlords' expectations of rapid economic growth and fast returns from the potentially rich lands of Antrim and Down. A delicate balance

[61] *Mont. MSS*, pp 32-7; T.C.D., MUN. P/24/4.

[62] *Cal. S.P. dom., 1635*, pp 573-4; Brereton, *Travels*, p. 129; Millsop, 'State of the church', ch. 2; Blair, *Autobiography*, pp 70-76.

[63] *Cal. S.P. Ire., 1633-47*, p. 291.

between the wished-for and the possible, as dictated by the physical landscape and demographic structure, was to shape the economic environment of east Ulster.

IV

THE ECONOMIC
STRUCTURE

LIKE ANY PRE-INDUSTRIAL economy, that of east Ulster in the early
seventeenth century was dominated by agriculture. The shape of the
agricultural economy was, in turn, moulded by the inputs of land,
labour, capital and also by historical forces. However, the predominant
element was the physical landscape, which, as has been shown above,
was difficult to modify significantly. Woodland could be cleared but the
level of technology in drainage and manures was so low that change in
the landscape depended primarily on the input of the labour force. But
the labour force in Antrim and Down during the early seventeenth century was relatively small and unevenly distributed thus limiting the
possibility of change.

Other considerable difficulties also existed which inhibited the introduction of new agricultural practices to east Ulster. In particular, many
of the major changes in the early modern agriculture of England and
Scotland, such as liming and ley grazing, were both capital and labour
intensive but in east Ulster supplies of capital for investment in
agriculture were limited because the backgrounds of many of the settler
landlords were such that they had little access to sizeable amounts of
capital. As a result the agricultural improvements in contemporary
England and Scotland were not matched in east Ulster.

The dynamics of change in the agricultural economy of east Ulster —
land, labour and capital — operated within a well-defined historical
context of landholding units and agricultural practices. The agricultural
techniques of the native Irish in the sixteenth century had evolved to suit
the environment of local areas within Antrim and Down. Ploughing by
tail is a case in point. It was well suited to poor stony soil, such as that of

county Down, because when the plough hit a stone the horse's tail would be pulled causing it to stop. A collar, on the other hand, would make the horse less sensitive to such obstacles and result in the light wooden ploughs which were used sustaining serious damage by being repeatedly pulled over obstacles. Other native Irish agricultural practices were also adopted by the settlers until pressures from improving landlords dictated otherwise. This continuity of practice was aided by the large number of native Irish who were retained as tenants by the new landowners and continued to practice traditional agricultural techniques. Agricultural production and practice was also affected by the degree of evolution of the market economy and the presence of fairs in the different regions of east Ulster since bulky and perishable goods, such as grain, could only be profitably produced if they could be marketed regularly and locally to avoid costly transport. All these factors were considered significant by those who were involved in the settlement of Ulster in the early seventeenth century and were included in the Instructions given to John Rowley, the agent for the Irish Society in Londonderry, requiring him to assess rents 'having a respect to the goodness or barrenness of the soil, the nearness of the town and the largeness of the balliboes'.[1]

In the light of all these variables it is clear that agriculture should be discussed in regional terms and not as a blanket activity. In map 4 an attempt has been made, by plotting all extant references to agricultural activity, to identify the agricultural regions of east Ulster in the late sixteenth and early seventeenth centuries. The nature of the sources makes it difficult to draw precise agricultural regions for early seventeenth-century Ulster because the absence of probate inventories and manorial records used extensively by English agrarian historians for this purpose means that only tentative regions can be suggested. Lack of information about rural industrial activity also clouds the picture of definite areas of agricultural activity. In most areas, however, there was little diversification from the agricultural base of the economy but there was some development of domestic industry such as textiles. Linen was shipped from Carrickfergus in the late sixteenth century and although this had risen appreciably by the 1630s the quantities exported were still

---

[1] T.W. Moody, J.G. Simms (eds), *The bishopric of Derry and the Irish Society of London*, i (I.M.C., 1968), p. 86.

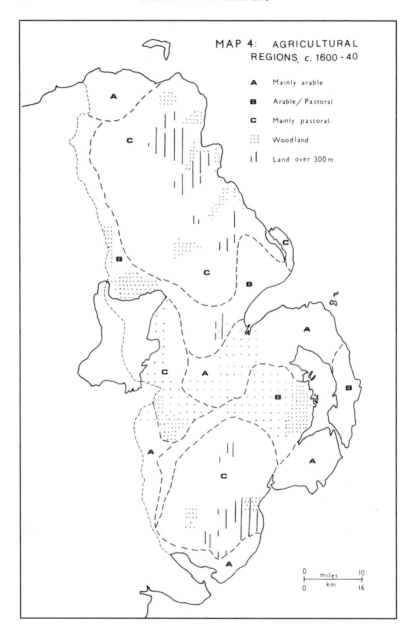

MAP 4: AGRICULTURAL REGIONS, *c.* 1600 - 40

A   Mainly arable

B   Arable / Pastoral

C   Mainly pastoral

Woodland

Land over 300 m.

0   miles   10
0   km   16

small.[2] Textile technology was poorly developed, a constant subject of complaint among contemporaries who wanted to introduce 'mechanical arts' to the natives, and so it was yarn and unprocessed wool which tended to be exported from east Ulster rather than finished cloth.[3] Tanning was also practised to a limited extent in the countryside but this was restricted to areas which had a supply of oak bark, hides and running water. A tannery was established at Toome, in south Antrim, during the early years of the seventeenth century by the Waring family, who later expanded their business to Waringstown and Derriaghy in mid-Down.[4] These diversifications were relatively minor in comparison with the fishing industry. Fishing was of particular importance since, in return for a small capital investment in boats and nets, the catch, once marketed, provided much needed cash in the rural economy. Fishing was widespread in east Ulster, the most important areas being the Copeland Islands off the north Down coast, the west Down coast around Groomsport and the Newry area, where the Bagnall family held the customs of fish. Inland, the river Bann and Lough Neagh were fished for salmon and eels respectively.[5] All these activities were rarely practised by themselves and were usually supplementary to agriculture. It is significant that when Thomas Richardson was attacked at Newry in 1641 he lost not only his fishing boat and nets but also a farm.[6]

Apart from these limited diversifications from agriculture in east Ulster, agriculture in the region was itself a very diverse activity determined by the local balance between pastoral and arable farming on a number of holdings in east Ulster. This pattern of local variations can be broadly classified in three ways: predominantly stock-raising areas, mixed stock and arable areas, and woodland areas.

It is necessary to consider these areas individually, beginning with the stock-raising regions. While some areas of the central upland masses of Antrim and Down produced grain for local consumption, high rainfall

[2] C. Gill, *The rise of the Irish linen industry* (Oxford, 1925), p. 7; SP63/259/46 ii; V. Treadwell, 'Irish financial administrative reform under James I: the customs and state regulation of Irish trade' (Ph.D., Q.U.B., 1960), app., 3, 5.

[3] B.L., Add. 39853, f 13; Harley 3292, f 29.

[4] McCracken, *Ir. woods,* p. 83; P.R.O.I., Ferguson MSS, xii, p. 3.

[5] *Ham. MSS,* p. 55; SL 19, no. 66; SP63/255/84; *Cal. S.P. Ire., 1633-47,* p. 199; *Civil Survey,* x, p. 64; for trade in fish to Scotland *Cal. Scot. P., 1586-8,* pp 55-6; *Cal. Scot. P., 1595-7,* pp 224-5.

[6] T.C.D., MS 837, f 12.

and poor drainage made tillage difficult in these regions and they tended to specialise in the raising of cattle. Sir Josias Bodley, who ventured into mid-Down in 1602, found that Newry, to the south of the Down uplands, could produce 'nothing but lean beef and very rarely a mutton' and in Antrim the uplands there were described in 1610 as not improved by husbandry except grazing cattle and a little oats.[7] The ports of Strangford, Ardglass, and Newry, which lay near the Down uplands and exported the goods from this area, were principally concerned with animal products rather than those of tillage. In the 1620s for example the Down ports exported a significant number of oxen and cows as well as quantities of hides, although they do not seem to have produced any substantial quantity of barrel beef. Carrickfergus, on the other hand, exported large quantities of barrel beef, and very considerable quantities of hides suggesting that there may have been more activity in the processing of agricultural products in south Antrim than in Down.[8]

The second category incorporates the low-lying regions of north Down, south Antrim, the east coast of Lough Neagh, the Bann valley and the Route in north Antrim all of which practiced agriculture in which arable farming played the greater part. The fertile barony of Lecale in east Down had even become a major exporter of grain by the 1620s, exporting the largest quantity of oats in Ireland in 1622 and 1628. These ports were closely followed in quantity of oats exports by Carrickfergus. There was a strong sixteenth-century tradition of tillage in south Antrim as Rowland White's comment in the 1570s that there were five or six hundred ploughs around Carrickfergus demonstrates.[9] Again in south Down a 1575 rental of the Bagnall estate shows that tenants in the low-lying areas to the south of the Mourne mountains paid up to 20 per cent of their rent in services associated with arable husbandry including ploughing and reaping and this same arable component of agriculture was also able to supply the mill at Newry with 541 pecks of wheat and rye.[10] This tradition of paying rent in grain in arable areas, which had arisen because it was difficult for tenants to market

[7] Anon, 'Bodley's visit to Lecale' in *U.J.A.*, 1st ser., ii (1854), p. 75; P.R.O.I., Ferguson MSS, ix, p. 85.

[8] P.R.O.N.I., T2860/13; P.R.O., CO/388/85, I am indebted to Dr David Dickson for this reference. This pattern was also true in 1613/15, Leeds City Library, TN/PO7/1 (1-4).

[9] SP63/31/31.

[10] Bodl., University College MS 103, ff 121, 123.

their small grain surpluses while merchants wanted to deal in large quantities, continued into the seventeenth century. Thus on Sir James Hamilton's estate one tenant paid 40 barrels of oats and 45 barrels of barley as part of his rent and in Antrim John Shaw of Carncastle also paid part of his rent in grain as did Archibald Stewart in the Route.[11] But even in these predominantly arable parts of east Ulster, tillage cannot be rigidly separated from livestock farming, since even in arable areas horses were required for ploughing and as a means of transport, and cattle and sheep were needed for manure.[12]

A third area of agricultural activity was practised in the woodlands. Small villages developed in the less dense woodland and in these areas livestock could be raised and incomes supplemented by domestic industry. A description of the Down woodlands in 1566 recorded that some areas were mainly underwood with 'no great oak and neither great building timber'.[13] This was the result of the pollarding of woodland to prevent the horns of cattle catching on branches which meant that the grazing of pigs and cattle prevented regeneration of the woodland. But since population in most of these woodland areas was low agricultural activity there was limited.

While agricultural regions provide a useful way of looking at the rural economy of east Ulster it would be misleading to over-emphasise regional specialization. The balance of the elements in the agricultural economy varied from place to place, as appendix B i shows but no area, whatever its physical limitations, could afford to specialise excessively. Even in the Mourne mountains a limited amount of corn was grown despite the unfavourable environment.[14] Every area had to produce a wide range of goods since marketing and communications were poor and the interchange of bulky goods such as grain was correspondingly difficult. A survey of farms on one estate, that of the Agnew family, which lay to the west of Larne on the edge of the Antrim uplands gives a more accurate indication of the workings of the agricultural economy

[11] P.R.O.N.I., T671/3, p. 4; T 549/1A; D2977, 8 Mar. 1624, Antrim to Archibald Stewart.

[12] On horses, J. Thirsk, *Horses in early modern England* (Reading, 1978).

[13] A.C. Forbes, 'Some legendary and historical references to Irish woods and their significance' in *R.I.A. Proc.*, xli, sect. B (1932-3), p. 33; P.R.O.I., Ferguson MSS, ix, p.85.

[14] R.M. Young, *Historical notices of old Belfast* (Belfast, 1896), p. 50.

at local level.[15]

The survey demonstrates that single farmsteads held in severalty provided the landholding framework within which farming took place, and this appears to have been typical of most areas in east Ulster. The maps of the Clandeboy estate made by Thomas Raven, for example, and the surviving leases of individual farms in the earl of Antrim's estate reveal that land was normally granted to individual persons.[16] The practice of holding in severalty was also common among the native Irish. One instance is a lease made by Rory Oge MacQuillan to three men which stated that the land was to be divided unequally between them and that it was to descend to their heirs with no alienation or reallocation.[17] There appears to have been little subdivision and individual holdings remained in the hands of the same family for considerable periods of time, as seen when the commissioners who fixed the boundaries of Iveagh were able to discover farms which had been held by families 'time out of the mind of man'.[18] Holding in severalty persisted because landlords were unwilling to divide the responsibility for rent payment among a number of men, preferring to keep it in the hands of one man who was easily held accountable. In general, it was within a framework of family farms, which were held and inherited in severalty, that the agricultural activity of east Ulster took place. There were exceptions to this pattern and at times it was necessary that some land be held jointly, for example, if the land was poor and needed more than one family to work it. The earl of Antrim did make a number of joint leases for poor land but although two men were bound for the rent, the earl was unwilling to allow joint occupancy. The lands of Glencorp, in north-east Antrim, for example, were leased by two men but were to be held 'by two equal moities'.[19] Other types of land also had to be held in common, for example bogs and poorer grazing land to which cattle from communities could be moved during the corn growing season to prevent cattle disturbing the growing crop.[20]

[15] Tabulated in appendix B, ii.

[16] P.R.O.N.I., T811; D556/10; D 2977, 4 Aug. 1637, Antrim to John Oge O'Muldany.

[17] S.R.O., GD97/1/314B.

[18] *Inq. Ult.*, appendix; on inheritance customs, see pp 157-8, 162 below.

[19] P.R.O.N.I., D2977, 4 Aug. 1637, Antrim to Gilgrove and John McDerogh; D2977, 23 July 1637, Antrim to Alexander and Donell McGee.

[20] On bogs: P.R.O.N.I., D1838/55A/83; Down Survey maps; on common grazing: P.R.O.I., Lodge MSS. Wardships and alienations, i, p. 133; P.R.O.N.I., T815.

The extent of individual holdings varied considerably but in the case of the Agnew lands holdings tended to be small, between five and thirty acres. This was due in large measure to the location of the estate near Larne, one of the main ports of entry for settlers, which created heavy demand for land there. The Raven maps for north Down also show demand for land near the coast since the smallest farms were found in the coastal areas with the largest holdings further away from the coast.

The pattern of agricultural activity on Agnew's lands was mixed, being a combination of livestock and arable. Of these, the better developed was probably the livestock sector, even though the livestock population on the estate was small, and cattle were especially scarce. Contemporaries varied in their estimates as to what constituted an adequate supply of cattle for an Irish farm. One writer of the 1550s had argued that each settler in Ireland should have at least eight cows and a horse, but a later plan suggested that a ratio of twenty cows to one plough was necessary, and by the early seventeenth century thirty sheep and cows were recommended for a seven acre holding which was also to produce at least one acre of corn.[21] By any of these standards the numbers of cattle on Agnew's lands were small, an average of only 0·2 cows per acre. This situation arose from the very low cattle population in sixteenth-century Ulster of which there is ample evidence. On the strength of this scarcity, Sir Ralph Lane, a late sixteenth-century expert on fortification, argued that the Antrim Scots could be cut off from the earl of Tyrone by building forts which would restrict their movements and hence they would not leave Antrim 'for fear of the loss of their cows, which they love as their lives, and far better than him [Tyrone]'.[22] Even when a herd was of little practical use, such as the 50,000 cows of Sorley Boy Macdonnell's herd, of which only 1,500 gave milk, it was retained because of the scarcity and hence high value of cattle.[23] The low cattle population in sixteenth-century Ireland led to settlers being advised to bring their own livestock, since during the early stages of the settlement before fields were properly cultivated cattle were of considerable importance to the settlers for manure as well as for food.[24] Robert Blair, for example, recorded that 'an abundance of people and

---

[21] SP62/1/22 i, ii: B.L., Add. 31878, f 73; Royal MSS, 18A, lxv, f 1ᵛ.
[22] *Cal. S.P. Ire., 1598-9*, pp 384-5, 421.
[23] SP63/112/41.
[24] SP63/256/17.

cattle' came from Scotland and the earl of Abercorn, a Tyrone settler, brought over large numbers of cattle to manure his estate.[25] As a result of the movement from Scotland the cattle population of east Ulster increased rapidly. Cattle also had an important place in east Ulster trade in the early years of the settlement when few markets existed since cattle were easier to move long distances than was grain. By the 1620s east Ulster exported about a third of total Irish cattle exports, mainly through the Down ports and even in the 1630s much of the trade of Bangor and Donaghadee, which had handled about a quarter of Irish cattle exports in 1628, was in cattle 'that are brought from other parts by reason of the aptness of transportation'.[26] The cattle shortage in the early stage of the settlement led to a system of coring on the Agnew estate by which cattle were brought from as far away as Larne to be pastured on land which required manuring.

It was not only cattle which were in short supply during the early stages of the settlement but also horses so that on Agnew's lands the average number of horses per holding was only 2·6 which was not enough to form a plough team.[27] This scarcity of horses had also been a feature of the sixteenth-century Ulster economy. During one raid on a Magennis camp in 1600 for example, Lord Mountjoy, the army commander in Ulster, seized 1,000 head of cattle but only fifteen or sixteen horses, and an earlier raid in 1599 had seized only ten or twelve horses.[28] This shortage of horses constituted a continual source of complaint in the early seventeenth century. As late as 1642 Robert Munroe, the commander of the Scots forces in Ulster, complained that in county Down horses were so scarce that he had to use oxen for carriage, and earlier in 1631, despite strenuous attempts, James Montgomery had been unable to borrow a horse anywhere in county Antrim.[29] Such a shortage was a source of concern to the central administration because it gave rise to

[25] B.L., Cotton Titus X B, f 407*; Blair, *Autobiography*, p. 57; *Reg. P.C. Scot., 1610-13*, p. 478.

[26] B.L., Harley, 2138, f 176; D. Woodward, 'The Anglo-Irish livestock trade of the seventeenth century' in *I.H.S.*, xviii (1972-3), pp 489-523.

[27] A.T. Lucas, 'Irish ploughing practices' in *Tools and tillage*, ii (1974-6), pp 67-83; E.E. Evans, 'Some problems of Irish ethnology: the case of ploughing by tail' in C. Ó Danachair, *Folk and farm: essays in honour of A.T. Lucas* (Dublin, 1976), pp 34-5.

[28] *Cal. S.P. Ire., 1600*, p. 26.

[29] Gilbert, *Contemp. hist., 1641-52*, i, p. 423; H.M.C. *Various*, v, p. 140; SP63/245/82i.

transport and communications problems and in 1637 Sir John Coke, one of the English secretaries of state, decreed that the replenishing of the horse population was 'a business of much importance' for Ireland.[30] For the settlers the problem of the horse shortage was more apparent than real since the demand for horses was acute only for spring and winter ploughing. A measure of this demand is the pattern of horse thefts in east Ulster which showed 48 per cent of thefts in Down and 54 per cent of Antrim thefts occurred at times of ploughing in May and August.[31] This seasonal shortage could be overcome by groups of tenants pooling equine resources and it is likely that the fifteen horses held by Alexander Dunlop on Agnew's estate represents the pooling of a number of tenants' horses. Pooling made considerable sense particularly since it was of limited value for each tenant to keep a full team of horses for only one or two ploughings when horses required stall feeding with hay during winter, a product which was labour intensive in production. Since deep ploughing was only necessary to break in new land much cultivation could be, and was, done by spades. Evidence of this is provided by the corn ridges on Richard Bartlett's map of Inishloghan, near Lisburn, which are probably spade ridges and not produced by horse and plough.[32] A further aspect of the horse industry was the attempt by some landlords to produce thoroughbred horses in east Ulster by setting up studs. One such landowner was Lord Conway and by 1641, Throgmorton Totesbury, who lived near the town of Antrim, had three two year old colts of 'my lord Conway's Spanish horse'.[33]

The third element in the livestock sector on the Agnew estate, sheep, was of considerable importance since much of the land was well suited to sheep rearing. Sheep not only produced wool but also, and perhaps more importantly in this context, large quantities of rich manure. It is significant that the farm with the highest number of sheep on Agnew's land, that of Thomas McCoy, also had a higher quantity of grain than was usual for a holding of its size on the estate.

In comparison with the livestock element in the agricultural economy

---

[30] SL, 13, no. 166/2, 170; SL24/25, no. 183.

[31] J.F. Ferguson (ed.), 'The Ulster roll of gaol delivery' in *U.J.A.*, 1st ser., i (1853), pp 261-6.

[32] *Ulster maps, c. 1600*, p. 11.

[33] E. Bewick, *Rawdon letters*, n.p. 1819, p. 90; *Cal. S.P. dom., 1631-3*, p. 101; *Cal. S.P. Ire., 1625-32*, pp 515-6; SP63/257/25, 46.

the arable sector was less well developed on Agnew's land. The quantity of arable land on any farm depended on labour supply and on the production of manure by cattle and sheep. Since the animal population on the estate was low, manure supply to fertilize corn land was also limited. The human population, and therefore labour supply, was also relatively low and hence only crops requiring little labour were grown on the Agnew lands, as indeed elsewhere. Charles Monck, the surveyor of the customs in the 1630s noted this when he observed of the arable lands of Clandeboy that 'the country itself consists wholly of oats which they have little labour'.[34] Given this situation it is not surprising that grain production was low. Contemporary official estimates of how much land in Ireland should be under grain varied from a sixth to a tenth but generally favoured a high figure since arable husbandry was believed to have a 'civilising' influence. It was held that by being labour intensive and thus absorbing any surplus mobile population, arable farming promoted social stability.[35] Agnew's lands produced only 0·2 bolls per acre of corn, probably oats, and 0·2 pecks of barley per acre. It was rare for any holding to exceed this figure and if any did it can usually be explained by the presence of large numbers of sheep producing high quality manure.

Agrarian techniques and the degree of agricultural improvement varied considerably over east Ulster as can be illustrated by reference to manuring practices. Lime was not introduced into east Ulster in the early seventeenth century despite its extensive use as a fertilizer in southwest Scotland, but cattle dung was used in most parts of east Ulster and in some areas it was customary to enrich it by mixing it with brine. In places where it was available seaweed was used extensively.[36] Many of the traditional Irish agricultural practices survived and were only changed by pressure from improving landlords, but in the promotion of agricultural change the role of landlords varied considerably in different parts of east Ulster. Men who had resided in England for long periods of time, such as the second earl of Antrim, or those who employed English land agents, such as George Rawdon, agent on the Conway estate, attempted to introduce English style improvements. One attempt to introduce such changes was made when the earl of

[34] B.L., Harley 2138, f 176; on the labour force see ch. 3.

[35] B.L., Royal MSS 18A, lxv, f 1ᵛ; B.L. Royal MSS 18A, liii, f 10.

[36] G. Boate, *Ireland's natural history* (London, 1652), p. 100.

Antrim re-leased most of his estate in 1637 and included clauses in the leases obliging his tenants to assist 'the general good of the settlement by burdening them to plant [trees] and bound their holding so near as may be to the manner of England'.[37] The earl of Antrim also made attempts to control spoilation of his woodlands as did Lord Conway, and on Conway's lands remission of rent was allowed to encourage building and the upkeep of farms.[38] Lord Cromwell attempted to improve his lands in the Downpatrick area by draining bogs as George Rawdon likewise did on the Conway estate.[39] The first earl of Antrim also attempted to modernize agricultural practices on his estate to the extent that the Commission enquiring into the state of Ireland in 1622 could report that he had 'banished that barbarous custom by holding all his tenants to the fashion of English ploughing'.[40]

Others whose contact with English norms were less frequent once they had settled in Ireland were less enthusiastic about this type of improvement, and in 1615 the lord deputy, Sir Arthur Chichester had to warn two south Down settlers, Marmaduke Whitechurch and Sir Edward Trevor, of the penalties incurred by allowing continued ploughing by tail on their lands.[41] Sir James Hamilton did equally little to improve the agricultural practices on his estate and this led to Charles Monck's complaint that on Hamilton's estate he found 'little difference or change in the country either in building or enclosing' and Sir Arthur Magennis's land in mid-Down was similarly still 'wild country, not inhabited, planted or enclosed'.[42] In reality, whatever the landlords' attitude or plans the problems of estate development were of such a scale that no individual could hope to achieve significant short term improvement. Estates were large and frequently, as in the case of Trevor and Whitechurch, widely scattered, and this made the plans of the improving landlord difficult to implement. Thus, despite the best efforts of the earl of Antrim, the sheer size and the initially backward state of his lands

[37] SL, 17, f 151.
[38] *Cal. S.P. Ire., 1625-32*, p. 515; for example of clauses to control spoliation, P.R.O.N.I., T529/1A, D2977, 31 Jan. 1621, Antrim to James Oge McHenry, D2977, 1 May 1634, Antrim to Archibald Stewart; *P.R.O.I., Chancery Bills, L45*.
[39] SL, 14, f 166; *Cal. S.P. Ire., 1625-32*, p. 541.
[40] B.L., Add. 4756, f 68.
[41] Bodl., Clarendon MSS ii, no. 106.
[42] B.L., Harley 2138, f 176; Brereton, *Travels*, p. 132.

defeated his attempts to make substantial agricultural improvements.[43]

The state of the rural economy of east Ulster outlined above together with the lack of improvement in the early seventeenth century caused a number of flaws to develop in the economic structure which at times could be tried to crisis point. The most significant of these weak points was the almost total lack of economic activity other than agriculture, which left no fall back in the event of harvest failure when there would be insufficient grain or livestock surplus to be marketed to pay rent and other dues. Some indication of the panic that could be caused by even the possibility of a harvest failure was demonstrated at Bangor in 1624 when, although most of the grain from the surrounding area had already been gathered, a heavy rain threatened to destroy the late harvest at Bangor. The inhabitants of the parish fasted and prayed all day for a change of weather and when it came the whole community worked for two days without break while the minister, Robert Blair, and two neighbouring ministers fasted and prayed until all the grain was gathered.[44] The failure of the harvest also had longer term effects since seed corn normally reserved for the next year's sowing had to be eaten, thus decreasing the probability of a good harvest in the ensuing years. Successive poor harvests, such as those in Antrim between 1636 and 1639, meant tenants were unable to pay rent, land went out of cultivation as tenants left, and ultimately land values fell. The growing poverty in south Antrim in those years was sufficiently serious to cause the remission of part of the royal subsidy.[45]

A good harvest was necessary to meet the growing demands of a wide range of groups on the economy, but especially the landlord's rent. Initially rents were low in order to attract settlers but from the late 1620s they began to rise which meant that a greater surplus had to be sold to raise enough money. A second development also made an increased harvest surplus necessary. In the early years of the settlement many landlords were prepared to accept part of their rent in kind. Thus John Shaw, a tenant of the earl of Antrim paid as rent one and a half barrels of meal, two fat veals and £13. 13s. 4d., and on the Adair estate John Stein

[43] SL, 18, no. 69.

[44] Blair, *Autobiography*, pp 62-3; W.D. Killen (ed.), P. Adair, *A true narrative of the . . . presbyterian church in Ireland* (Belfast, 1866), p. 11.

[45] SP63/256/89; SP63/255/24. R. Gillespie, 'Harvest crises in early seventeenth century Ireland' in *Ir. Econ. and Social Hist.*, xi (1984) pp 5-18.

and James Wallace paid twelve fowls, ten ducks, ten stones of butter and eight days work as part of their rent.[46] This did not necessitate a large harvest surplus provided there was sufficient to pay these dues but there was a change in the 1630s when more landlords demanded all their rents in cash. All the leases made by the earl of Antrim during the re-leasing of 1637, for example, commuted all food renders to cash. This meant that the surplus produce from farms had to be marketed, but since it was difficult to sell small quantities of produce to merchants because of the shortage of specie a larger surplus was necessary. On one occasion, John Hamilton, brother of Sir James and agent on his estate, gathered all his brother's tenants together 'showing both to him[self] and to them what was due by every[one] of them, which they promised to pay with all the haste they could, praying to forebear them for some short time so that they might sell some of their commodities at some fairs which were near'.[47] Rawdon recognised the problem of marketing small quantities and offered to act as intermediary for all the tenants in marketing produce to merchants who were unwilling to deal in small quantities.[48]

Obligations to the landlord were not the only ones which the tenants had to meet. There were also demands by the established church in the form of tithes and given the high number of non-conformist presbyterians in east Ulster, tithes were a contentious issue.[49] In 1635, for example, a serious dispute flared between Mr Gwillam, vicar of Blaris, and his parishoners who withheld their tithes. Gwillam took the case to Dublin where it was tried before the bishop of Derry, John Bramhall, who granted a process against those withholding the tithes.[50] In some cases the problems which tithe collection posed were so great that many clerics in the diocese of Down and Connor did not try to collect them 'for fear of scandal'.[51] Clergy, like landlords, sought to collect their dues in cash, even though the arrangements for tithe collection in

---

[46] P.R.O.N.I., T549/1A; LPC 1333; T1531/1/1; D929/F1/33, 34; DI04/33/5/1.

[47] P.R.O.N.I., D1071B/B/1, p. 28; *Reg. P.C. Scot., 1625-7*, p. 591; P.J. Bowen, *The wool trade in Tudor and Stuart England* (London, 1962), p. 204.

[48] *Cal. S.P. Ire., 1625-32*, pp 516-17.

[49] Blair, *Autobiography*, p. 104; P.R.O.N.I., T2171/1, D552/B/2/1/7.

[50] SP63/255/62, 64, 66, 69, 70.

[51] *Cal. S.P. Ire., 1633-47*, p. 87; H. Leslie, *A treatise of the authority of the church* (Dublin, 1637); *Mont. MSS*, p. 55; *Ham. MSS*, p. 34.

Ulster drawn up in 1615 had stipulated that they were to be gathered in kind. On at least one occasion a cleric refused payment in kind but an appeal to the bishop's court for collection in cash was not upheld.[52]

A third major claim on the resources of east Ulster was the direct and indirect demands of the crown. The direct demands were for payments towards the support of the army and through royal subsidies each of which were often heavy. Between 1628 and 1632 Antrim and Down paid £6978. 19s. 5d. towards the maintenance of the army, a higher figure than any other part of Ulster.[53] The impact of royal taxation can best be shown from subsidies levied on the counties in 1635. A commission chosen from non-residents of the county was appointed to assess each barony, the assessment being apportioned among the residents of that barony. Despite these precautions severe inequalities arose. The earl of Antrim complained that on his lands 'few of those who have indifferent good estates in that county are come off reasonable free and some of the poorer sort of them the most part are cessed very near to as much as they are really worth'.[54] Indirect taxation was imposed by the government in the form of soldiers quartered on the land which generated considerable discontent and animosity towards the government. In January 1627 the earl of Antrim complained that too many soldiers were billeted on his tenants and this was followed within a month by a more general complaint by most of the Antrim landholders. By May, Lord Conway had also complained that too many soldiers were stationed on his land 'to the disheartening of my tenants' and requested that some soldiers should be sent to the coast.[55] The quartering of troups was disruptive and soldiers consumed much of the tenants' harvest surplus required for the rent. The effects were worst in poor harvest years, such as the late 1630s, when quartering was heavy in east Ulster due to the Covenanter disturbances.[56]

Given these demands it was difficult for tenants to accumulate any reserves of capital. At times when savings were necessary in rural society, such as for the provision of a dowry or the expansion or acquisition

[52] SP63/254/168.

[53] SL, 1, ff 8, 32.

[54] SL, 15, no. 215. This form of taxation was generally acknowledged to be in equitable, bearing more heavily on tenants than on landlords, *Cal. S.P. Ire., 1625-32*, pp 461-2. Strafford, *Letters* i pp 238, 407.

[55] *Cal. S.P. Ire., 1625-32*, pp 203, 206, 237.

[56] SP63/258/92 ii.

of a holding, cash was often not available. In one case, Quentin Moore, a tenant of Lord Cromwell, had to sell part of his farm to provide a jointure of £40 for the future wife of his second son.[57] The main capital outlay which any settler had to meet was in the initial acquisition of his land, which Robert Blair estimated was between £200 and £300 in the 1630s. This could be obtained by selling the home farm in England or Scotland or borrowing money there and one settler's wife even sold her jointure in England to provide her husband with capital. Landlords could also help by staggering the rent or allowing it to remain a year in arrears.[58] One tenant who experienced the problem of finding sufficient capital to establish his holding wrote to Rawdon shortly after acquiring his land that he had stocked it with cattle and was about to plough it 'but I want money and must get it now at the right time of year'.[59]

Attempts to save were frustrated by a shortage of specie in the rural economy. In part, this was a result of a general shortage of coin in Ireland which arose because there was no mint there and, in contrast to the general Irish situation, there was little movement of coin into east Ulster from Scotland or England. Out of twenty-three seventeenth-century coin hoards found in east Ulster only six contain Scottish coins and a similar number English coin.[60] The central administration had banned English and Scottish coin in Ireland for fear that Irish coin, which contained a third less silver than its English or Scottish counterpart, would be rejected in the face of the purer specie. This situation produced unease among English and Scottish settlers who were reluctant to accept Irish coin lest they should be defrauded. Thus, when Ever Oge Magennis sold lands in south Down to a Dublin lawyer, Sir Jerome Alexander, Alexander insisted that payment be made in 'pure silver or gold coin'.[61] Given the shortage of specie and the lack of confidence in it, it is not surprising that a considerable amount of foreign coin was used as tokens in everyday transactions and that complex credit mechanisms evolved within the rural economy to facilitate trade.

[57] P.R.O.N.I., D1556/16/1.

[58] SL, 22, no. 134; S.R.O., RH11/45/5; P.R.O.N.I., D671/D8/1/48A.

[59] SP63/256/17.

[60] I.D. Brown, M. Dolley, *A bibliography of coin hoards of Great Britain and Ireland* (London, 1976); E.M. Jope (ed.), *An archaeological survey of County Down* (H.M.S.O., 1966), pp 454-7.

[61] P.R.O.N.I., D671/D8/1/24.

The forms of credit used by settlers were twofold, consisting of direct loans for large transactions and, for smaller items, indirect loans in the form of delayed payment for goods or services.[62] In the case of direct loans the main security was land in the form of a mortgage. For example, John Worsley, a Nottinghamshire man and tenant of the Bishop of Dromore, granted part of his tenancy to one John Cope 'for money lent'. Similarly in 1630 Alexander Houston, a tenant on Adair's estate in mid-Antrim, mortgaged part of his leasehold to the earl of Antrim for £128.[63] Smaller sums changed hands with lesser security. In 1638 for instance, on the death of one Antrim settler, John Temple, it was found he owed £29. 19s. 0d. to his neighbours on 'IOU's'.[64] Promises to pay became the principal means of borrowing small sums and many became a medium of exchange themselves because of the shortage of coin. Thus settlers such as Josiah Welsh, the minister of Templepatrick, accepted and dispensed promissary notes for cash and a number which he owned had passed through other assignees before reaching him.[65] A second important way of paying debts when small change was scarce was indirect credit whereby debts were allowed accumulate until there was enough to warrant the payment of a large sum. This method was risky for the creditor as it meant that in some cases debts were outstanding for a number of years. In 1636, for example, William Bourke had to petition the lord deputy for an order to compel a number of inhabitants of Antrim and Down to pay sums ranging from £2 to £35 for aqua vitae which they had bought on credit.[66]

In many respects the rural economy was precariously balanced, the demands were high and the base narrow. The use of credit was based on confidence and when this began to decline in the mid-1630s a crisis loomed for the rural economy of east Ulster.[67] In the early part of the century the economy of east Ulster had expanded rapidly. The trade of Carrickfergus rose as is evident from the customs returns which increased from £63 in 1603 to £264 in 1623-4 and the Down customs rose

---

[62] B.A. Holderness, 'Credit in English rural society before the nineteenth century' in *Ag. H.R.*, xxiv (1976), pp 79-80.

[63] *Cal. S.P. Ire., 1625-32*, p. 538; P.R.O.I., D15237.

[64] P.R.O.I., RC9/1, p. 41.

[65] P.R.O.N.I., T284.

[66] Bodl., Rawl. C439, f 213.

[67] Some people even distrusted bills of exchange. B.L., Add. 18824, no. 8.

similarly from £125 in 1603 to £260 in 1623-4. After the revision of customs valuations in the 1630s the rise was more spectacular; Carrickfergus increased to £306 in 1631-2 and the Down ports to £361. After 1635 however, the customs returns for east Ulster, and Ireland generally, began to fall.[68] This can be attributed largely to the slowing down of the rate of population increase, since the expansion in the economy in the early years of the settlement had been mainly due to increased labour inputs. A further cause of decline was a series of bad harvest in Antrim and Down during the late 1630s which had two main effects. First, the reduced supply of grain meant that markets and fairs functioned less efficiently and the limited amount of coin available circulated even more sluggishly. On Lord Conway's estate the agents took rent 'in such coin as is not current here [Ireland] yet good enough for the north' and distresses of rent were made since tenants had no coin to pay.[69] The second effect of poor harvests was a rise in discontent. Crime in east Ulster in 1613 tended to be concentrated in the winter months, especially December to February, during which time food was in short supply since the produce of the autumn harvest was running low and the spring harvest had not yet been gathered. A poor harvest would have accentuate this trend.[70] Other evidence of seasonal variation in crime such as the activity of woodkern supports this and some of those who rebelled in 1641 were probably like one north Antrim deponent who rose 'after the husbandry failed'.[71]

Economic matters were not the only contributors to the crisis of the late 1630s as political factors also played a part. The attempt by the lord deputy, Thomas Wentworth, earl of Strafford, to increase his grip on the localities came to a head in east Ulster in May 1639 with the attempt to control the presbyterians by requiring them to take a strict oath of loyalty, known as the Black Oath, to the established church and king. To enforce the taking of the oath the army was used and local volunteers called up. This involved quartering on tenants who, in a year of poor

---

[68] Figures from Treadwell, 'Financial administration'. Tables A-C; SL, 24/25, no. 174; B.L., Lansdowne 156, f 314.

[69] SP63/255/84; *Cal. S.P. Ire., 1625-32*, pp 515-16.

[70] J.F. Ferguson (ed.), 'The Ulster roll of gaol delivery' in *U.J.A.*, 1st ser., i (1853), pp 261-6; J. Thirsk (ed.), *The agrarian history of England and Wales*, iv (Cambridge, 1967), p. 620, table 21; *Cal. S.P. Ire., 1625-32*, p. 217-18; K. Wrightson, J. Walter, 'Dearth and social order in early modern England' in *Past and Present*, lxxi (1976), pp 22-42.

[71] T.C.D., MS 838, f 30.

harvests, had little to spare for the army. Sir Edward Chichester, brother and heir to Sir Arthur, complained to the earl of Ormonde, the military commander, that the 'poor people . . . are so much impoverished that they can no longer subsist, and the plantation which was here begun and brought to some perfection is now so much ruined as there is little hope to recover it'.[72] The calling up of local forces placed a further strain on the rural economy since it removed farmers from their holdings, and this had frequently given rise to complaint in the past. The earl of Antrim, for example, complained in 1629 that his tenants were greatly troubled at having to leave their farms five times a year to attend the sessions at Carrickfergus.[73] A requirement to attend for military service was even more serious since musters were usually called in the early spring when the campaign season opened.[74] Since this was the time of ploughing and sowing, men were taken away from their holdings at a crucial time, as happened in the late 1630s.

The rural economy was also severely damaged in a more spectacular way by political events. The imposition of the anti-presbyterian Black Oath caused many tenants and labourers to flee to Scotland for fear of persecution and in a finely balanced economy of which labour was an integral part this was disastrous. Sir Edward Chichester complained that many tenants from his lands around Carrickfergus had fled to Scotland carrying with them 'their horses, cows, sheep and what else they have and leave their corn standing in the ground, by which means Scotland will be well victualled and stored . . . however these parts are left miserably poor and the country growing waste'.[75] In parts of county Down the population declined so much that the harvest of 1640 could not be reaped because of the shortage of labour. The disturbances which followed the Black Oath were not, as some commentators believed, controlled from Scotland, but were rather the consequences of heavy quartering of troops in east Ulster which combined with a bad harvest resulted in a shortage of food and seed corn.[76] The crises of the late 1630s were, in part, the consequence of

---

[72] Bodl., Carte 1, f 379.

[73] *Cal. S.P. Ire, 1625-32*, pp 515-16; H.M.C., *Various*, v, p. 135.

[74] For example the muster of 1640; Steele, *Tudor & Stuart proclam.*, ii, no. 335.

[75] SL, 19, no. 92; P.R.O.N.I. D1071B/B/1, pp 39-40. It is significant that a proclamation of 1639 forbidding Scots in Ireland returning to Scotland was issued at harvest time, B.L., Egerton 2533, f 111ᵛ.

[76] SP63/258/92 ii.

the structure of the rural economy with all its problems of credit, inadequate development of tillage, and hence a very erratic, although usually sufficient, food supply, and the failure to develop even partial alternatives to agriculture.

To this point this analysis has concentrated on what can be described as the 'fixed factors' of the east Ulster settlement: the landscape, the population structure, and the attitudes of the settlers, together with the result of the amalgamation of these three — the economic structure. These features formed the basis of the distinct social structure and organisation of the east Ulster settlement. The pivot of that social structure was the landowner, and the next two chapters will examine how his desires and attitudes were circumscribed by his relations with other groups, especially with his tenants, and more importantly, with the central administration.

V

CENTRAL GOVERNMENT
AND LOCAL INTERESTS

WITHIN THE LIMITS imposed by the physical landscape and the
economic and population structures, relationships between the three
main groups of actors in the east Ulster settlement, the central government, the landlords and the tenants, developed slowly. In many ways it
was the relationship of the major landholders of Antrim and Down to
the central administrations in Dublin and London which played the
greater part in shaping the settlement. The relationship of landlord and
administrator was symbiotic since seventeenth-century legal theory
placed all land and its rights in the hands of the king who had the disposition of them. In reality it was the Dublin administrators who controlled
the granting of lands and the level of the rents which were paid for them,
and the rights which went with them, and in this way the landholders of
east Ulster were dependent on other royal services, such as the courts, to
resolve disputes, and the army, for protection in times of serious
trouble. In return the central government expected the greater landlords
to act as its agents, to enforce its instructions and maintain law and
order in the counties. It is the aim of this chapter to examine how this
relationship worked in practice.[1]

---

[1] Important studies on this problem in an English context are: P. Clarke, *English Provincial Society* (Harvester, 1977); T.G. Barnes, *Somerset 1625-40: a county government
during the personal rule* (Cambridge Mass., 1961); M.E. James, 'The first earl of
Cumberland and the decline of northern feudalism' in *Northern History*, i (1966), pp
43-4; A.H. Smith, *County and court* (Oxford, 1974).

I

In a colonial situation, such as east Ulster, it was necessary for the crown to establish its right to grant lands to settlers as securely as possible since an English statute of 1440 (18 Hen. VI, c.6) had deemed it necessary for the crown to prove its title to any land before granting it. Failure by the crown to establish title firmly prior to making a grant could have serious repercussions for the settlers. The case of the island of Rathlin, which had been inadvertently left out of a patent to Sir Randal Macdonnell in 1603, but included in 1604, provides an example of the problems which could arise, since title to Rathlin had not been proved in inquisition. In 1617 the crown's right to grant Rathlin was challenged by George Crawford, a landholder at Lisnorris in Kintyre, who claimed that the island was part of Scotland and not Ireland. Although Sir Randal won the long and expensive legal battle which ensued the dangers of unstable royal title were clearly demonstrated.[2]

The problem of crown title to Antrim and Down is a complex one. The right of the king to the lands of east Ulster rested on three supports: inheritance, church land, and the attainder of Shane O'Neill. The claim by inheritance derived from the medieval earldom of Ulster which had passed from the family of William de Burgh, fourth earl of Ulster, into the hands of Lionel, duke of Clarence, by marriage. By the marriage of his only child, Phillipa, to Edmund Mortimer, earl of March, the title subsequently passed into the Mortimer family. Two generations later the lordship passed to Richard, earl of Cambridge, grandfather of Edward IV and great great grandfather to Elizabeth I. The idea of the earldom of Ulster was still alive in the fifteenth century for in 1410 the clergy and nobles of Down 'with all the faithful and true liege people of the earldom of Ulster' petitioned the crown for protection from the Irish and Scots, and in the early sixteenth century the lordship was regarded as a living entity which had temporarily declined.[3] The royal claim to the lordship was pressed most forcibly in 1541 when an appeal from the lords of north Antrim, the McQuillans, who were under pressure from the Scots, 'hath called us [Henry VIII] to call to our own remembrance

---

[2] *Statutes of the realm*, ii, p. 306; P.R.O.I., Ferguson MSS, vii, pp 15, 36; *Cal. Carew, 1603-24*, pp 351-62; Marsh's Library Z1.1.13, no. 2.

[3] O'Laverty, *Down and Connor*, i, p. lxviii; *S.P. Henry VIII*, ii, pp 24-5, 59, 83; SP61/3/72.

both what great possessions in our own right appertain to us as all the lands appertaining to our crown and state there, the earldom of Ulster'.[4] This claim by inheritance was reinforced in 1542 when, as part of the wider policy of surrender and regrant, Conn O'Neill and Sir Arthur Magennis surrendered most of the lands of Ulster to Henry and were regranted them.[5]

The second claim to the lands of east Ulster originated after the rebellion of Shane O'Neill, chieftain of Tyrone, in the 1560s. The lords and captains of Clandeboy, the Glens of Antrim and the Route were accused of being 'at the command of the said traitor Shane O'Neill in this sharp and traitorous war by him levied against your Majesty', in the statute which attainted O'Neill in 1569 and their lands were duly declared forfeit.[6] There was some doubt however about the efficacy of the statute. Sir Henry Sidney, the lord deputy, was of the opinion that the military defeat of Shane was sufficient grounds to establish title to Antrim and Down but Elizabeth maintained that there was a distinction between the conquest of and the right to land.[7] For this reason the claim by inheritance was included in the preamble to the statute as a pedigree which was 'clear sound and unspotted'.

The third support of the crown's right to the land of east Ulster was based on the Irish statute, 23 Henry VIII, c.5, which had declared that all church land from that date automatically belonged to the crown and no inquisition was needed to prove this formally. Of the three claims this was the strongest since by the early seventeenth century it had been well tested and found reliable. A number of leases of church lands in east Ulster had been made in the sixteenth century by the crown and so title was well known.[8] In the first decade of the seventeenth century there was a natural reluctance by the crown to stress any wider independent title since it had not been tried and tested. Most of the early patents for land in east Ulster were simply royal confirmations of private deals, such as that between Hamilton, Montgomery and Conn O'Neill, or a recognition of the status quo, such as the grants to Sir Randal Macdonnell. By

---

[4] *S.P. Henry VIII*, iii, pp 302, 309.

[5] Ibid., p. 429; *Cal. pat. rolls Ire., Hen. VIII-Eliz.*, p. 79; for later surrenders and regrants, Perrott, *Chron. Ire., 1584-1608*, pp 43-4; *Fiants Eliz.*, no. 489, 4984-5.

[6] 11 Eliz. I, s.3, c.1 (1569) (Ir.); *Cal. Carew, 1603-24*, p. 456.

[7] D.G. White, 'Tudor plantations in Ireland before 1571' (Ph. D., T.C.D., 1969), ii, p. 246.

[8] For example, *Cal. pat. rolls Ire., Jas I*, pp 8, 10.

the 1620s however the crown had established sufficient control in east Ulster to be able to press its claim to inheritance, attainder and through the lands of the church there.[9] Although royal title to the lands of east Ulster had been worked out as a basis for royal authority there, the actual relationship between the government and the settlers had been less clearly defined. No guidelines were laid down for the organisation of the settlement such as the *Orders and Conditions* in the escheated counties and no clear policy of land distribution existed.

In late sixteenth-century England there was a certain reluctance by the administration to become involved in an Irish plantation scheme after the failure of the settlement in Munster[10] but James I's concern after 1603 was to establish stability in Ulster as rapidly as possible. Since north Antrim had been particularly unstable politically in the late sixteenth century it became James's first target. In the latter half of the sixteenth century the Scottish Macdonnells attempted to enlarge their interest in the area at the expense of the McQuillan sept who resisted these encroachments. Government policy had been to bolster up McQuillan as a buffer against Macdonnell and the O'Neills of lower Clandeboy and Sir Arthur Chichester, as the main government agent in Ulster by 1603, was intent on continuing this policy into the seventeenth century.[11] There was opposition to this, especially from Sir Randal Macdonnell, younger brother of James Macdonnell and son of Sorley Boy, who had held the Route by a grant from Elizabeth. Randal's personal claim to the Route and the Glens was dubious in English law as the lands of the Route should have passed to James Macdonnell's son, Gilleasbugh, on his father's death in 1601 and not to the claimant, Sir Randal. Nor was Sir Randal's claim to the Glens of Antrim any stronger, since the Glens were, as the result of a fifteenth century marriage agreement, the inheritance of the head of the Dunyveg branch of the Macdonnell family. In 1586, the Glens had been granted to Donal Gorm as chief, and later to his son, Angus, but by the late 1590s James Macdonnell, Angus's

[9] *Cal. pat. rolls Ire., Chas I*, pp 230-31, 504; SP63/229/93; SL, 24/25, nos 295, 302; *Mont. MSS*, pp 43-4.

[10] D.B. Quinn (ed.), 'A discourse of Ireland, *c.* 1599' in *R.I.A. Proc.*, xlvii, sect. C (1942), pp 154, 162.

[11] Bodl., Carte 31, ff 43, 73-4; Anon., 'Sir Henry Sidney's memoir of his government in Ireland' in *U.J.A.*, 1st ser., v (1857), p. 310; *Cal. S.P. Ire., 1600-01*, pp 333, 385, 418; *Cal. S.P. Ire., 1603-6*, p. 503.

cousin, had made himself *de facto* lord of the Glens. An attempt was made in 1602 by Angus Macdonnell, the chief of the Macdonnells of Dunyveg, to reassert his lordship but Elizabeth was unwilling to foment trouble in the Glens and the attempt failed.[12]

Chichester vehemently opposed the claim of Sir Randal Macdonnell to the lands of the Route and the Glens which had been strongly pressed at court by the earl of Mar. In the light of his experience of the activities of the Antrim Scots during the Nine Years War, which included the murder of his brother, Sir John, he had reason to fear the establishment of a Scots' power base in north Antrim. He also saw the difficulties which could result if a large quantity of land was concentrated in the hands of one man.[13] Chichester's own idea for a settlement, as expounded in his 'Notes of Remembrance' in 1607 and his reorganisation of the Monaghan settlement in 1605, was to make small grants of land to a few settlers and a number of trustworthy natives with the retention of the natives as tenants. This was the way he envisaged that the settlement of east Ulster should evolve. He argued in 1605 that land in Antrim should be distributed in small amounts to the 'ancient gentlemen' of the county and condemned the large grants of land which had already been made, arguing that they should have been made into small freeholds. He managed his own Antrim property in this way and applauded Sir James Hamilton for selling off his scattered property in small lots.[14]

Chichester, created lord deputy in 1605, showed concern about the large grants of land passed to Sir Randal Macdonnell, Sir James Hamilton, Sir Hugh Montgomery, Sir Edward Cromwell and others between 1603 and 1605 and complained to Sir Robert Cecil, James's principal secretary of state, that the king was making too many large grants of lands. James's reply came in the form of a reprimand and instructions to the lord deputy to pass the grants forwaded to him without

---

[12] K. Simms, 'Gaelic lordships in Ulster in the later middle ages' (Ph.D., T.C.D., 1976), pp 222, 239, 268; Hill, *Macdonnells*, pp 21-2; *Cal. Carew, 1575-88*, p. 438; G.A. Hayes McCoy, *Scots mercenary forces in Ireland* (Dublin, 1937), pp 276-80, 332; *Cal. S.P. Ire., 1601-3*, p. 445; *Cal. Scot. P., 1595-7*, pp 511-12.

[13] *Scots peerage*, v, p. 613; Hayes McCoy, *Scots mercenaries*, pp 318, 324; *Cal. S.P. Ire., 1600-01*, pp 333, 335.

[14] T.W. Moody, 'Ulster plantation papers' in *Anal. Hib.*, viii (1938), pp 281-6; T.W. Moody, *The Londonderry plantation*, (Belfast, 1939), p. 25; *Cal. S.P. Ire., 1603-6*, p. 502; B.L., Cotton Titus C vii, f 56; P. Roebuck, 'The making of an Ulster great estate' in *R.I.A. Proc.*, lxxix, sect. C (1979), pp 17-19.

question.[15] The king wanted to encourage stability and settlement in Antrim and Down and was prepared to make concessions to this end. In 1604, for example, the king was prepared to ease the terms under which Macdonnell was to receive a regrant of lands because Sir Randal had complained of burdensome terms.[16] What James probably had in mind was an Irish extension of his settlement in the Scottish Isles. In order to consolidate the plantation there it was necessary to restrict movement between east Ulster and the west coast of Scotland. The cheapest and best way to ensure this was to consolidate royal authority on the coasts of Antrim and Down by introducing English and Scots settlers and giving them the incentive of large estates with few obligations, save those of building.[17]

The result of this policy was a series of large estates over which the crown, although with established title, had little authority since it had devolved much of its power to the new landholders as a rapid way of establishing effective local government. No conditions, such as the *Orders and conditions* drawn up for the plantation of Ulster or the regulations for the later plantations in the midlands, to check the landholders' ambitions were laid down. The geographical isolation from the Dublin administration gave further encouragement to landowners to exploit the extensive rights and privileges which they had been granted. In particular many of the privileges minimised the role of royal officials on settlers' estates by limiting their function. Sheriffs, bailiffs, justices and escheators, for example, were virtually excluded from Sir James Hamilton's lands by a clause in his patent.[18]

There were those who through ambition, or other factors, reacted to this restriction of royal authority by availing of the opportunity to enhance their own local influence. In 1612, for example, Sir Hugh Montgomery refused to accept a royal warrant issued to two Scotsmen, James and Alexander Kennedy, for apprehending the murderer of their

[15] *Des. Cur. Hib.*, i, pp 462-3. This letter is undated but internal evidence, the references to the settlement of Monaghan and to a letter of the 23rd of the previous month (probably SP63/217/45), suggests early July 1605.

[16] Erck., pp 166-7.

[17] *Reg.P.C. Scot., 1613-16*, pp 717, 769-71. On James and the Isles, *Reg.P.C. Scot., 1599-1604*, p. 24; *Reg.P.C. Scot., 1604-7*, p. 89; D.J. MacDonald, *Clan Donald* (Loanhead, 1978), pp 252-3. For building and planting clauses, *Cal. pat. rolls Ire., Jas I*, pp 78, 125; *Ham. MSS*, app. 1; *Cal. S.P. Ire., 1603-6*, p. 502.

[18] *Ham. MSS*, app. 1, pp vii, xxv.

father; Montgomery arguing that the offence was caused by wilful resistance by the elder Kennedy, an offence which was not warrantable in Ireland, although it was in Scotland or England. It was later pointed out that the real motivation was an assertion of Montgomery's right to discipline his own tenants without external interference from royal officials.[19] A later example of the exertion of landlord rights occurred in 1627 when although Lord Conway's agent, Henry Spenser, was acquitted of manslaughter, Spenser's goods were declared forfeit to the king. Lord Conway objected strongly on the basis that all felons' goods belonged to him under the terms of his patent. The king capitulated and returned the goods to Spenser but not through Conway, making it clear to the lord deputy, Lord Falkland, that he was not doing this 'upon any nice construction of the Lord Conway's patent in that point' but for the sake of justice, Spenser being innocent.[20] Many of the settlers had risen rapidly on the social scale through the acquisition of extensive lands and rights as a result of the settlement and were determined to consolidate their new positions. Given this defensive attitude to their rights it was natural that royal officials and authority should be resisted. It was this idea which underlay the earl of Antrim's offer in 1635 to cess his own tenants for the subsidy, as he was trying to keep royal commissioners from entering his lands.[21]

The agents of royal authority who should have impinged on the settlers' lands most frequently were judicial officials. One way of minimising their influence was to make maximum use of the manorial courts which were under the control of the lord and therefore judicial officials were given little occasion to visit the settlers' estates. The earl of Antrim achieved maximum use of his manor courts by inserting a clause in his leases that

neither the said [tenant's name] nor his heirs or assigns nor any of their undertenants . . . shall commence any suit against any of the tenants of the said earl . . . for any debt, trespass or any other misdemeanour not exceeding the value of thirty nine shillings sterling in any of the sheriffs' courts of the county of Antrim but shall either compound the same by order of neighbour and friends or else commence such action in the Court Leet or Court Baron . . . under pain of forfeiture of ten shillings sterling for every such action so commenced.

[19] *Cal. S.P. Ire., 1611-14*, pp 234, 241.
[20] *Cal. pat. rolls Ire., Chas I*, pp 259, 321; *Cal. S.P. Ire., 1625-32*, p. 301.
[21] SL, 15, no. 234.

Other landlords, such as Sir James Hamilton, also included similar clauses in their leases in order to minimise royal interference in the running of estates.[22] The success of such actions is reflected in the geography of the gaol deliveries from east Ulster since all the cases presented from the well consolidated estates of Hamilton, Montgomery and the earl of Antrim would have been outside the jurisdiction of the manor courts. The areas from which most cases came to royal courts, such as chancery, were the poorly consolidated and inadequately run lands of Sir Edward Trevor, the Magennis family and Sir Edward Cromwell where manorial courts did not function.[23]

As well as attempting to limit the powers of royal judicial officials by replacing their functions by landlord-controlled institutions, individual lords also took more spectacular action in resisting the powers of local government officials. The sheriff of Antrim, Cahall O'Hara of Crebilly, complained in 1627 that it was impossible to carry out any of his duties on the earl of Antrim's estate without the earl's express permission. The earl claimed the right to approve all warrants affecting his lands or tenants and any attempt to execute a warrant without his permission resulted in the sub-sheriff being placed in the stocks. Indeed the earl attempted to manipulate the law to his own ends threatening one man with 'a bellyfull of law' at the 1627 quarter sessions in Carrickfergus. He also attempted to have the Antrim quarter sessions moved to his own estate at Oldstone so that he could increase his influence, pleading in mitigation that it would be less inconvenience to his tenantry.[24]

Not only were the agencies of central government resisted by this settler attitude but the rights of other centralised groups such as the church were eroded in some areas. In the case of Newry the local landlord, Henry Bagnall, refused to admit officials of the church courts to his estate claiming that when the lands were granted in the sixteenth century to his grandfather, Sir Nicholas Bagnall, marshall of the army, the grant had included all the rights and immunities of the medieval monastery of Newry. He also claimed all the churches and ecclesiastical jurisdiction on his lands as his personal property and the 1622 visitation

---

[22] P.R.O.N.I., D2977; LPC 133; T549/1A; T761/3, p. 4.

[23] This point is further developed below, pp 157-8. There is a similar distribution for cases brought to the court of common pleas (T.C.D., MS 2512).

[24] SP63/245/821, i-v.

observed of his territory that:

two other bishops immediate predecessors were in possession and farmed several
parcells of this living to several persons but the bishops being in England shortly
after his presentment soldiers were sent to take up the tithes and two of the
bishops' farmers being found upon their journey in the Newry were committed
and kept prisoners until they were forced to quit and surrender their possession.
The now bishop thereafter petitioned to the Judges of Assize and had order to
the sheriff to put and keep him in possession. That there being one who dwelled
at the Newry and tenant to Mr. Bagnall, would neither put him in possession,
nor give him his order back again; that he had such order appears under his
hand, and under the hands of the other justices of the peace; as may be seen there
are no tithes received by any clergyman, nor cure served, nor presentment of
recusants made, no way given to the Ecclesiastical Courts, nor to the bishops' officers, and the confusion is within the bounds of no less than sixteen miles upon
the sea coast. Mr. Bagnall has given several commissions to several persons to
keep several spiritual courts, whereof, some of them were laymen and several
persons have fled from the censure of the bishops spiritual courts in these
bounds, and there they have immunity and escape deserved censures because the
apparitors would not, nor durst not, cite any person in these bounds.[25]

In a more discreet way there was also a refusal by many other
landlords to recognise the church's authority as nonconformist
religious groups flourished in parts of east Ulster under local patrons. A
sympathetic attitude by the earl of Antrim towards catholicism, for example, promoted its survival in north Antrim, and in north Down tacit
support for presbyterianism by Sir James Hamilton helped its establishment there.[26]

Thus two groups developed conflicting aims over the settlement of
east Ulster. The government had established its authority over Antrim
and Down by proving crown title and, as will be shown below, developing a system of local officials there to safeguard its rights. On the other
hand however the rapid social rise of most of the new settlers made them

---

[25] O'Laverty, *Down and Connor*, i, pp 14-15; SP63/254/4; *Cal. S.P. Ire., 1625-32*, p.
644; B. Bradshaw, *The dissolution of the religious orders in Ireland under Henry VIII*
(Cambridge, 1974), p. 159. Bagnall also claimed all secular fines levied on his land,
P.R.O.I., Thrift MSS, no. 255.
[26] On Antrim's catholicism C. Giblin, *The Irish Franciscan mission to Scotland*
(Dublin, 1964); SL, 1, f 67; SL, 10, ff 131, 172; *Cal. S.P. Ire., 1615-25*, pp 324-37. On
Hamilton's presbyterianism, Blair, *Autobiography*, p. 58; M. Perceval Maxwell,
'Strafford, the Ulster-Scots and the Covenanters' in *I.H.S.*, xviii (1972-3), p. 547.

anxious to consolidate their new found position and exploit such concessions as had been made to them. In this situation conflict was inevitable as the central administraton attempted to assert its control over the localities as for example when in the early years of the settlement a crisis developed over the collection of customs. In the sixteenth century the collection of customs in Antrim and Down had been left in local hands. The customs of Carlingford and Newry were held by the Bagnall family and those of Ardglass, Strangford and Lecale had been leased to the earl of Kildare. At Carrickfergus two-thirds of the customs revenue was leased to a succession of constables of the town at a rent of £10, the remaining third going to the corporation.[27] This arrangement was disrupted by the growth of new port towns in east Ulster, such as Bangor and Donaghadee, and by the decision in 1613 to farm all the Irish customs to a group of financiers. In order to farm the customs the crown had to resume all the grants which had been made to individuals. The customs revenues of east Ulster had been farmed to Sir James Hamilton who was reluctant to surrender them even after being ordered to appear before the privy council.[28] However the success of the administration in resuming grants in other areas, especially the case against the corporation of Dublin in king's bench during 1613, convinced Hamilton that it was wise to do a lucrative private deal with the farmers of the customs, a deal he concluded in December 1616.[29]

Others, less astute than Hamilton, were not prepared to lay down their rights so easily. The countess of Kildare retained the family interest in Lecale as part of her jointure, leasing it to four merchants and although she was ordered by the Dublin administration to surrender her claim or submit to a committee of judges she refused to do either. The countess was persuaded to make a lease of the customs to the customs farmers for her life at £70 per annum but pressure on the family over this issue was not relaxed and after the countess's death her son, George, earl of Kildare, was summoned to the exchequer and forced to surrender his claim. Roger Langford, a minor Antrim landowner who held part of

[27] *Cal. pat. rolls Ire., Eliz.*, p. 154; V. Treadwell, 'The Irish customs administration in the sixteenth century' in *I.H.S.*, xx (1977), pp 407, 408; V. Treadwell, 'The establishment of the farm of the Irish customs' in *E.H.R.*, xciii (1978), pp 580-89.

[28] *Cal. pat. rolls Ire., Jas I*, p. 201.

[29] H.M.C., *Various* , viii, p. 191; *Acts privy council, 1615-16*, pp 277, 347; V. Treadwell, 'Irish financial administrative reform under James I: the customs and state regulation of Irish trade (Ph.D., Q.U.B., 1960), p. 242; *Cal. S.P. Ire., 1615-25*, p. 128.

the Carrickfergus customs on a lease from the crown, which was not due to expire until 1626, also remained stubborn. In July 1619 the king, whose patience was wearing thin, ordered the settlement of outstanding grants, by *quo warranto* proceedings if necessary. Under this pressure Langford surrendered his lease for a composition of £323.9s.4d. This however did not finally resolve the problem of the Carrickfergus customs for one-third of the revenue still belonged to the corporation and it was not until 1638 that the crown purchased this.[30]

Before the late 1620s there was little attempt to attack the powers of the new landlords apart from occasional forays against some of them. In 1618 for example, Sir James Hamilton was required to produce all his patents for a detailed examination of his privileges but no action was taken against him. Four years later he was attacked by the attorney general, Sir William Pyres, for abusing the rights granted to him but again he was acquitted. Within the next ten years the government summoned Sir Edward Chichester, the earl of Antrim and Rowland Savage on similar charges but gained no convictions. Hamilton was again summoned to the exchequer in 1639 on a charge of illegally holding an admiralty court at Groomsport but by pleading his patent of 1622 he was acquitted.[31] The 1630s however saw a more concerted policy of establishing royal authority in the localities implemented by the new lord deputy, Thomas Wentworth. The contrast between royal policy in the administration of east Ulster in the 1630s and the earlier decades is best seen in the case of the position of the church.

The control of the church and its wealth in the localities was an important issue because as well as being a spiritual body it was also an important political agent in the counties. This point is illustrated in a letter of 1601 containing the queen's instructions for the appointment of a new bishop of Down and Connor which directed that he should have enough learning 'to instruct our people and sufficiency to govern them to the continuance of their duty and loyalty to God and us, their gracious sovereign'.[32] Thus it was essential that the central administration

[30] Treadwell, 'Irish financial administrative reform', p. 243; P.R.O.I., Ferguson MSS, xxvi, p. 132; *Cal. S.P. Ire., 1633-47*, p. 190; P.R.O.N.I., D671/D3/1/3; A. Knox, *A history of county Down* (Dublin, 1875), p. 434.

[31] P.R.O.I., Ferguson MSS, xxvi, pp 58, 91, 95, 145; Bodl., Carte 30, f 234ᵛ; *Ham. MSS*, pp 30-31.

[32] *Cal. pat. rolls Ire., Eliz.*, p. 589.

controlled benefices and the lands that went with them in order to ensure that suitable candidates were appointed to cures. There was concern that benefices might fall into the wrong hands and the archbishop of Canterbury, William Laud, wrote of his fear 'that my earl of Antrim should get the advowson of the benefices, if he could, is no wonder to me, for being a recusant . . . [he] . . . might make great use of them'. The danger of private patronage was clearly shown in 1623 when Lord Clandeboy presented Robert Blair, a radical Scots presbyterian, to the living at Bangor from which Blair openly defied the ideas of the established church.[33] Despite the importance of this issue the government was unwilling to confront the lords of east Ulster who held the rights of presentment and church lands as part of their estate. The late sixteenth and early seventeenth centuries saw the granting of church lands to the local landlord on long leases, a policy much favoured by the first three seventeenth-century bishops of Down and Connor.[34] By the late 1620s the original rents were no longer realistic and there was an attempt by the church to resume these lands and so in 1627 the newly presented dean of Down, Henry Leslie, petitioned the king to annul a 1589 lease to the earl of Kildare of the church's lands in Lecale. Legal advice was sought which declared that the charter of 1610, which had reorganised the dean and chapter of Down, gave the church the right to these lands and the dean was given permission to proceed against the earl in the king's name but there is no evidence that he did so.[35] It was not until 1636 that any systematic campaign to recover church lands began when the lord deputy, Wentworth, established a commission to recover church lands in the diocese of Down and Connor. Many landowners resisted this move. Lord Clandeboy, for example, claimed that the lands of Black Abbey, which lay in his estate, were not the property of the church even though they had been found to be church land by an inquisition of 1623. It required a king's letter of June 1639 to compel Clandeboy to surrender the lands but only on a promise of a sixty year lease of them.[36] By October 1639 the government was pressing the

---

[33] Laud, *Works,* vii, p. 59; Blair, *Autobiography*, p. 78.

[34] J.B. Leslie, H.B. Swanzy, *Biographical succession lists of the clergy of Down* (Enniskillen, 1936), p. 8.

[35] *Cal. pat. rolls Ire., Chas. I,* pp 494-5; *Cal. S.P. Ire., 1625-32,* p. 328.

[36] P.R.O.N.I., DI04/5/1, ff 82-92. Sir Edward Chichester also came to a personal arrangement.

claims of the church through a series of court cases against the earl of Antrim and Lords Clandeboy, Ards, Cromwell, Iveagh and Sir Edward Trevor. As a result of these moves the revenues of the bishoprics of Down and Connor were increased by 243 per cent.[37] A similar campaign was mounted against lay impropriations, the right of local landowners to present to livings, which had also been granted by bishops to the local gentry in the first two decades of the century. Bishop Todd, for example, made over all rights to courts and presentment to livings in north Antrim to Sir Randal Macdonnell in 1610.[38] Wentworth waged the campaign for the recovery of impropriated livings with equal ferocity to that for the recovery of lands but with less success.[39]

This systematic attempt by Wentworth to reassert royal authority in the localities was characterised by a probing into the affairs of landowners through the Commission for Defective Titles and the court of wards. Both of these activities depended on the reform of the system of tenure in east Ulster; the conversion of common socage, a relatively light form of tenure with no obligation of wardship, escheat or license of alienation, to knight service which held all these obligations and was financially more lucrative to the crown.[40] Most of those who acquired their east Ulster lands in the sixteenth century, such as the Macdonnell and Bagnall families, held their lands by knight service, as did most of the native landowners such as the O'Neill family and Cahall O'Hara. In contrast the newcomers, Hamilton, Montgomery, Chichester and Conway, for example, were all granted their lands in common socage as part of the plan to induce settlement.[41] As a result of this Dublin administrators became concerned over low levels of revenue produced by east Ulster and the display of resistance to royal authority arising from the concessions granted in the early years of the settlement. In 1631, for instance, the crown rent from Antrim was £211.7s.4d. and that of Down £483.0s.11d. whereas the average rent from an escheated county was

[37] *Cal. S.P. Ire., 1633-47*, p. 226; E.P. Shirley, *Papers relating to the Church of Ireland, 1631-9* (London, 1874), pp 14-16.

[38] T.C.D., MS 1059, ff 161-5.

[39] Shirley, *Papers*, pp 2-3, 14-16.

[40] For a detailed explanation of this, see H.E. Ball, *An introduction to the history and records of the courts of wards and liveries* (Cambridge, 1953), p. 75, n. 6; J.C.W. Wylie, *Irish land law* (London, 1975), pp 56-7.

[41] *Cal. pat. rolls, Ed. VI*, iv, pp 387-90; *Cal. pat. rolls Ire., Jas I*, pp 93-4, 102; Erck, pp 281-4. For landlord reaction to the different tenures, see Hill, *Plantation*, p. 81.

£736.18s.0d.[42] Advice had been taken from the attorney general as to the legality of imposing an annual composition on Antrim and Down similar to that in the Leix-Offaly settlement but this scheme was never implemented.[43] These problems of finance and of asserting royal authority were attacked by Wentworth through the Commission for Defective Titles which granted new patents to landowners, thus increasing crown rent as well as royal control by changing socage tenures to knight service. In May 1637 the first patents under the commission were passed for east Ulster.[44] Rents were increased considerably, in the case of Sir Hugh Montgomery by 320 per cent, and substantial renewal fines were imposed on the settlers for new patents, £103.17s.8d. in the case of Montgomery.[45]

Reactions in east Ulster to the calling in of old patents, and hence of rights, were mixed. Some who held their lands or part of their lands by conveyance, such as Sir Hugh Montgomery, Robert Adair in mid-Antrim and Bernard Ward in east Down, took advantage of the commission to have their titles to land secured by obtaining a formal patent.[46] Others, mainly native Irish, showed considerable concern at the move as they feared that they were to be evicted from their lands and a formal plantation made. In a lease dated December 1637 between Conn Magennis of Newcastle and Arthur Hill, the insecurity of title was reflected by a clause stating 'that if hereafter it shall happen all or any part of the premises to be evicted, recorded or otherwise taken away from the said Arthur Hill . . . by way of plantation or any other way' he was to be compensated.[47] Some settlers intent on protecting their rights from royal encroachment evaded the commission. The earl of Antrim, for example, feared the repercussions of not passing a patent under the commission but did not want his rights eroded and so convinced Wentworth that he was about to acquire a patent from the commission although he never actually did so.[48]

---

[42] SL, 1, f 29. There were, however, fewer arrears in the crown rent from east Ulster. In 1620, 4·9 per cent of the total Ulster arrears was from Antrim and 9·2 per cent from Down and only £15 was considered 'doubtful', N.L.I., MS 8013 IV.

[43] N.L.I., MS 8013 III, no. 8; Bodl., Carte 61, f 142.

[44] SP63/256/33.

[45] N.L.I., MS 15584.

[46] P.R.O.I., Lodge MSS, Records of the rolls, vi, pp 10, 28, 40, 42, 99, 118, 254, 337.

[47] P.R.O.N.I., D671/D8/1/55A.

[48] Laud, *Works,* vii, pp 391, 445; SL, 17, no. 236.

Royal authority in east Ulster should have been enhanced by the creation by the commission of more tenures in knight service since these would give royal officers, such as the escheator and officers of the court of wards, an increased role in east Ulster and increase royal revenues through feudal incidents. In the late sixteenth and early seventeenth centuries Antrim and Down landowners had attempted to avoid feudal incidents, the payment for wardship, alienation, and marriage, as far as possible. They had attempted to avoid wardship by 'enfeoffing' land to use which involved a father placing the use, though not the ownership, of his lands into the hands of a group of men whom he could trust, usually close relations. This meant that when a landowner died his estates could not be taken into wardship if his son was a minor since he was not possessed of his lands on his death.[49] Hence the crown could not grant the lands to a stranger who might strip the lands of its assets during the minority of the heir. When the heir came of age the lands would be conveyed to him by the group of feoffees and the only claim of the crown would be the payment of a relief.[50]

Attempts had also been made to avoid alienation fines, the fine paid to the supreme owner of land, the king, before it could be alienated. The officer responsible for the levying of these fines and detection of breaches in the alienation procedure was the escheator who used a series of inquisitions returned to chancery to gather his information.[51] Antrim and Down came under the jurisdiction of the escheator for Ulster, George Sexton, a secretary to the lord deputy, who was appointed escheator in 1605.[52] Much of his own estate, which he had accumulated piecemeal from Magennis and Conn O'Neill, lay in Down. Sexton's acquisitions were of dubious legality as he had used his position as escheator to ignore the normal procedures and purchase land at advantageous rates. An inquisition taken at Downpatrick in April 1632 revealed that Sir Arthur Magennis had alienated land to Sexton on 29 November 1617 for which no fine was paid. In 1623 it was revealed that

[49] Bell, *Courts of wards,* pp 3-4, 13-14; for examples, P.R.O.I., RC9/1, no. 3; *Cal. S.P. Ire., 1611-14,* p. 321; *Cal. pat. rolls, Ire., Chas I,* pp 520, 545.

[50] This situation could cause problems if the reconveyance was not made but only one case of this in east Ulster, over Bagnall's lands, is known, P.R.O., C3/332/15.

[51] Bell, *Court of wards,* pp 38-45; SP63/216/4.

[52] *Cal. pat. rolls, Ire., Jas I,* p. 86; SP63/232/23; *Cal. S.P. Ire., 1608-10,* p. 79; *Cal. S.P. Ire., 1611-14,* p. 443.

Magennis had alienated further land illegally to Sexton and a pardon granted to Sexton's heir after his death in 1632 detailed six further alienations which were previously unrecorded.[53] With this calibre of supervision evasion of feudal incidents was easy. What was required was a general tightening of royal authority and administration in the localities, a process which had begun in east Ulster in the late 1620s and was later intensified by Wentworth.

By the late 1620s a number of reforms made in the local organisation of the court of wards by the central government, including the reorganisation of the escheatorships and the creation of central commissioners, began to affect east Ulster. In 1627, for example, commissioners from the reformed court of wards were inquiring into wardships in Down and in at least one case 'they did press to see if a wardship could be found'.[54] One of the features of this new regime was the more efficient way in which the crown's rights over land, such as alienation fines, wardship and liveries, were ascertained by inquisition. In the earlier part of the century there does not appear to have been any attempt made by the escheator to keep track of feudal rights and in the late 1620s a series of inquisitions in east Ulster detected unlicensed alienations of land which had remained hidden for up to eleven years. For example, one inquisition taken at Carrickfergus on 18 May 1628 uncovered an illegal alienation made thirteen years earlier by Shane McBrian O'Neill.[55] Another series of inquisitions taken by Ballymena and Carrickfergus between 23 August 1634 and 18 March 1635 revealed well over one hundred cases of illegal alienations, undetected wardships or liveries unsued which had been concealed by the earl of Antrim.[56] So great had been the

---

[53] *Cal. pat. rolls Ire., Jas I*, pp 194, 304-5; *Cal. pat. rolls Ire., Chas I*, pp 233, 604; T.C.D., MS 644, f 120; *Inq. Ult.*, Down, Chas I, no. 30; P.R.O.I., Lodge MSS, Wardships and Alienations, i, p. 131; P.R.O.N.I., D765/5. Sexton spent most of his time in Dublin. J.T. Gilbert, *A history of the city of Dublin*, ii (Dublin, 1859), p. 171.

[54] H.M.C., *Various*, v, pp 124-5, 130; on this point generally, V. Treadwell, 'The Irish court of wards under James' in *I.H.S.*, xii (1960-61), pp 15-24; H. Kearney, 'The court of wards and liveries in Ireland' in *R.I.A. Proc.*, lvii, sect. C (1955), pp 32-7; the 'revival of feudalism' in Caroline England is yet unstudied but two articles are of value, H. Leonard, 'Distraint of knighthood: the last phase' in *History*, lxiii (1978), pp 23-37; G. Hammersley, 'The revival of the forest laws under Charles I' in *History*, xlv (1960), pp 85-102.

[55] P.R.O.I., Lodge MSS. Pardons of alienation, i, pp 169, 170.

[56] *Inq. Ult.*, Antrim, Chas I, no. 14, 25-105, 109, 110; P.R.O.I., Lodge MS. Pardons of alienation, i, pp 174-7; T.C.D., MS 644, ff 86-9.

backlog of business of wardships and alienations by the 1620s that one inquisition post mortem held in Down on 17 September 1627 had to establish ownership of the land of Donagh Magrory who had died in August 1599.[57] Something of the impact of the reforms of the 1620s and 1630s is illustrated by the case of William Adair of Ballymena who died on 4 November 1626 for within just five months his lands had been surveyed by the commissioners from the court of wards.[58] Personnel changes aided the increased efficiency of the administrative structures of the court of wards as the inefficient George Sexton was replaced in April 1629 by two escheators for Ulster, Edmund Perceval, a cousin of the Dublin clerk of wards, and Jonas Querle.[59] As a result of these administrative and personnel changes the business of the court of wards mounted rapidly in east Ulster from the mid-1620s to reach a peak under the administration of Wentworth in the 1630s.[60]

This extension of central government influence into Antrim and Down through officials of the reformed court of wards disturbed some of the greater landowners who were often zealously protective of the 'rights' which they had acquired. In 1634 Arthur and Mabel Bagnall at Newry attempted to avoid wardship by nominating guardians for their son, Nicholas, should they die before he attained his majority but they failed in an attempt to have this arrangement recognised at law.[61] Many east-Ulster landlords simply refused to acknowledge that the Dublin administration had any control over their lands and refused to pay the semi-feudal dues demanded of them. On the death of Edward, Lord Cromwell, in 1609, for example, the earl of Kildare claimed part of Cromwell's lands and requested an inquisition to determine the rightful heir. The inquisition upheld the rights of Thomas, son of Edward Cromwell, and levied on him a livery of £100 but Thomas delayed payment, presenting a number of excuses and asking for more time. This was not an isolated case and by 1617 evasion of payment of liveries had become so widespread that the exchequer ordered all liveries to be paid within six days of the return of an inquisition post mortem to chancery

[57] *Inq. Ult.*, Down, Chas I, no. 6; T.C.D., MS 648, f 143.

[58] *Inq. Ult.*, Antrim, Chas I, no. 4.

[59] *Liber mun. pub. Hib.*, i, pt 2, p. 58; Sexton died in Mar. 1631, B.L., Add. 4820, f 239; P.R.O.N.I., D765/5; H.M.C., *Egmont*, i, pt i, pp viii-xi; *D.N.B.*, sub-nomine.

[60] Appendix C.

[61] P.R.O.I., Lodge MSS, Wards and liveries, i, p. 29.

on pain of forfeiture of the land in question. Within a week Cromwell paid his livery.[62] The reaction of others to the demands of central administration were less guarded. The earl of Antrim, for example, by 1635 owed the king £1000 in alienation fines which he refused to pay.[63] Sir James Hamilton, on the other hand, was more subtle and responded to the increased presence of Dublin officials by attempting, using his influence with the king through an old friend, James Fullerton, to have escheators barred from his estates.[64] Increased government efficiency in the administration of the counties of Antrim and Down was not welcomed by most landlords and the Dublin administration realised that it would be impossible to keep landowners under coercion for long. Landlords had to be encouraged to see the county, rather than their individual estates, as the main unit of political life. Such a transformation they hoped would be brought about by the county based machinery of local government.

Antrim and Down had had, at least in theory, the territorial and administrative organisation for English style local government since medieval times. The central figure in this local government was the sheriff who was responsible for carrying out the day-to-day administration of local government and for enforcing the decisions of the central administration in the county. This meant receiving and implementing royal writs, including those for elections, collecting royal revenue from his county and presiding over the quarter sessions. He had to be acceptable to the local gentry and also had to wield substantial local power which central govenment could, hopefully, harness. This explains the appointment of Shane McBrian O'Neill as captain or sheriff of Lower Clandeboy in 1583 since he was 'chief of his name'.[65] All the sheriffs of Antrim in the early seventeenth century were drawn from the major landed families of the county as were most of those of county Down.[66] A few county Down sheriffs, James Peckham and Piers Pulbereigh, for instance, were not landed proprietors there but were appointed due to

[62] P.R.O.I., Ferguson MSS, xi, pp 180, 181, 183, 222-3, 257-8, 262; Lodge MSS, Wardships and alienations, i, p. 96.
[63] Strafford, *Letters*, i, p. 517. By 1639 he owed £700 to the court of wards and £400 to the king, Strafford, *Letters*, ii, p. 358.
[64] N.L.S., Denmilne MSS, 5, no. 135.
[65] *Fiants Eliz.*, no. 4201.
[66] P.R.O.N.I., D302; Anon, 'High sheriffs of the county of Antrim' in *U.J.A.*, 2nd ser., xi (1905), pp 78-83.

court influence or were nominated by Down landowners. This effective limitation of the office of sheriff to a few men of considerable local influence meant that given the small pool of settlers available there was a shortage of acceptable candidates and some men held office a number of times. Sir Hugh Clotworthy, for example, was sheriff of county Antrim three times between 1600 and 1641 and the Hill family held the office twice.

In practice the greater part of the routine work of the sheriff was carried out by sub-sheriffs who, although not among the first grade of county society, were still substantial landowners and carried weight within their own local community.[67] In 1641, for example, the sub-sheriffs for county Down were Sir Conn Magennis of Newcastle, Daniel Oge Magennis of Glasscoe, Edmund McBrien Oge Magennis of Iveagh, Captain Patrick Owney of Kilwarlin and Michael Grave of Newry, all men of some importance but not in the upper ranks of landed society.[68] Prior to the authorisation of sub-sheriffs the sheriff was assisted by influential local men as in 1584 when one of the conditions of a grant to Sir Arthur Magennis was that he would assist the sheriff in his duties.[69]

The sheriff was also aided in the enforcement of the law by the justices of the peace.[70] In the sixteenth century the functions of the justice of the peace in east Ulster had been carried out by the governor of Clandeboy but by the early seventeenth century the office was made distinct through the efforts of the lord deputy, Sir Arthur Chichester, who saw the need for a body of reliable men to enforce law and order in the localities.[71] The main role of the justice of the peace was the routine maintenance of law and order in his own locality. Where necessary this included preventing disorder before it occurred by taking recognisances for the peace from potential malefactors such as Sorley James Macdonnell, nephew of the earl of Antrim, and 'other traitorous rebels

[67] A sheriff was allowed to appoint, at his own expense, four sub-sheriffs for each county who were to live not less than twelve miles apart, (10 Car I, s.2, c.25.(Ir)).

[68] T.C.D., MS 837, f 12.

[69] P.R.O.I., Thrift MSS, no. 114; Ferguson MSS, xii, p. 15.

[70] The J.P. in Ireland was a sixteenth century development deriving from two medieval English statutes applied to Ireland by 10 Hen. VII, c. 22; cf. R. Frame, 'The judicial powers of the medieval keeper of the peace' in *Ir. Jurist*, n.s., ii (1967), pp 319-22, 326. For instructions to J.P.s, *Desiderata Curosia Hib.*, i, p. 20.

[71] For example, taking pledges for good behaviour, G.A. Hayes-McCoy, *Scots mercenary forces in Ireland* (London, 1937), p. 252; SP63/217/67.

in Scotland' who arrived in Antrim during 1617. The possibility of a breach of the peace arose and so a justice of the peace, Sir Fulke Conway, demanded that Sorley's uncle enter into recognisances of the peace for his nephew.[72] However, most of the work of the justice of the peace was done not as an individual but as one of the body of justices at the quarter sessions. The sessions, which met at least four times per annum and sometimes more frequently, were summoned by the sheriff and met in the county towns; Carrickfergus in Antrim, and, initially, Newry in Down, although this was moved to Downpatrick in the 1630s.[73] The workings of quarter sessions can be seen in 1641 when the sheriff held five sessions in county Down to deal with rebels. A jury was impanelled and sworn and then 'writs were legally indicted before a lawful jury' against the accused. Since the quarter sessions felt the rebels' offence was too great to be dealt with locally, writs were issued against the rebels to appear at a Dublin court.[74]

Justices of the peace were appointed by a commission of the peace, issued to each justice after he took the Oaths of Supremacy and loyalty as a justice of the peace, and after there had been consultation with established J.P.s and the assize judges who knew the counties.[75] An indication of the structure of the commission for east Ulster is provided by a list of the mid-1620s.[76] The commission was small, only thirteen members for each county and the possibilities for expansion, as seen by the compiler of the list, were limited to three more men in Antrim and six in Down. In an English context this was a very small grouping. Cheshire for example, had between sixty and eighty people on the commission until 1625, after which it fell to about forty-five. The reason for the low figure in east Ulster, as for the office of sheriff, was the limited number of gentry available to fill places since if he was to impose his authority in the localities the justice of the peace had to be a substantial landholder. Significantly a number of the 'declining' families such as the Savages and the Russells were not included in the list of possible appointees to

[72] P.R.O.I., Ferguson MSS, xi, p. 242; *Acts privy council, 1615-16*, p. 632; *Cal. pat. rolls Ire., Jas I*, p. 314. For other examples, B.L., Harley 2138, f 175; R. Bolton, *A justice of peace for Ireland* (Dublin, 1638), bk i, pp 229-46.

[73] Bolton, *Justice*, bk ii, p. 1.

[74] T.C.D., MS 837, ff 3-7.

[75] Bolton, *Justice*, bk i, pp 5, 7-8; *Cal. S.P. Ire., 1611-14*, p. 434.

[76] T.C.D., MS 672, f 186ᵛ.

the commission of the peace although a number of prominent native Irish families, such as Sir Henry O'Neill in Antrim and Sir Hugh Magennis in Down, were included. Support from an important landed magnate in a locality was necessary to ensure that a person became a justice of the peace. In this way Archibald Stewart, the land agent of the earl of Antrim, became a justice of the peace, as did Henry Spenser, an agent on the Conway estate and the commission to Archibald Edmonston was due mainly to the influence of his brother in law, Lord Clandeboy.[77]

The main way in which officials for central government directly impinged on the counties on a regular basis was the visitation of the justices of assize which acted not only as a law court but also as the watchdog of central administration in the counties and as apologist for central government policy in the localities. During the late sixteenth century there had only been sporadic assizes in east Ulster but in the early seventeenth century the assize circuit was remodelled and assizes became more regular.[78] There is definite evidence that assizes operated in east Ulster in 1605, 1609, 1611, 1612, 1613, 1615, 1616, 1619, 1624 and 1625, demonstrating a regular pattern of visitation.[79]

The assizes dealt with both criminal and non-criminal cases but since most minor cases were dealt with at the quarter sessions the business of the assize was relatively light. The assize judges operated through the local jury, of about sixteen men, who provided the information against the accused who was then called to the bar, judged and, if necessary, sentenced by the judge. In non-criminal cases the assize represented the Dublin courts in the counties by dealing with such cases as a lord sueing for distraint of a tenant's goods or for payment of rent or as arbitrator in

---

[77] H.M.C., *Various*, v, p. 130.

[78] For example, *Cal. pat. rolls Ire., Eliz.*, p. 25; SP63/171/21; *Fiants Eliz.*, no. 5769.

[79] For the sixteenth century circuit, SP63/171/21; and the remodelling, *Cal. S.P. Ire., 1603-6*, pp 321, 323; for various assizes, *Cal. S.P. Ire., 1603-6*, p. 321 (1605); SP63/226/96 (1609); P.R.O.I., Ferguson MSS, ix, p. 15 (1611); Thrift MSS, no. 255 (1612); Ferguson MSS, ix, p. 103 (1613); *Cal. S.P. Ire., 1615-25*, pp 65, 127 (1615, 1616); H.M.C., *Egmont MSS*, i, pt i, pp 50, 53 (1617); P.R.O.I., Ferguson MSS, ix, pp 145, 147, 186, 222 (1619, 1622, 1624); Blair *Autobiography*, p. 78 (1625). In England assizes were normally held twice per annum (J.S. Cockburn, *A history of the English assizes* (Cambridge, 1972), pp 23-4). A similar order existed for Munster and Connacht (*Cal. S.P. Ire., 1608-10* p. 154) but in Ulster the norm was one visit per year (J.F. Ferguson, 'The Ulster roll of gaol delivery' in *U.J.A.*, 1st ser., i (1853), pp 260-61.)

cases of disputed land. This was more convenient than going to Dublin but it was by no means cheap as the petition of Ferdoragh Magennis to the lord deputy in 1636 stated that he had spent £20.8s.0d. to take a case on tithes to the Down assize.[80]

The system in Antrim and Down appears to have been reasonably efficient. The return of fines from the Lent circuit of 1616 by the sheriffs of Antrim and Down showed Down returning £541.6s.8d. and Antrim £452.15s.6d. which represents the second and fifth highest in the country.[81] Yet the incidence of litigation per head in east Ulster, as measured by the gaol delivery rolls, was not significantly higher than other Ulster counties so the high sums probably reflect an effective judicial system. It was not, however, perfect for much depended on the actions of juries in returning people for trial. Such actions were not always reliable and the lord deputy complained in 1627 that the common law was being threatened by the inhabitants of Antrim and Down who would not find bills of indictment against suspects no matter how strong the evidence was.[82] The power of the local community was stronger in some cases than that of the judicial system and in cases such as recusancy many jurors refused to present their neighbours. Those jurors who refused to present recusants, such as John Magennis of Corage, county Down, or Brian Oge Magennis, were referred to Star Chamber in Dublin to be dealt with.[83] The bias of the local community was feared by two members of the Russell family, small but significant Old English landowners in Lecale, who were accused in 1628 with Dr Duinegan, titular bishop of Down, of recusancy. They agreed to a trial but asked that the jury should not be drawn from county Down for they had enemies there.[84]

The assize had an ecclesiastical counterpart in the episcopal visitations which were held in east Ulster in 1622, 1634, 1636 and

---

[80] Bodl., Rawlinson C439, ff 100, 123, 129ᵛ, 216, 227. Judges of Assize operated under five separate commission; that of Assize allowed them to deal with ejectments, *Nisi Prius* allowed civil matters, in which points of fact but not points of law could be determined, to be dealt with, Oyer and Terminer with treasons, felonies and trespasses and of Gaol Delivery which allowed them to deal with prisoners in gaols. They also sat as Justices of the Peace.

[81] SP63/234/18e.

[82] *Cal. S.P. Ire., 1625-32*, p. 220

[83] H.M.C., *Egmont MSS*, i, pt i, pp 50, 53.

[84] *Cal. S.P. Ire., 1625-32*, p. 330.

1638.[85] On these occasions the bishops could transmit royal ecclesiastical policy to their clergy, mainly through the visitation sermon.
In 1638, for instance, Bishop Leslie of Down and Connor preached his
sermon at Lisnagarvey on the evils of the Scottish Covenant and condemned laity and clergy for not enforcing tighter controls on non-
conformity.[86] It was also a chance for the bishop to take stock of the
state of his diocese and ensure that ecclesiastical discipline and courts
were operating as efficiently as possible.

The nature of certain administrative problems meant that they were
best dealt with at a local level and so the central administration devolved
a certain amount of power to local lords. The earl of Antrim, Lords
Conway and Hamilton and Sir John Clotworthy, for example, were
made responsible for the apprehension of malefactors on their own
estates and they were allowed to construct gaols to which suspects could
be committed by the seneschal of the manor court, usually the lord's
agent, and the gaol delivered at the assize.[87] The government also allowed the licensing of alehouses to be dealt with locally. Thus, in Antrim
and Down, John and James Clotworthy, the sons of Sir Hugh, were
licensed to control the sale of wines and spirits but by 1635 this system
was replaced by an assize of alehouses conducted by local justices of the
peace, as was the practice in England.[88]

Much of this system of local government worked less efficiently than
it might have done in Antrim and Down because of a lack of effective
administrative personnel to run it and because of resistance to some of
its activities by the landed gentry of east Ulster. Although most
landlords wanted local offices for their prestige value they were less than
enthusiastic about carrying out their duties. Problems also emerged as
the counties lacked a group of professional administrators to fill the role
of legal officers. The office of clerk of the peace for example was a vital
one. The clerk had to draw up most official legal documents and act as
clerk to the quarter sessions and so required a sound legal training.[89]
This office in Ulster was held from 1603 to 1612 by George Sexton and

[85] P.R.O.N.I., T975/1; H. Leslie, *A treatise of the authority of the church* (Dublin,
1637); ibid., *A full confutation of the Covenant lately sworn* (London, 1639).

[86] Ibid., pp 2-3.

[87] *Report on manor courts*, H.C. xv (1837), pp 291, 300, 303-4, 508; most of these
rights had disappeared in England, Cockburn, *Assizes*, pp 27, 86.

[88] *Cal. pat. rolls Ire., Chas I,* p. 450; SL, 15, no. 234; 10, 11 Chas I, s.4, c.5.

[89] Bolton, *Justice*, bk ii, p. 6.

after this jointly with Mathew Ford.[90] There is no evidence that either of these men had any legal training, and Sexton's administrative record as the escheator would not inspire confidence in his ability to be an efficient, impartial clerk of the peace. The sort of problem which this lack of trained personnel could cause was illustrated in 1637 when the estate of Turlough McManus was escheated after his conviction for manslaughter. The attainder had been certified in the office of the clerk of the exchequer but nothing could be done to resume the lands because of faulty information provided by the clerk of the peace in Down.[91] The shortage of settler personnel meant that natives were often employed in some minor offices. This frequently generated confusion, because many natives were not fully acquainted with the niceties of common law practices. In 1634, for instance, Henry Spencer of Inishloughlin brought an action of ejectment against Francis Hill of Castlereagh and three of his tenants for the townland of Clontokelly and judgement was given for him. On an appeal to chancery in November 1634, it was revealed that the sub-sheriff involved, Rory McEver Oge Magennis, had failed to serve notice of the case to be commenced against Hill because he did not know he had to and so the suit was void.[92]

By 1641 the central government had begun to make an impact on the power blocks which King James had allowed evolve by his large east Ulster grants of land and exceptional powers to ambitious men in the first decade of the seventeenth century. The administration had to feel its way delicately in its relations with the east Ulster landlords but by 1620 the crown was surer of the royal title to Antrim and Down than it had been in 1605. Furthermore, by the 1630s the crown's representatives for collecting revenue and monitoring land transactions in the counties were working more effectively than a decade previously. The judicial administration was working as efficiently as could be expected given the limited local resources it had and judicial officials, such as the justices of assize, were frequently present in east Ulster. Yet little of this administrative consolidation impinged on the major landowners. They resisted attempts by central government to erode their rights, the earl of Antrim being accused in 1638 of wanting to be a Count Palatine because

---

[90] *Liber mun. pub. Hib.*, i, pt ii, p. 173.
[91] P.R.O.I., Ferguson MSS, xii, p. 383.
[92] P.R.O.I., Thrift MSS, no. 114.

of his successful resistance of royal encroachment.[93]

II

The settlers were not the only group in Antrim with which the central administration had to deal. There were also the native Irish and the remnants of the late sixteenth century settlement by catholic Scots from the Isles in the Glens of Antrim. This latter group were often considered synonomous with the Irish and Sir Arthur Chichester once described them as 'very savage and heathenish, speaking Irish, wavering and uncertain, better affected to this [Irish] nation than to us, liking their manners and dissolute living better than our justice'.[94] Both groups, Scots and Irish, were viewed by the central government as potentially disloyal and hence usually treated equally. In 1601 the view of Sir Francis Stafford, who was the government's main source of information on Ulster during the 1590s, of the Ulster natives was that they were 'perfidious, ungrateful and apt to wind with every innovation' and not to be trusted.[95] Yet, Stafford hoped for the reformation of some natives, especially O'Hanlon and Magennis. His assessment of the native Irish was founded on the view that gaelic society was basically unstable, being controlled by ambitious, overmighty lords who acted as tyrants towards their followers. The late sixteenth century solution to the problem had been an attempt to diminish the powers of the gaelic lords in east Ulster by reducing their landholding and making their title to land dependent on the queen. This, it was argued, would lessen their powers and their influence over their followers so that the lord would no longer be guaranteed an army to follow him into rebellion.

The sixteenth-century idea of a reformation by making the tenant less dependent than hitherto on his lord and hence stopping the 'tyranny' of the greater sixteenth-century lords, was carried into the seventeenth century and as late as 1610 Chichester was still committed to this policy of 'breaking the faction of great men in this kingdom'.[96] In March 1605 Chichester issued a proclamation decreeing that all the inhabitants of Ulster were free, natural and immediate subjects of the king and not the

---

[93] SL, 10, f172.
[94] *Cal. S.P. Ire., 1601-3*, p. 245.
[95] Ibid., p. 117-18.
[96] SP63/229/108.

natural followers of any lord', confirmed the policy of land redistribution in Monaghan and began settlements along similar lines in Cavan and Fermanagh. A new concept of the nature of the lord's relationship with his tenants evolved which emphasised the contractual nature of the relationship. The 1604 patent to Sir Randal Macdonnell stipulated that *every* tenant should be a free suitor to the manor court, a clause not included in the patent of 1603 because by 1604 both Chichester and Sir John Davies were becoming worried about the control which Sir Randal was exercising over his tenants. Chichester even advocated that on the Macdonnell estate freeholders responsible to the queen should have been created earlier to balance the powers of Sir Randal.[97] The manor court was a substitute to creating freeholders since it was a way in which the tenant could enforce his contract with the lord.

By the early seventeenth century the only major native Irish family left with a substantial power base in east Ulster was that of Magennis. Conn O'Neill had already been reduced to a third of his previous territory in north Down by the settlement in 1605 with Hamilton and Montgomery and in Lower Clandeboy the problem of the natives had been solved in the late sixteenth century by dividing the lands between the two contenders Shane McBrian O'Neill and Neale McHugh O'Neill. After Neale's death his share was split between his two sons Neale Oge and Hugh O'Neill. This left the O'Neill septs of Clandeboy so fragmented that they had little power and thus could safely be ignored by the administration and in eastern Down the power of the McCartans was severly weakened by the sale of half their land to Lord Cromwell in 1605.[98] The method which Chichester used to limit the power of the Magennises was the 1606 Commission of Defective Titles.

Since the early seventeenth century the reality was that the only good claim to land was by grant from the crown and although Sir Arthur Magennis held his lands of the crown by patent, it could be argued that this was now invalid by virtue of rebellion. Thus it was in Magennis's interest to have his title confirmed and so, about June 1605, he actually requested a surrender and regrant of his lands.[99] The lord deputy and council seized the opportunity to limit Sir Arthur's power and so

[97] Erck., p. 137; A.B. Grossart (ed.), *The work of Sir John Davies,* iii (London, 1876), p. 127; SP63/215/15; *Cal. S.P. Ire., 1603-6,* p. 502; Bodl., Carte 62, f 556.
[98] Erck., pp 191.
[99] SP63/217/47.

appointed thirteen of his most substantial freeholders to hold their lands directly from the crown. The scheme was completed by 10 January 1609 and forwarded to Magennis, who was to divide the lands under the supervision of Sir Robert Jacob, the solicitor general, who was to ensure that Magennis received no more land than that stipulated by the order of January 1609.[100] As Jacob saw it, the essence of the scheme was that it 'will so weaken him [Magennis] and raise up so many opponents against him that he will never be able to make any strong party if freeholders patents shall once be made and the country quiet but two or three years'. This view was strongly endorsed by Lord Deputy Chichester who felt that it would keep Sir Arthur and his dependants within the rule of the common law and ensure that the crown rent was paid.[101] On 10 December 1609 the commission was issued to receive the surrender of the lands of Iveagh, the surrender being made on 8 June 1610. As soon as the surrender had been made the king issued a letter on 26 June which was a warrant to pass the patents for the settlement which were issued between 10 December 1610 and 22 February 1611.[102]

A second method of bringing the natives to 'civility' lay in government education of the new generation of the greater lords' sons which would bring them up in 'English ways'. Arthur Magennis, son of Sir Arthur, for example, was sent to England by the Irish Privy Council in order to be educated properly 'to do his majesty and his country service . . . being a gentleman of more than ordinary note in his country, and on whom a fair inheritance is likely to descend'.[103] He was sent by the Privy Council to Oxford where he was to have an 'honest and religious' tutor but three years at Oxford appears to have had little effect on him if we are to judge from the report of the Privy Council that 'the time he has spent there has in no way bettered him in those things which we specially desired nor had sorted to that effect as was expected'. Undeterred, the Council placed him at the Middle Temple to complete his education and a year later he returned to his father's lands at the king's command.[104]

[100] *Cal. pat. rolls Ire., Jas I.*, pp 394-6; *Cal. S.P. Ire., 1608-10*, p. 469.

[101] SP63/226/69; SP63/229/106, i, 104; *Cal. S.P. Ire., 1608-10*, p. 193.

[102] *Cal. S.P. Ire., 1608-10*, pp 469, 487; *Cal. pat. rolls Ire., Jas I*, pp 181, 190-91, 193, 195; P.R.O.I., Ferguson MSS, xii, pp 187-8.

[103] *Acts privy council, 1613-14*, p. 308.

[104] Ibid., *1618-19*, pp 157, 181, 490; H.F. MacGegge (ed.), *Register of admissions to the Middle Temple*, i (London, 1949), p. 490.

The education of some natives had a greater measure of success as is seen from one gaelic poem of *c.* 1630 which referred to Sir Henry O'Neill of south Antrim as a man of great education and knowledge of English law and learning.[105]

One way of measuring the degree of acceptance of the new system of local government by the native Irish is the use made of its institutions to resolve disputes, especially over land. In the later sixteenth century the way in which landed disputes were settled was by arbitration by the local community who knew the traditional boundaries or, in more complex cases, such as the dispute in the 1580s and 1590s over the division of Lower Clandeboy, by bringing in an independent arbitrator, in that case the lord deputy.[106] The new order provided an alternative method of procedure, a case in a local court such as the quarter session of assize or in chancery. Fifty bills of pleadings in chancery relating to Antrim and Down in the early seventeenth century have survived and of these about a quarter involve a native Irishman as a litigant. It cannot be argued that the settlers dragged the Irish into the courts since two thirds of these suits were pursued entirely by natives. Given that a case in chancery was usually a last resort, the procedure being long, complex and costly, this is a high figure. Measured in this way acceptance of the new order was, therefore, quite widespread. The native Irish generally resorted to the common law over a wide range of matters including theft and murder.[107] One particularly good example of the faith of the native Irish in the common law occurred when the Gilmores of Ballinclamy were attacked by the inhabitants of Hollywood shortly after the outbreak of the 1641 rebellion. They did not retaliate but Bryan O'Gilmore, 'who was chief of the Irish which lived there upon', went to the local justice of the peace, Lord Clandeboy, who issued a warrant to prevent O'Gilmore's tenants from being molested.[108]

Thus by 1641 the central administration had brought the native Irish under its control. In many ways it was an insignificant triumph for the natives were declining in importance as they were forced to sell and

---

[105] *Lr. Cl. Aodha Buidhe,* no. 23.

[106] C. McNeill (ed.), 'The Perrott papers' in *Anal. Hib.*, xii (1943), p. 10; Perrott, *Chron. Ire., 1584-1608,* p. 36; *Inq. Ult.*, p. xliii.

[107] J.F. Ferguson (ed.), 'The Ulster roll of gaol delivery' in *U.J.A.*, 1st ser., i (1853), pp 261-6.

[108] T.C.D., MS 838, f 247.

mortgage their lands to meet increasing debts. The real problem, the growing power of settler landed society in the face of attempted centralisation by the Dublin government, remained unsolved.

VI

RURAL SOCIETY

THERE WAS NO SINGLE 'rural society' in early seventeenth-century east Ulster but rather a number of different status and cultural groups each of which had its own concept of society and of its place in it. The distinctions which existed between different social groups were, it appears, so much a commonplace to contemporaries that they rarely articulated their ideas of the social hierarchy. Yet these concepts dominated rural society in east Ulster throughout the early seventeenth century. These concepts were broadly founded on ideas common to settler and native, a hierarchy of status in which each man had his place in 'a great chain of being'.

I

In early modern England, social theorists, such as Sir Thomas Smith or Thomas Wilson, built their classifications of society around the theme of the ownership of land. This is hardly a surprising criterion in an inflationary age when land was the main source of wealth and political power and also the principal way of storing accumulated capital. The crucial social distinction lay not principally in the amount of land held but in the relationship between the holder of land and his immediate superior since if the immediate superior was the king then the landholder was deemed to belong to 'landed society' and all others were relegated to a lesser social stratum. In an English context Edward Gwynn described his family to Sir Simon Archer in the early seventeenth century as 'anciently noble', yet they had only acquired their knighthood a few years previously. It was, rather, the holding of land directly from the king for generations which created their nobility in his

113

eyes.[1] Sir Francis Bacon had no hesitation in drawing a line between 'gentry', who held their land by royal patent, and 'peasantry', who held their land by lease and, in an Irish context, Sir Henry Sidney, the lord deputy, referred, with his English perceptions, to Shane O'Neill, and his 'peasants'.[2] Those who were not 'owners' of the land were, in law, workers. A gentleman, for example, was in law a husbandman if he did not hold land from the crown. So John Shaw of Ballygally was described on a lease of 1634 as a 'gentleman' yet in more formal legal documents, such as his grant of denization, he was deemed a farmer.[3]

Above this relatively well-defined social barrier of landholding a man's status could be fixed by his position in the peerage, the size of his landholding, his income or a combination of these. Below this barrier, however, the situation was much more complex. Different cultural groups within east Ulster society had their own ideas of the detail of social order and stratification. The native Irish, for example, remained a distinct group retaining their own customs and communities into the early seventeenth century. Distinctive gaelic Irish customs such as fosterage continued to play a part in forming social bonds, as is clear from the 1652 deposition of Gilcroney McItalter of Culfreightin, in north Antrim, who 'stayed with . . . Ferdorach Magee for security of his life, he having been fostered to his mother's brother and tenant of his mother's kindred'.[4] The traditional rights of gaelic society did not disappear with the settlement but were remembered into the early eighteenth century when Seamus O'hUid, a descendant of one of the bardic families of Clandeboy, claimed rights in ten townlands in mid-Antrim from Cormac O'Neill, the descendant of the O'Neills.[5] The native Irish also retained their own ideas of stratification and continued to use them in the seventeenth century. Unlike the practice of the non-'landed' elements of English and Scots society, an Irishman's status was not regulated by the value of his lands or his education, but on the basis of

[1] K.B. McFarlane, *The nobility of later medieval England* (Oxford, 1973), p. 6.

[2] J.R. Lumby (ed.), *Bacon's history of the reign of Henry VII* (Cambridge, 1902), p. 71; SP63/16/35.

[3] T. Westcote, *A view of Devonshire in 1630* (London, 1848), p. 58; P.R.O.N.I., LPC 1339; W.A. Shaw, *Letters of denization and naturalisation* (Huguenot Society, Lymington, 1911), p. 331.

[4] T.C.D., MS 838, f 66. On fosterage in Antrim and Down in the sixteenth century, SP63/208/5i, *Desid. cur. Hib.* i, p. 85.

[5] S. Ó Ceallaigh, *Gleanings from Ulster history* (Cork, 1951), pp 95-6.

his lineage. As Sir John Davies, the attorney general, observed 'though their portions were never so small and they themselves never so poor . . . yet they did not scorn to descend to husbandry or merchandise or to learn any mechanical art or science'.[6] This bound the Irish into a distinct group so that even those who were apparently almost totally integrated into settler society, such as the anonymous native Irish author, of the *War in Ireland*, could refer to the Irish in the 1640s as 'my countrymen'.[7] The settler element on the other hand, did not form one cohesive group since the Scots and English differed from each other in significant respects. The amount of land required to attain the status of 'gentleman' in Ulster differed between these two groups, the Scots level being lower because Scots gentry at home were relatively poorer than their English counterparts. Similarly differences in literacy rates, which were slightly higher among the English, reflect differing attitudes to education among the different gentry societies.

Despite these variations some general statements can be made about the nature of social organisation in early seventeenth-century east Ulster. The social order was by no means as egalitarian as some advocates of colonization suggested.[8] It was a society in which a man's title was important, for it decreed how much respect and obedience he was due. A visible sign of this was the funeral of Viscount Ards in 1636 which was organised so that the mourners followed the coffin in order of their social rank and, in the case of a less spectacular activity, the taking of the Covenant at Holywood in 1644, the social order was demonstrated by the order in which men were allowed to sign.[9] Such a system of social regulation was strongly approved of by the central government which saw it as promoting stability and ordering society. The central administration had actually attempted in 1608 to regulate the status of servants in Tyrone by ordaining that all those under fifty years who did not possess goods valued at £6 were to be compelled to labour and those who

[6] See appendix D, i, ii; G. MacNiocaill, 'A propos du vocabulaire social Irlandaise du bas moyen âge' in *Etudes Celtiques*, xii (1971), pp 512-46; H. Morley, *Ireland under Elizabeth and James the first* (London, 1890), p. 292; *Advertisements for Ire.*, p. 43.

[7] E. Hogan (ed.), *A history of the war in Ireland* (Dublin, 1873), p. 4.

[8] For example, Sir Robert Gordon, 'Encouragements for such as shall have intention to be undertakers . . .', Edinburgh. 1625, in D. Laing (ed.), *Royal letters, charters and tracts relating to the colonisation of New Scotland, 1621-38* (Bannatyne Club, Edinburgh, 1867).

[9] P.R.O.N.I., D627/1; T 776.

did not have a one-eighth share in a plough were ordered not to employ servants but to labour themselves. In a less extraordinary way the law attempted to regulate the status of various groups by limiting their rights so that a servant, for example, could not carry arms unless accompanied by his master.[10]

In a colonial setting, such as east Ulster, there were problems in assigning a man to his place in the social order. Many had risen in material terms from their old place in society by migration and there was no tradition of a family's place in the social order such as Sir Thomas Smith recorded in English society when he observed 'we do not call any man a yeoman till he be married and have children and have as it were some authority among his neighbours'.[11] In the absence of other criteria the main factor in assigning an individual to his place in the social hierarchy was his wealth, as measured by the value of his land.[12] In the case of the earl of Antrim's estate in 1638 the rent which a gentleman paid for his lands generally lay between £9 and £20 while a yeoman's rent fell below this, and rents paid by the Irish were more erratic.[13] Other lesser factors also determined status, the most important of which was tenure since it demonstrated the security of economic position in a society where land was the main source of wealth. Under certain circumstances, tenure became even more important than land value. In a rental of the north-west part of the earl of Antrim's estate made in 1641, the average rent paid by a yeoman was £16·2 while that of the next social group, the husbandman, was £18·6.[14] In some cases the differences in rent were considerable, the lowest yeoman paying £8 against £11 paid by the lowest husbandman. These differences are explicable in terms of tenure, for while all the yeomen held their lands directly from the earl all

[10] *Cal. Carew, 1603-24*, p. 29-30. The lowest status of employer in east Ulster was a yeoman, T.C.D., MS 838, f 257; R. Bolton, *A justice of the peace for Ireland* (Dublin, 1633), bk 1, p. 22; Stone, *Crisis*, pp 21-35.

[11] L. Alston (ed.), *De Republica Anglorum* (Cambridge, 1906), p. 45. On the problem generally, M. Smith, 'Pre-industrial stratification systems' in N. Smelser, S.M. Lipsett (ed.), *Social structure and mobility in economic development* (London, 1966), pp 141-76; K. Wrightson, 'Aspects of social differentiation in rural England, 1580-1660' in *Jnl peasant studies*, v (1977), p. 35.

[12] For this point, T.C.D., MS 838, ff 30-37; Bodl., Carte, 61, f 354; Strafford, *Letters*, ii, p. 219.

[13] See appendix D, i.

[14] B.L., Harley 430, ff 111-15ᵛ.

but one of the husbandmen were sub-tenants.

Other, less tangible, factors also played a part in placing a man in the social hierarchy. There was, for example, a correlation between a man's status and degree of literacy although the exact connection is unclear. East Ulster literacy rates were much lower than those of contemporary England as only 29 per cent of deponents in 1641 in Antrim and 43 per cent in Down could sign their names, but this low level may well be the result of the pattern of migration rather than a product of the social structure.[15]

Thus the main factors controlling a man's place in the social hierarchy were the value of his lands and the tenure by which they were held, both of which were in the control of his landlord. Since landlords' leasing policies varied considerably over Antrim and Down, the social structure must also have varied from estate to estate. One way of attempting to assess this variation is to examine the type of arms held by the tenants as recorded on the muster roll of *c*. 1630, since the criterion for the allocation of arms purchased by the landlord was the man's social status.[16] This was demonstrated when the 1560 Commission for Musters in Ireland ordered that arms were to be noted according to a man's status and in Scotland a muster was called after O'Doherty's rising in 1608 ordering men 'to provide themselves with arms according to their rank'. In the case of Scotland the point was underlined in 1626 when the Scottish Privy Council went as far as to lay down arms appropriate to each rank.[17] The correlation between arms and status holds up well among the settlers on the earl of Antrim's estate, where, for example, Randall Buithill, one of the largest landowners, was also the best armed.[18] On some estates, such as those of Dalway and Clotworthy, there was a total

[15] Appendix D, i, ii, iii. On the measurement of literacy, R.S. Schofield, 'The measurement of literacy in pre-industrial England' in J. Goody (ed.), *Literacy in traditional societies* (Cambridge, 1968), pp 319, 324; L. Stone, 'The educational revolution' in *Past and Present*, xxviii (1964), pp 43-4.

[16] B.L., Add. 4770. For an outline of the mustering system, R.J. Hunter, 'The settler population of an Ulster plantation county' in *Donegal Annual*, x (1971-3), pp 124-6; for landlords purchasing arms, *Cat. pat. rolls Ire.*, *Chas I*, p. 201; Steele, *Tudor and Stuart*, ii, no. 260.

[17] H.M.C., *15th Report*, appendix 3 (Halliday MSS), p. 84; *Reg. P.C. Scot.*, *1607-10*, p. 79; ibid., *1625-7*, p. 419; For English examples see 4 & 5 Philip & Mary, s.1, c.2 (Eng.); Stone, *Crisis*, p. 28; M. James, *Family, lineage and civil society* (Oxford, 1974), pp 37-8.

[18] B.L., Add. 4770, f 161ᵛ; P.R.O.N.I., LPC 1031; LPC 1059; T549/3.

lack of arms due to the landlord's incompetence but generally the picture is clear.[19] On the Adair estate in mid-Antrim, 79 per cent of all the armed men had simple weapons such as a sword, pike, halbert, or a combination of these, the other 21 per cent holding more complex weapons, such as muskets or other guns. At the time of the muster, Adair was pursuing a policy of consolidating his newly acquired lands by leasing large proportions on good terms to those who could afford them and hence creating quite a sizeable upper stratum of tenants with a much broader base of sub-tenants. On Adair's lands 16·5 per cent of armed men held complex weapons such as snaphances as did 20·2 per cent of Viscount Ard's estate in north Down, whereas on Lord Clandeboy's lands in north Down the pattern was different, since only 7 per cent of the armed men had the most advanced weapon, the snaphance. From the beginning of the settlement Clandeboy had shown a reluctance to create a large stratum of well-off tenants for fear that they would pose problems for him later and thus a group of 'gentlemen' never grew up there.[20]

In this evolving society, where status was important and in the gift of the leasing policy of the landlord, there was a considerable amount of physical movement as tenants moved from one area to another in search of upward social mobility. John Shaw of Greenock, for example, came to Down with Sir Hugh Montgomery and received a grant of four townlands in the Ards, but by 1622 he had moved to the earl of Antrim's land at Ballygally, where he had a larger holding. William Edmonston also came to Down with Montgomery, who granted him the townland of Ballybrian, but by 1609 he had seized the chance of moving upwards socially by acquiring the lands of the Braid, in south-east Antrim, from John Dalway and subletting part of his Down lands.[21] Some of the native Irish also managed to rise socially as a result of the landlords' power to determine the social structure of their estates. The O'Hara family of Crebilly, county Antrim were such a group. In the sixteenth century the O'Hara influence in Antrim was slight and Loughguile, which was to become their seat in the seventeenth century, was in the hands of the McQuillans in 1556. During the late sixteenth century

---

[19] Appendix D, iv. For discussions of arms see C.G. Cruikshank, *Elizabeth's army*, 2nd ed. (Oxford, 1966), pp 113-16.

[20] T.C.D., MUN.P/24/4; *Ham. MSS*, p. 36.

[21] *Mont. MSS*, p. 52; *Ham. MSS*, p. xiv; P.R.O.N.I., LPC 1339; T815; S.R.O., GD97/1/328.

Cahall O'Hara attached himself to the rising family of Macdonnell and by 1611 was rewarded by a lease of four townlands, including Loughguile, from Sir Randal Macdonnell. O'Hara's position was further strengthened in 1629 when he interrupted the passage of a new patent to the newly created earl of Antrim by demanding these lands as his right and to avoid lengthy disputes Antrim conceded the point. O'Hara had added to his lands by the purchase of part of the church land of Kells from Sir Arthur Chichester, and also part of the lands of Crebilly, to make him one of the most important native landholders in east Ulster by 1630.[22]

Landlord influence could cause downward social mobility as well as promotion. Landlords could, for example, offer grants of lands which were still occupied by the native Irish to new settlers and thus relegate the natives into the position of subtenants. In 1635, for example, Sir Patrick Agnew granted part of his lands, on which the family of Ó Gnímh were living, to Captain Alexander Dundas, forcing Ó Gnímh downward to the level of a subtenant.[23] A similar reversal of fortune was suffered by Carbery McCann 'chief of his name', who had to leave his lands in the barony of Orier, county Armagh, which had been reallocated under the plantation scheme, to become a subtenant to Conn O'Neill in Down.[24]

Other factors, such as the expansion of a new family, could also create downward mobility among the native landholders. The expansion of the Macdonnell family in north Antrim during the late sixteenth century, for example, pushed the McQuillan family downward on the social scale. The process began in the mid-sixteenth century as the Macdonnells began to expand their power in north Antrim and by 1555 the McQuillans had already lost the castle of Dunluce to Sorley Boy Macdonnell and by 1568 their power was further eroded as two of their southern strongholds, Ballylough and Ballybeg, had been occupied by another temporarily resurgent power, the O'Neills of Clandeboy. In an attempt to create a buffer to the expansion of Scottish power, the Dublin administration tried to prop up McQuillan by partitioning the lands of the Route in north Antrim between him and Sorley Boy, but this

[22] On the O'Hara genealogy, L. McKenna, *The book of the O'Hara* (Dublin, 1951), pp xiii, xxi; *Cal. Carew, 1575-88*, p. 438; *Cal. S.P. Ire., 1574-85*, p. 577; *Cal. Carew, 1515-74*, pp 261-62; *Cal. pat. rolls Ire., Jas I*, p. 94; *Cal. pat. rolls Ire., Chas I*, p. 504.
[23] S.R.O., GD 154/509/5.
[24] R.J. Hunter, 'Plantation in Armagh and Cavan', p. 318.

restriction of Macdonnell expansion only created more discontent. The legal recognition of the expansion of Macdonnell power by granting all the land of north Antrim to Sir Randal Macdonnell in 1603 meant the complete extinction of the McQuillan influence there, although in 1608 they were compensated by a grant of the tough of Clangartity in mid-Antrim. By 1619 Rory Oge McQuillan had sold these lands, probably due to increased indebtedness, to Faithful Fortescue who in turn sold them to William Adair. Rory Oge had to live for the remainder of his life on a royal pension and a number of loans from Adair.[25]

Each of these social groups, landlord and tenant, native and settler, had different aims and ambitions which they pursued within the framework of the social stratification outlined above. To appreciate fully the fabric of colonial society in east Ulster it is necessary to distinguish the various social groups, and examine them individually. Landlord society and tenant society, although complementary to each other were very different and each will now be examined separately.

II

The acquisition and development of land was the primary pre-occupation of the socially ambitious at the upper level of Ulster society in the early seventeenth century. Initially the desire for land was contained by grants of territory in east Ulster but by the 1620s land hunger was growing again and settlers from Antrim and Down began to cast their eyes elsewhere. As early as 1609 a number of east Ulster settlers, including Moses Hill, Sir Edward Trevor, Sir Fulke Conway, Lord Cromwell, and John Dalway, had expressed interest in acquiring land in the infant scheme for the plantation of Ulster, but none of them succeeded.[26] In 1626 Lord Cromwell attempted to obtain lands in the plantation of Longford, but was unsuccessful and again in 1636, when proposals were made for a plantation of Connacht, he petitioned for lands.[27] Similarly, in the 1630s the second earl of Antrim attempted to

---

[25] G. Hill, 'The MacQuillans of the Route' in *U.J.A.*, 1st ser., ix (1861-2), p. 63; D.B. Quinn (ed.), 'Calendar of the Council Book, 1581-6' in *Anal. Hib.*, xxiv (1967), p. 138; *Cal. S.P. Ire., 1509-73*, pp 245, 377, 494; Hill, *Macdonnells*, p. 198, n.15; N.L.I., Harris Collectena, vol. 18, f 216; *Cal. S.P. Ire., 1596-7*, p. 181; *Cal. Carew, 1575-88*, pp 427-8; *Cal. Carew, 1601-3*, p. 490; *Cal. S.P. Ire., 1603-6*, p. 503; *Cal. pat. rolls Ire., Jas I*, pp 114, 363, 367; *Inq. Ult.*, Antrim, Jas. I,no. 1; E. Suffolk R.O., HA12/A2/3/11a-b.

[26] *Cal. S.P. Ire., 1608-10*, pp 366-8.

[27] *Cal. S.P. Ire., 1625-32*, p. 164; Bodl., Carte 64, f 3; SL, 14, f 273.

enlarge his estate by requesting that the lands between the rivers Bush and Bann, which his father had surrendered in 1610, be regranted to him, but he was unsuccessful.[28] Others achieved rather more. Sir John Clotworthy, who held lands around Antrim town, succeeded in enlarging his estate by acquiring most of the lands of the Draper's Company in county Londonderry.[29]

Land could be acquired in three ways, by purchase, by royal grant or by mortgage, each method being employed according as opportunity and circumstances dictated. At the end of the Nine Years War the land market in east Ulster was favourable to purchasers. The finances of the few sixteenth-century settler landholders were poor since most of them had been badly hit by the war. Sir Henry Bagnall, whose father, Sir Nicholas, established himself at Newry, had had his estate attacked by O'Neill, who had burnt his mills and caused tenants to flee. Sir Henry's own finances were in poor shape as he was owed considerable sums by the crown, £4,591 in 1595, for his services as marshal of the army.[30] Thus by 1601 the estate was in poor condition and Sir Henry's widow, Mabel, complained that the profit from the estate was small and some parts of it, such as Narrow Water were being run at a loss.[31] The native Irish had fared little better. The uncle to Conn O'Neill, early seventeenth-century lord of Clandeboy, was imprisoned in Carrickfergus Castle for debt by Sir Arthur Chichester in 1598 and Conn's father, Niall McBrian McFertogh O'Neill, was described in 1600 as 'a beggar who yesterday, being with us [Chichester and his forces], was not able to eat without the queen's entertainment'. By 1603 Conn himself was severely in arrears with the crown rent on his land and even after the sale of part of his lands in the early seventeenth century Conn was still continually in debt.[32] Sir Hugh Montgomery, the purchaser of a third of O'Neill's land, claimed that he had given Conn £2,000 and 'beside this, Conn has received continual and daily benefits from me in money, horses, clothes and other provisions of good value and also has been

[28] SL, 10, pt i, f 172; SL, 10, pt ii, f 22.

[29] Moody, *Londonderry plantation*, p. 446.

[30] SP63/185/21; SP63/181/27; SP63/198/8; *Cal. Carew, 1589-1600*, p. 116; SP63/183/34; H.M.C., *Salisbury MSS*, vi, pp 393-4.

[31] *Acts privy council, 1600-01*, pp 250, 279; SP63/208/4.

[32] *Cal. S.P. Ire., 1600-01*, p. 85; P.R.O.I., Ferguson MSS, ix, p. 3; SP63/102/22.

chargeable unto me in divers other disbursements'.[33]

This was a situation ripe for purchase and speculation. The older inhabitants of east Ulster needed cash and the new settlers could muster it. Sir Hugh Montgomery for example borrowed part of the money required to purchase O'Neill's lands in Edinburgh and the rest came from a mortgage on his Braidstane lands. Sir Arthur Chichester, who purchased land in Antrim, raised £1,700 in bonds from London and elsewhere and Sir Fulke Conway sold his English lands as well as his wife's jointure to raise money for Antrim lands.[34] Ex-army officers, such as Sir Edward Trevor and Lord Cromwell, who purchased land found their army pensions, payable only in Ireland, an important source of capital. Sir Edward Trevor had a pension of £96.14s.0d. per annum, which he used to build up piecemeal a scattered estate in Down, and Sir Hugh Clotworthy had £91.5s.0d. as captain of the king's boats on Lough Neagh.[35] Others such as Moses Hill, who built up a considerable but scattered estate in north Down, indulged in more questionable activities to raise cash for land purchase, Hill acquiring some of his initial capital in a fraud over whiskey supplies to the army.[36] Many of these early acquisitions of land in east Ulster, such as the purchases by Sir James Hamilton and Sir Hugh Montgomery in north Down and Lord Cromwell in Lecale, were given the seal of respectability by being confirmed with a royal patent.

The second method of acquiring land was by direct grant of a patent from the crown and this means of acquisition was much availed of in the early years of the settlement. To obtain a patent a king's letter had to be produced which specified the value of the lands to be granted, although after 1610 it was required that the actual lands be specified in the letter. Once the king's letter was produced in chancery an inquisition was arranged to determine the values of the lands to be granted and when this was returned to chancery the patent was issued under the great seal. This system appeared to protect the interests of all, but the crown's concern to establish stability of landholding in east Ulster meant that

[33] J. Maidment (ed.), *Letters and papers relative to Irish matters from the Balfour MSS* (Abbotsford Club, Edinburgh, 1837), p. 274; *Mont. MSS*, pp 69-70.

[34] *Mont. MSS*, p. 35; G. Robertson, *A genealogical account of the principal families in Ayrshire*, iii (Irvine, 1825), p. 235; B.L., Cotton Titus B X, ff 410-11ᵛ; SL, 24/25, no. 351.

[35] *Cal. pat. rolls Ire., Jas I*, pp 101, 105, 142, 147, 367, 373.

[36] *Cal. S.P. Ire., 1601-3*, p. 509.

inquisitions were frequently dispensed with and *non-obstante* clauses came to be used extensively.[37] The general system of granting land was thus open to abuse by those who could manipulate it. The events surrounding the king's letter granted to Thomas Ireland, a London merchant, provide an illustration of the manipulation of the system by one settler, Sir James Hamilton.[38] On 6 December 1604 Thomas Ireland paid £1,678.6s.8d. for a letter entitling him to a grant of unspecified land to the value of £100 per annum which he assigned to Sir James Hamilton on 26 February 1605.[39] On this letter Hamilton obtained three large tracts of land in Antrim and Down and fragments in Meath, Mayo, Wexford, Galway, Dublin and other counties, including much church land. These large tracts were officially valued at £179.10s.11d. per annum, although worth considerably more. In reality the Dublin administration had little concept of land values and quality in east Ulster, since the only valuation prior to the early seventeenth century had been made in 1550 and even it was not comprehensive.[40] The administration relied on native Irish juries whose ideas of the annual value of land were shaped not by ideas of economic rent but by the symbolic render paid to the superior lord, so that the result was usually a gross underestimation of the true values of the land.[41]

The system of simply granting unspecified lands to a certain value in the king's letter, much used in the early years of the seventeenth century, was open to considerable abuse since there was no way, short of a complete search of the patent rolls, of ensuring that the letter had not already been exhausted when it was presented for the making of a grant. Checking was difficult since record keeping in early seventeenth-century Ireland was grossly inefficient, there being no central repository for official documents.[42] Thus, king's letters which had been previously used could often be put through the system a second or third time without detection. Hamilton, for example, used the letter to Thomas Ireland to pass five separate books of land and another letter, acquired in a similar

[37] See pp 15-17.
[38] Erck, pp 244, 83-4, 194; for Ireland's identity, *Cal. border papers, 1595-1603*, p. 680.
[39] Erck, pp 194-6, 210, 213-18.
[40] P.R.O.I., RC9/1, Ed. VI, no. 1.
[41] SP63/165/31 and below on native views of 'rent'; Erck, p. 213.
[42] H. Wood, 'The public records of Ireland before and after 1922' in *R. Hist. Soc. Trans*, 4th ser., xiii (1930), pp 20-22.

way in 1605 from one John Wakeman, was still being used by Hamilton to pass land grants in the 1620s. Hamilton's activities might have remained secret but for a personal dispute which flared up in 1617 between himself and Sir Hugh Montgomery, his neighbour, and John Wilkinson, the recorder of Coleraine. As part of the legal case which ensued Wilkinson brought Hamilton's excessive grants to the notice of the lord deputy, Oliver St. John, who having ordered a list of Hamilton's lands to be drawn up found all of them approved by royal letters.[43] Suspicions, however, were aroused, and Hamilton's further land acquisitions were monitored so that when, in 1623, he attempted to pass a grant of lands of St. Mary's abbey, near Dublin, on the Wakeman letter it was stopped.[44] Further investigations into Sir James's activities carried out by Wentworth, after his appointment as lord deputy, led to a case in the court of exchequer as a result of which the crown resumed lands to the annual value of £79.10s.11d. which had been granted on the Wakeman letter after it had been exhausted.[45] Hamilton was not alone in his manipulation of this system of royal grants for John Bramhall, the bishop of Derry and close friend of Wentworth, complained to Archbishop Laud that many landlords in Down were manipulating royal grants to acquire church land. They 'first found offices to entitle the king to this land and tithes . . . [then] . . . they passed them by patent from the crown, the bishops sometimes conniving', he complained, and in this way two notable Dublin speculators, John King and Thomas Hibbotts, acquired large grants of church land in Down.[46]

The third main method by which land could be acquired was mortgage. The traditional form of mortgage in sixteenth-century Ireland was the indenture of defeasance. This involved registering the debt, or principal of the mortgage, in a court of record, usually a staple court, which then issued a memorandum of the transaction called a statute staple and required the loan to be guaranteed by a transfer of lands to the mortgagee.[47] One mortgage on the lands of Kearney in Lecale, for example, recited that Patrick Savage had mortgaged the lands from Dowltagh

[43] Bodl., Corpus Christi 279, ff 155ᵛ-6; *Ham. MSS*, p. 29-30.

[44] *Acts privy council, July 1621-May 1623*, p 421; P.R.O.N.I., D1071B/B/1, pp 29-30.

[45] T.C.D., MS 804, ff 231-2; *Cal. S.P. Ire., 1615-25*, p. 402.

[46] Shirley, *Ch. of Ire., 1631-9*, p. 71; Erck, pp 83-4, 24, 61-2.

[47] For example, P.R.O.N.I., D671/D8/1/27, 28.

Smith for £90 and that the land was to be given to Savage in peaceable and quiet possession.[48] On the repayment of the principal the indenture of defeasance became void and the land was reconveyed to its original owner.[49] This system was clumsy and could lead to disputes over the value of improvements during the mortgage or the degree of damage done to the land. Furthermore, tenants and small owners were reluctant to part with their land since it was their only source of income, and people were generally reluctant to mortgage until it was really necessary.

By the early seventeenth century the custom of mortgaging had begun to change. Security for loans was no longer taken by physically possesing land but simply by granting the rents of any piece of land to the mortgagee by means of a deed of rent charge and the rent from the lands also acted as a repayment of the loan. In February 1634, for example, Ever Oge Magennis made a bond with Sir John Trevor for £300, in October the agreement for the passing of the rents of land was made and the deed of rent charge was drawn up in December. A similar agreement was made in 1635 between Robert Adair of Ballymena and a group of men, including James Edmonston of the Braid, in which the rent of a group of townlands was granted to the consortium until Adair's debts of £2,500 were paid.[50] The new system was easy to use at a time when most landlords were in urgent need of cash, either to invest in lands or, as in the 1630s, to redeem part of their debts and it was also closer to the English and Scottish practices of mortgaging than the older custom.[51] This new custom gained wide acceptance in east Ulster, so that by the 1630s only five out of two hundred and twenty seven entries in the register of the statute staple, the record of mortgages under the old custom, refer to east Ulster at a time of heavy mortgaging by Antrim and Down landholders.[52] This new ease of mortgaging meant that more mortgages were taken out, mainly by the declining landlords, especially the native Irish. However repayments of the principal had to be made within twenty-one years, which many native landowners failed to do,

---

[48] P.R.O.N.I., D552/B/1/1/38.

[49] For example, P.R.O.N.I., D929/F1/1A.

[50] P.R.O.N.I., D671/D8/1/23, 25b; D929/F4/1/33; *Cal. S.P. Ire.*, 1625-30, p. 538.

[51] C.F. Kolbert, N.A.M. McKay, *A history of Scottish and English land law* (London, 1977), p. 319. The statute of frauds (10 Chas I, s.2, c.3 (Ir.)) gave mortgages increased legal security.

[52] B.L., Add. 19843 ff 3ᵛ, 7, 33, 94, 110ᵛ; P.R.O.N.I., D552/B/1/1/34, D929/F4/1/5.

especially after the outbreak of rebellion in 1641. Failing repayment, land passed permanently to the mortgagee and in this way men such as Jerome Alexander, a Dublin lawyer, could build up considerable landed estates in Down.

There were considerable legal problems with all these methods of acquiring land. A patent, for example, only granted the lands it named and in a period when townland names and boundaries were uncertain weaknesses could be found in most land grants, a fact which Wentworth and his Commission for Defective Titles exploited. Men pryed into each other's grants hoping to find weaknesses which could be capitalized on. The question of title to the fishings of the Bann, for example, was reopened in 1628 by Sir Arthur Forbes, a Longford planter who had searched Sir Arthur Chichester's land grants and found irregularities.[53] As a result of this situation most east Ulster settlers feared that loopholes could be found in their titles. John Dalway, a settler from near Carrickfergus, articulated this fear in the parliament of 1613-15 when he noted that no act had been passed to confirm land titles, and therefore feared that settlers 'should be left prey to lawyers'; a phrase to which Sir John Everard, a prominent Pale lawyer, took exception.[54] As a reaction against this insecurity, as well as against fears of central government encroachment, landholders began to consolidate their estates, including the rights and privileges annexed to the land, since these were the key to the position which they had carved out in the new social order created by the settlement of east Ulster.

III

The physical consolidation and development of a newly acquired estate required, in essence, three elements: capital for initial investment, tenants to work the land and a reliable system of estate management since the success of the new venture would depend on the proper management of these new assets. The initial capital investment in newly acquired land, particularly in building, was heavy. Sir James Hamilton, for example, claimed that of £2,260 which it cost him to purchase and operate the Bann fisheries, one-fifth was spent on buildings and general

---

[53] *Cal. pat. rolls Ire., Chas. I*, pp 40-3.
[54] *Commons jn. Ire.*, i, p. 34.

improvements.[55] Costs for building varied considerably on individual estates in east Ulster. At the lower end of the scale, the building at Dalway's Bawn, to the north of Carrickfergus, in 1632 cost £32, exclusive of materials, for each of the four flankers and John Dalway himself included a clause in a sublease of the lands of the Braid, in southeast Antrim, that a house was to be built costing at least £300. At the other end of the scale, Killeleagh castle probably cost nearer the £1,200 paid by a Tyrone settler, Sir William Stewart, for his 'fair strong castle of stone and lime'. After a house had been built, ancillary buildings such as mills, costing about £30 each, and barns, had to be constructed so that a figure of £600 was not an unrealistic estimate for initial investment in building on an estate.[56]

The raising of this initial capital was a major problem given the backgrounds of the east Ulster settlers. Most had little or no land in England or Scotland from which money could be raised, or else their estates were not large enough to provide the sums required. Even if money could be raised in Scotland or England, as Montgomery and Chichester managed to do, there were problems in moving it to Ireland. In 1601 a proclamation was issued forbidding the movement of sterling to Ireland, which was still in force in 1612, as it was feared that if too much pure English coin was moved to Ireland it would result in a loss of confidence in the more debased Irish coinage.[57] The instability of the Irish coinage in the early years of the seventeenth century further retarded the movement of English or Scottish coin to Ireland as evidenced by the few hoards containing English or Scottish coin which are known from Antrim or Down. As late as 1629 base money, which should have

[55] T.W. Moody, J.G. Simms (eds), *The bishopric of Derry and the Irish Society of London,* i (I.M.C., 1968), pp 51-2.

[56] A.T. Lee, 'Notes on bawnes' in *U.J.A.*, 1st ser., vi (1858), p. 131; P.R.O.N.I., D1255/3/32, box 175; R.J. Hunter, 'A seventeenth century mill at Tyrhugh' in *Donegal Annual,* ix (1970), pp 238-40; Perceval Maxwell, *Scottish migration,* pp 132-7; W.R. Scott, *The constitution and finance of English, Scottish and Irish joint stock companies,* ii (Cambridge, 1910), pp 338-43.

[57] J. Thirsk, J.P. Cooper (eds), *Seventeenth century economic documents* (Oxford, 1972), pp 602-3; B.E. Supple, *Commercial crisis and economic change, 1600-41* (Cambridge, 1959), pp 179, 181, 187, 189, 194, 231, 250; Irish coin could not be moved to England without permission, *Cal. S.P. Ire., 1625-32,* p. 479; *Cal. S.P. Ire., 1611-14,* pp 238-9. These difficulties were compounded by the problems of obtaining and redeeming bills of exchange in east Ulster because of the small merchant community there.

been called in after 1603, was still circulating in east Ulster.[58] This coinage problem meant that if money was to be spent in east Ulster it had to be raised mainly in Ireland.

Sources of capital in early seventeenth-century Ireland were meagre and this point is particularly evident when we compare the position of the landlord there with his counterpart in England. There the landlord had access to local merchant communities with substantial cash balances on hand which could be lent to finance rural development. Such stable merchant communities with large cash balances never developed in east Ulster as most east Ulster merchants were too mobile to be effective financiers of rural development. As a result most of the capital to generate economic growth had to be found by the settlers from their own resources.

In the absence of a stable merchant community the main sources of capital were the profits from land speculation, and most east Ulster settlers indulged in some speculation in the early years of settlement to obtain capital to develop their lands. Sir Hugh Montgomery, for instance, was dealing in church land at Clogher, county Tyrone, as early as 1612.[59] The best example of a speculator however was Sir James Hamilton, whose background as the son of an impoverished Scottish cleric meant that he had few external resources to draw cash from. He had, however, a number of important personal contacts in Ireland, such as the Munster settler Richard Boyle, and in the English court, Sir James Fullerton, a former Trinity College colleague. As a result Hamilton's influence was considerable, as was evident from his threat to stop a grant of lands to Trinity College, Dublin, if he did not receive the farm of them.[60] In 1604-5 he used his contacts and influence to obtain grants of land scattered over Ireland and then, concentrating his activities on the large block of land he purchased in north Down, sold much of the scattered land to build up a reserve of capital. He also speculated in land in various parts of Ireland, acquiring titles by royal grant or by finding flaws in other grantees' titles which were subsequently sold to build up

---

[58] Steel, *Tudor & Stuart proclam.* ii, nos 162, 172, 173, 177; H.M.C. *Various*, v, p. 126; I.D. Brown, M. Dolley, *A bibliography of coin hoards of Great Britain and Ireland* (London, 1976), passim.

[59] S.R.O., RH 15/91/59/122.

[60] J.W. Stubbs, *The history of the University of Dublin* (Dublin, 1889), p. 33; *Lismore papers,* 1st ser, iii, p. 221.

cash reserves. In April and May 1606 he concentrated his landed interests further by selling most of his lands in county Antrim to Sir Arthur Chichester, the remainder he set up as fee farm grants, probably with high entry fines, while he sold his Meath lands to a Dublin official, Sir James Carroll. By 1614 he had also acquired lands in Longford which were later surrendered to the crown for a pension of £250 per annum and he also attempted to acquire lands from the imprisoned Kerry chief, Florence McCarthy Mór, in return for a pardon, but failed.[61] This judicious land speculation could yield a considerable return but in the long term the opportunities in this area were limited and erratic and so many settlers had to turn to steadier sources of income to replenish their capital reserves.

The main source of steady income for east Ulster landlords consisted of the resources of their own estates. In the early years of the settlement of Antrim and Down it was necessary to exploit the newly acquired lands to the maximum to build up a capital base for further development. Some settlers, such as Sir Arthur Chichester, leased much of their land at low rents and on long leases but with high entry fines in order to raise large sums of money quickly. Normal estate management in England fixed the entry fine at ten years purchase but in east Ulster it was usually substantially longer.[62] Long leases also had the advantage that long-term improvements to land and buildings could be farmed out by clauses in the lease. Other manipulations of tenurial arrangements could have the effect of providing a substantial income. Arthur Hill, for example, used the rack rent, a flexible system of rent assessment which meant rent could be increased annually, so that by 1632 he had raised his income from a small part of his lands to almost £1,000 per annum.[63] Since a patent granted not only land but also rights and privileges

[61] T.M. Healy, *Stolen waters* (London, 1913), pp 74-5; Erck, p. 191; H.M.C. *Various*, iii, p. 156; *Acts privy council, 1613-14*, p. 471; D. McCarthy (ed.), *The life and letters of Florence McCarthy Mor* (London, 1867), p. 395; P.R.O.I., Chancery Bills BB 16; SL, 14 no. 201; H.M.C., *Hastings*, iv, p. 160.

[62] P. Roebuck, 'The making of an Ulster great estate: the Chichesters, barons of Belfast and viscounts of Carrickfergus' in *R.I.A. Proc.*, lxxix, sect. C (1979), pp 17, 23; E. Hopkins, 'The releasing of the Ellesmere estates' in *Ag. H.R.*, x (1962), pp 14-28; P.R.O.N.I., T965/21; T712/3; T1030/4.

[63] Brereton, *Travels*, p. 128; *Mont. MSS*, p. 55; E. Kerridge, *Agrarian problems in the sixteenth century and after* (London 1969), pp 46-7.

associated with land most landlords exploited these rights as well as the land itself. The patents to Sir Randal Macdonnell granted not only only lands in north Antrim but

also power to have and hold the like, courts leet, view of frankpledge, hundreds, lawdays, assizes, assizes of bread, wine and beer, waifs and strays, goods and cattle of felons and fugitives, deodans, knights fees, wards, marriages, escheats, reliefs, heriots' free warrens, parties, customs . . . with power also to him and his heirs to hold courts baron within each manor, and every tenant therein to be a free suitor at such court; to appoint seneschals in and for each manor and the said suitor and seneschals to do all things customary to be done in any courts held in any other ancient manor.[64]

Other profitable rights and customs could also be associated with land, such as the woodland rights of house boot, plow boot, hedge boot and fire boot. And one deed between James Hamilton and Sir Thomas Phillips of the priory of Coleraine also included the right of one day's fishing on the river Bann

the Monday next after the feast of St John the Baptist in every year, in which day, all fish taken in the river do of right belong to the said priory, one salmon every day, yearly, from time to time, for ever of all the fisher(men) which shall fish in said river, during the fishing time; which salmon do likewise belong to said priory.[65]

All these rights could be profitably exploited, but the generators of the largest and most regular sources of income were the manor courts. Fines were levied on all tenants at meetings of the courts and most landlords, such as Sir Henry O'Neill, charged ten shillings for each action begun in his courts while those who did not take their disputes to the manor courts were fined a larger sum.[66] Landlords guarded these judicial rights because of their economic value, and only sold them in times of debt. Alienation of such rights was, in fact, unusual and when lands were sub-let the rights and profits of the courts were usually retained by the grantee. In 1609, for example, when John Dalway sold the lands of the Braid, in south-east Antrim, to a Down settler, William Edmonston, he

[64] Erck, p. 274, on this point generally, J.C.W. Wylie, *Irish land law* (London, 1975), pp 296-7.
[65] Erck, pp 191, 231.
[66] P.R.O.N.I., D929/F2/3/9; D929/F3/3/15, 31.

retained his judicial rights. Similarly in his 1606 grant of lands to Sir Hugh Clotworthy, Sir Arthur Chichester retained the manor courts of the lands and the right to receive homage fines from all Clotworthy's tenants.[67] The profits which manor courts yielded made them a source of dispute, one long running clash in the 1630s between Sir Edward Conway and another south-west Antrim landowner, Hercules Langford, centred on the right to collect the profits of the manor court of four townlands.[68] Other courts, such as the market courts, also produced considerable profit and the landlord's right to a proportion of all grain ground at the manor mill was profitable and could be leased or sold for cash, as was done by the earl of Antrim. There were however limits to the exploitation of these rights. The shortage of tenants in east Ulster meant that a landlord had to shepherd carefully those which he had acquired and not exploit them excessively. Sir Hugh Montgomery was even prepared to defy the wishes of the king in 1618 because he could not 'happily wrong such tenants as are come to inhabit with me and I have set rights unto'.[69]

Capital could also be built up by exploiting the natural resources of an estate, mainly wood and iron. An English legal decision of 1568 had made most minerals, other than gold and silver, the property of the landlord and this had opened the way for exploitation. In much of east Ulster mineral rights were farmed out by landlords in order to raise cash quickly. The salt pans and coal mines of Bonamargy, in north Antrim, were leased by the earl of Antrim jointly to his agent, Archibald Stewart, and to Henry Maxwell, the son of the archdeacon of Down, while the coal rights of Islandmagee were leased by Sir Arthur Chichester to Moses Hill.[70] Minerals such as iron, which could be exploited quickly, and without heavy capital investment, were particularly appreciated. Since iron works were not capital intensive, needing only a hearth where ore could be smelted between layers of charcoal, they developed in areas where timber, ore and water were all found in close proximity.[71] Most east-Ulster ironworks were small even by Irish

[67] H.M.C., *Various*, v, p. 128; P.R.O.N.I., T815; D207/16/9.

[68] SP63/256/96.

[69] P.R.O.N.I., T549/2; D1838/55A/83; N.L.S., Denmilne MSS 6, no. 8.

[70] P.R.O.N.I., D778/4; D778/1/1; D2977; 12 Sept. 1639, earl of Antrim to Archibald Stewart and Henry Maxwell.

[71] G. Boate, *Ireland's natural history* (London, 1651), ch. XVII; E. McCracken, 'Charcoal burning ironworks in seventeenth and eighteenth century Ireland' in *U.J.A.*,

standards: the one at Six Mile Water in south Antrim had only three hearths which produced twenty-one hundredweight of iron per week as compared with ironworks in Cork which had ten times that capacity.[72] Although works were small they were usually very profitable. Thus Simon Richardson, an agent on the Conway estate, around Lisburn, informed his employer that although it would cost £1,000 to set up ironworks on the estate they would yield that much profit within the year making Killultagh, a heavily wooded area, 'a good, pleasant and flourishing country'.[73] The development of iron works in east Ulster was restricted by the reduction in woodland by 1640, the problems in transporting large quantities of iron and the lack of skilled workers, which remained a problem even though some settlers, such as Lord Cromwell, imported skilled iron workers.[74]

The source of income which east Ulster landowners principally relied on was the rents paid by the tenants on their lands. In 1627, for example, Lord Cromwell depended so much on tenant's rents that he was unable to pay his debts until rents were collected, and similarly in 1641 some Antrim landlords were unable to pay for arms which they wished to purchase in Scotland because rents had not been paid before the outbreak of rebellion.[75] Income from rents was doubly vital because, since demense farming was rarely practised in east Ulster due to problems of recruiting labour, landlords had to purchase their own food in the markets.[76] The vital role of rent in income meant that tenants had to be selected carefully to ensure that they had the means to pay the required rent and that they would not flit, leaving large arrears. Landlords had few remedies against obstinate tenants for tenants' goods which were distrained could not be sold but only held as a pledge for their debt. Sir James Hamilton advised Trinity College, Dublin, that on the basis of experience on his own county Down lands, tenants for its estate should

3rd ser., xx (1957), pp 123-38; ibid., 'Supplementary list of Irish charcoal burning ironworks' in *U.J.A.*, 3rd ser., xxviii (1965), pp 132-5.

[72] D.R. Hainsworth (ed.), *Commercial papers of Sir Christopher Lowther* (Surtees Society, Newcastle upon Tyne, 1977), p. 72; T. Ranger, 'The career of Richard Boyle, first earl of Cork in Ireland' (D. Phil., Oxford, 1959), p. 148.

[73] *Cal. S.P. Ire., 1625-32*, p. 516; ironworks were established there by 1626, *Cal. pat. rolls Ire., Chas I*, p. 276.

[74] Hainsworth (ed.), *Commercial papers*, pp 67-9, 70-3; B.L., Add. 4770, f 264.

[75] *Cal. S.P. Ire., 1625-32*, p. 271; *Reg. P.C. Scot., 1638-43*, pp 499-500.

[76] *Cal. S.P. dom., 1631-3*, p. 387.

be 'men of good substance and means' but on the other hand they were not to be too powerful, so that they might become overmighty and troublesome. Hamilton observed: 'I had rather let it [land] to such honest men of meaner ranks, who if they do not pay me their rent shall, whether they will or not, permit me to fetch away their distress'.[77] Moreover, because of the shortage of capital landlords were dependent on their tenants to develop the estates. Development was promoted by including improvement clauses in the lease — such as the condition to plant trees included in most of the earl of Antrim's leases. If these improvements were to be realized landlords had to make sure that they limited their choice to tenants with some capital, and they had the opportunity to vet prospective tenants when they petitioned for land.[78] Once appropriate tenants had been found the landlord had to offer them incentives to stay with him lest more favourable terms elsewhere would persuade them to defect to another landlord. Even then defections did occur as can be seen from the instances of William Edmonston and James Shaw, who both came to Down to settle under Sir Hugh Montgomery but who within a few years had both moved to larger and better tenancies offered by John Dobbs and the earl of Antrim respectively.[79] Since land was plentiful and tenants scarce, lords also had to offer services in addition to land to retain satisfactory tenants. These included protection, both physical and legal, forums, such a manor courts, for settling disputes and help with marketing tenants' goods by creating local market centres.[80]

In order to offer these non-material benefits the landlord was obliged to develop techniques to manage them and also ways of rent collection. Landlords, however, were frequently non resident, but land agents were used on most estates as an effective substitute for the lord.[81] Since the agent was concerned with the running of the estate he had to be a trusted man, and was often a member of the landlord's family. Sir James Hamilton, for example, used two of his brothers as agents on his lands and his son used a younger brother. The agent on Sir Randal

[77] T.C.D., MUN/P/24/4-5.
[78] SP63/255/80, 105; SP63/256/42.
[79] *Mont. MSS*, pp 52, 57; P.R.O.N.I., T1030/41; T815.
[80] This point is examined in more detail below, pp 153-8.
[81] P.R.O.N.I., T1030/4,41 for requirements of agents on lands if the landlord was absent.

Macdonnell's estate in the early years of the settlement was John McNaughton, whose mother was apparently a sister of Sir Randal's father, Sorley Boy, and Sir Fulke Conway employed his brother-in-law, Sir William Smith, to manage his land around Antrim town.[82] If no immediate relative was available to act as agent others were pressed into service as for instance, after the death of Sir William Smith in 1632 when Sir Edward Conway, Sir Fulke's nephew and heir, selected one of his English servants, George Rawdon, to manage his Irish lands in the knowledge that Rawdon had been trained in estate management by the agents of Conway's lands.[83]

The agent was the key to a well run estate and, hence, considerable care was taken with his welfare. In 1627 for example when Henry Spenser, one of the assistant agents on Sir Edward Conway's estate, was accused of murder, Conway intervened on his behalf. He informed Lord Deputy Falkland that if Spenser was convicted 'my right may suffer as much as his. The interest I have in him and the much good I have heard of him move me to proceed further by way of caution than I hope there is any need to'.[84]

The agent's brief was a wide ranging one since he had to deal with all his employer's affairs, moving about between the estate, Dublin and London. In 1635-6, for example, George Rawdon spent no more than five months in Ireland, the rest of the year having been devoted to Conway's Irish business in England.[85] On the estate itself the agent's work was supervisory since much of the work, such as rent collection, was done by local men acting under the agent's instructions.[86] He spent most of his time in dealing with legal matters presiding over the manor courts, engaging in law suits over ownership, defining the boundaries of

[82] P.R.O.N.I., T808/2758; *Ham. MSS*, p. 12; A.I. Macnaughton, *The chiefs of Clann Macnachtan and their descendants* (n.p., 1951), pp 62-3; G. Hill, 'Gleanings in the family history of the Antrim coast' in *U.J.A.*, 1st ser., viii (1860), p. 134; *Cal. S.P. dom., 1631-3*, pp 376, 378, 387.

[83] *D.N.B.*, sub. George Rawdon; M. Beckett, *Sir George Rawdon* (Belfast, 1935), pp 16-17; *Cal. S.P. dom., 1627-8*, p. 496; *Cal. S.P. dom., 1631-3*, pp 240, 273-4, 310, 318, 325, 361, 382.

[84] B.L., Add. 11033, ff 95-95ᵛ.

[85] Rawdon's movements may be reconstructed from *Cal. S.P. dom., 1634-5*, pp 377, 393; *Cal. S.P. dom, 1635*, pp 3, 137, 436, 454, 490, 602, 606; *Cal. S.P. dom., 1635-6*, pp 269, 315, 338, 357, 540-46; SP63/255/24, 62, 66.

[86] SP63/255/24, 104; *Cal. S.P. dom., 1635*, p. 426; *Cal. S.P. Ire., 1625-32*, p. 541.

the estate, ensuring that patents were passed and carrying out the legal paperwork resulting from land acquisition.[87]

Since the bulk of the land agent's work was legal the main framework through which he managed the estate was a legal one, the manor. The manorial framework was vital to the successful development of any estate in east Ulster, a fact appreciated by landlords, for Sir Randal Macdonnell insisted that a clause be inserted into his 1604 patent dividing his large estate into several manors. He was allowed:

to divide the said territories into several different precincts, each to contain 200 a[cres] at least, and to give different names to each division, that so they may become manors . . . to hold courts baron and appoint seneschals.[88]

The manor courts were a vital instrument in regulating the affairs of the estate and in resolving local problems and they also acted as a central clearing house where records, such as leases, could be enrolled for reference.[89] The keeping of such records was of prime importance since the lease was the central document controlling landlord-tenant relations and had to be produced in order to prove that it had been breached. Thus the manor court not only secured the landlord's legal position, but because of the profits of the manor courts was also an economic asset, and also provided a dispute-settling forum for tenants.

Through the agent and the manor courts, landlords consolidated their hold on the estate and its rights and began to make then economically viable. This, however, was a long-term process, and there were considerable problems. Shortage of tenants meant that the men to whom landlords were forced to lease land were far from the ideal advocated by Sir James Hamilton. Sir James himself had a number of troublesome tenants and one even encouraged one of Hamilton's neighbours, Sir James Montgomery, a younger son of Sir Hugh, to encroach on Hamilton's lands. Another tenant of Sir James, Brian Oge O'Flynn, was far from being the ideal prompt payer of rent since he was

[87] Beckett, *Rawdon*, p. 19; SP63/256/88, 96; G. Hill, *The Stewarts of Ballintoy* (reprint) (Ballycastle, 1976), pp 8-9. Hence many were also J.P.s, see p. 98.

[88] Erck, p. 137. The king's letter for the patent did not contain this clause (Erck, pp 166-7). Manors could only be created by royal permission, Kerridge, *Agrarian problems*, pp 17-18; Wylie, *Irish land law*, pp 14, 20, 65.

[89] For example, P.R.O.N.I., T761/3, p. 5; N.L.W., Cross of Shaw Hill MSS, Deeds no. 174.

twenty-two years in arrears by 1629.[90] Rent collection was an unpredictable business on even the best regulated estates. Many unforseen circumstances, such as bad harvests, could reduce the tenants ability to pay rents as in 1636, when the poor harvests, coupled with a shortage of coin meant that rents were particularly difficult to collect. A local rent collector on the Conway estate wrote in April 1636 to the agent, George Rawdon, informing him that if the May rent could be collected by Christmas it would be a major achievement.[91] The normal remedies of ejection or distraint were rarely used because of the difficulty in finding new, suitable tenants and landlords were also reluctant to prosecute tenants in arrears since the debts helped to bind tenant to landlord. Thus incomes from an estate, although potentially substantial, could be unreliable and landlords were ill advised to depend on them totally.

This was especially true in the early stages of the settlement when tenants were still being recruited and payments of rent were often irregular. Sir Randal Macdonnell for example, petitioned, in 1605, for a renewal of his grant and an abatement of the crown rent because of 'the poorness and dispeopling of his country' and a plea was made in 1605 by a group of native Irish for an abatement of homage money, Sir Arthur Chichester describing one of the group, Henry O'Neill of Killileagh, county Antrim, as very poor with many dependants.[92] As a result, most of the east Ulster landholders suffered financial problems in the early stages of settlement. Sir James Hamilton, for instance, despite his speculation, described above, had to mortgage part of his lands in Down to Trinity College, Dublin in 1614 and a further part in 1618.[93]

Despite all these problems estates developed rapidly. Sir James Hamilton estimated that the value of his north-Down lands increased fivefold in the early years of the settlement from about £100 per annum in the early stages, and Conway's land was valued at £2,000 per annum on Sir Fulke's death in 1624.[94] A more general picture of the wealth of

[90] P.R.O.I., Ferguson MSS, xx, p. 85; W. Mure (ed.), *Selections of family papers preserved at Caldwell* (Maitland Club, Glasgow, 1856), pp 93, 267.

[91] SP63/255/24, 104, 107, 112.

[92] *Cal. S.P. Ire., 1603-6*, p. 267; *Cal. S.P. Ire., 1606-8*, p.403; P.R.O.I., Ferguson MSS, ix, pp 84-5.

[93] T.C.D., MUN 1P/24/26, 27, 28, 52, 62.

[94] SL, 17, no. 38; *Cal. S.P. dom., 1623-5*, p. 412. This estimate was given as part of a defence during the claim of Daniel O'Neill on Hamilton's lands. Other sources (e.g. *Ham. MSS*, pp 48-59) suggest that it may have been higher but not appreciably so.

landowners is given by the assessment of the wealth of individual landlords for the subsidy in 1635. While the subsidy laid down a fixed sum for each county, the contributions by individual landlords were assessed on the basis of their individual wealth using the criteria set down in the Irish statute granting the subsidy (10 Chas. I.s I,c I). Working from the figures available it can be estimated that the mean wealth for east Ulster landowners was £3,705 per annum whereas on the long established and developed English estates the figure was £5,000.[95]

By the 1620s most estates in Antrim and Down had been sufficiently consolidated and developed to begin producing a significant profit. Sir Hugh Montgomery had begun, by 1619, to channel revenue from his Irish lands into purchasing land around Portpatrick in Wigtonshire, Scotland, the purchases continuing until at least 1628. Lord Cromwell also began to purchase lands in Nottinghamshire and Archibald Edmonston's lands in Antrim produced enough of a surplus by the late 1620s to redeem the mortgage on the family lands in Scotland. Sir James Hamilton also began to redeem earlier mortgages made on his lands during the 1620s.[96] This trend however was dramatically reversed in the 1630s.

The 1630s were a period when the effects of specie shortage were fully felt and prices were also rising rapidly so that Lord Conway, for example, complained that it had recently become expensive to live in Ireland.[97] Costs were also pushed up by non-economic factors, such as the Commission for Defective Titles, which raised crown rents. The costs of many of the legal disputes, begun as much as ten years before, were now becoming unbearably heavy. Sir Hugh Montgomery, for example, alleged that one case in London had cost him £1,400 and another case between him and Ever Magennis, a minor landowner in south Down, was fought 'until they were constrained by too much poverty, having no means to follow the said suit'.[98] By the 1630s further major

[95] Appendix E. For English landed incomes, Stone, *Crisis,* pp 324-34, 762.
[96] S.R.O., GD237/171/1/2, 4-8, 11, 50, 51, 54; RS1/18, f 301; RS1/27, f 135; P.R.O.I., D20559; *Acts privy council, July 1619-June 1621,* p. 210; ibid., *July 1621-May 1623,* p. 165; H.M.C., *Various,* v, p. 137; T.C.D., MUN P/24/54. Rents on church land in this period quadrupled in some cases, S. Millsop, 'The state of the church in the diocese of Down and Connor during the episcopate of Robert Echlin' (M.A., Q.U.B., 1979), table IVa, b.
[97] *Cal. S.P. Ire., 1625-32,* p. 530.
[98] N.L.S., Denmilne MSS 6, no. 8; P.R.O.I., Thrift MSS, no. 99.

expenses were incurred by many landholders arising out of family com-
mitments as the second generation settlers began to marry and large
dowries became a feature of east Ulster society as the settlers strove to
demonstrate their recently acquired wealth and social position. One
daughter of the earl of Antrim received a dowry of £2,700 and a
daughter of Sir Hugh Montgomery had a dowry of £600, 'a great sum in
those days' as the author of the *Montgomery Manuscripts* observed.[99]
This had the inevitable result of dragging landholders into debt. Personal extravagance also exacerbated this already difficult situation. One
illustration of this extravagance is that of the life of a courtier which was
pursued by the second earl of Antrim before the death of his father, the
first earl, in 1635. Court life was expensive involving a considerable
number of extravagances necessary to display one's social standing and
so by 1635 he had borrowed £10,000 at court as well as having lost
£2,000 at one session of nine pins. Forced to abandon the life of a courtier, he left the court for Ireland in 1638 in the hope of living more cheap-
ly there but this hope proved illusory. By 1640 the second earl had accumulated debts of £39,377, of which £12,944 had been borrowed in
England within the previous three years and £9,110 had been acquired in
Ireland. Antrim's creditors were already pressing for payment and he
was consequently forced to mortgage the entire barony of Carey, in
north-east Antrim.[100]

As a result of these heavy drains on their resources, most east Ulster
settlers had fallen into severe debt by the 1640s. Lord Cromwell for example, had a personal debt of £3,550 by 1642 and his creditors were also
pressing for payment. During the previous four years he had been stav-
ing them off by mortgaging part of his lands to pay debts, but the day of
reckoning was close. Others in a similar situation included Lord
Conway, whose debts in Ireland were slightly higher than
Cromwell's.[101] Most settlers were borrowing heavily, both locally, in

[99] P.R.O.N.I., D552/B/1/1/20, 21; *Mont. MSS*, p. 90; *Cal. S.P. dom., 1637-8*, p. 574; *Cal. S.P. Ire., 1625-32*, p. 459; on English levels of dowries see Stone, *Crisis*, pp 637-45.

[100] P.R.O.N.I., D2977, 17 Sept. 1667, 'A declaration of Andrew Stewart'; D2977, c.1640, 'An accompt of my lord of Antrim's debts due in England'. H.M.C., *4th Report*, appendix 1, p. 108; ibid., *5th Report*, appendix 1, p. 6; SP63/255/48; *Cal. S.P. dom., 1635*, p. 385; SL, 21, no. 3; H.M.C., *Denbeigh*, p. 60; Laud, *Works*, vii, pp 471, 531; SL, 18, no. 99; Strafford, *Letters*, ii, pp 248, 262-3; P.R.O.N.I., D671/D3/2/1, 13.

[101] Stone, *Crisis*, p. 779; H.M.C., *6th Report*, appendix 1, p. 172; SP63/256/38; SP63/258/45.

Dublin, and in Scotland. Sir Hugh Montgomery, apart from borrowing extensively from friends in Scotland, was also forced to mortgage most of the Scottish land that he had acquired in the 1620s.[102] The roots of these growing debts lay in the early years of the settlement when, in an endeavour to attract tenants and cash, landlords had leased land for long periods at low rents to gain the short term benefit of high entry fines. However, because of these long leases, rents could not easily be increased and so the inflated costs and accumulated debts of the 1630s hit hard. The earl of Antrim recognised this and in 1637 attempted to improve his rental by forcing his tenants, on the pretext that leases had to be renewed after his father's death, to surrender their old leases so that new ones at higher rents could be made. By November 1637 the process was complete, with only minor objections from one tenant, Cahall O'Hara, a large tenant near Ballymoney, and the rental was substantially increased. One lease which had been made to Brian O'Neill for 303 years at £30 per annum in May 1632, was replaced by a forty-one year lease at £63 per annum and another lease made in 1621 to John Shaw of Ballygalley at a rent of £13.13s.4d. was increased to £24 per annum.[103]

Rent levels were only part of the difficulty facing the settlers for there was a more general economic problem in east Ulster which affected the landlords' position, the shortage of specie and the associated problems of credit. The poor harvests of the 1630s considerably slowed up the circulation of coin in east Ulster since there was less surplus produce to market. In these circumstances rent payments became more difficult and infrequent and landlord income declined in consequence. This situation was exacerbated by increased difficulty in obtaining credit. The political crises and growing debts of the 1630s made east Ulster landlords a poor credit risk so that by 1638 the earl of Antrim could not even raise £300 credit in Dublin. Viscount Ards encountered a similar situation in 1640, and the problem spread even to local towns, such as Carrickfergus, where credit began to dry up by the 1640s.[104]

There were however, some who were well placed to take advantage of

[102] P.R.O.N.I., D671/D4/1/6a-c; D929/F4/11; P.R.O., C5/20/112; S.R.O., GD 237/175/1/41-2; RH11/45/4; GD237/174/32.

[103] P.R.O.N.I., D2977, Exercise book marked 'barony of Dunluce', p. 36; D282/1; T549/1A; LPC 1339.

[104] *Cal. S.P. Ire., 1625-32*, p. 428; Bodl., Carte 2, f 117; Carte 1, f 267ᵛ; Strafford, *Letters*, ii, p. 278.

this situation, having surplus cash available for investment. Those who had made profit from office or the church (as in the case of Alexander Colville, precentor of Connor), the law (as in the case of Jerome Alexander), or trade (as in the case of Arthur Hill), were seeking to invest their money in land. They capitalised on the indebtedness of many native landholders and first generation settlers by mortgaging land from them. The Hill family, which was later to assume the title Marquis of Downshire and become one of the leading landed families in eighteenth century Ireland, provides a good example of this phenomenon. The first settler, Moses Hill, built up a small scattered estate in north Down and south Antrim, which was inherited by his eldest son Peter. The real basis of the landed wealth of the family was, in fact, established by the younger son, Arthur, from Dublin, who built up a mid-Down estate by acquiring fragments of land from indebted natives and settlers by mortgage. The two parts of the estate were united on the death, without heir, of Peter Hill's son, Francis.[105]

The native Irish landowners fared no better than their settler counterparts in the difficult economic climate of the 1630s. The fortunes of the Magennis family of mid Down, for example, declined rapidly and they were forced to mortgage most of their lands to those settlers who had cash: Arthur Hill and Sir Edward Trevor, as well as Sir Jerome Alexander, a Dublin-based lawyer. As early as 1621 Donal Magennis, one of the minor branches of the family, entreated Sir Edward Trevor 'to lend him certain sums of money which he stood greatly in need of' and John Magennis 'having special occasion for money' also borrowed heavily from Trevor.[106] The O'Neill family of Killileagh, on the north shores of Lough Neagh, were little better off. On the death of Neill Oge O'Neill it was revealed that he was heavily in debt to a Scottish settler, Sir Robert McClelland of Bombie in Kirkubrightshire. Apart from jointure land for his wife, worth £250 per annum, and land worth £40 per annum for his son, all his lands were mortgaged to pay debts. His son, Sir Henry O'Neill, was later forced to mortgage the remainder of the estate

105 W.A. Maguire, *The Downshire estates in Ireland* (Oxford, 1972), pp 2-4; the process may be traced in detail in P.R.O.N.I., D671.

106 P.R.O.N.I., D671/D7/1/3A; T588/1 ff 19, 43, 44; P.R.O.I., Lodge MSS, Records of the rolls, v, p. 361; Ferguson MSS, xii, p. 93; Thrift MSS, nos 78, 84, 87, 107, 109; Harold O'Sullivan, 'The Trevors of Rosetrevor: a british colonial family in seventeenth century Ireland' (M. Litt., T.C.D., 1985), pp 25-59.

to pay debts, which as late as 1664 remained unpaid.[107]

The problem of debt was not confined to the native Irish or the settlers, for the small pockets of Old English landholders concentrated in Lecale were also in financial trouble. One of these landholders, Patrick Savage, had by 1636 mortgaged part of his lands to Viscount Ards, his father-in-law, as well as borrowing from him and also from a number of Carrickfergus merchants. Patrick's will, proved in 1643, revealed the true extent of his problems, with debts of £2,077.13s.0d. due and only £588 owed him. His lands were also heavily mortgaged, bringing in only £158 in 1645, a rental which fell to £118.17s.11d. by 1648.[108] Savage's experience was not untypical of the Old English group and by 1660 the eight important Old English families of the sixteenth century in Lecale had disappeared because indebtedness had forced them to sell their lands.[109]

The origins of the financial difficulties of the Old English and native Irish in east Ulster were rather different from those of the settlers. The underlying reason for this difference was the changed concept of land tenure which resulted from the colonisation. The sixteenth-century system of landholding in east Ulster did not centre on profit or on the concept of an economic rent for land but on a token render or 'ceart' to a lord who did not own any land. The land was held by family groups who paid this token sum, fixed by custom, and therefore theoretically immutable, to a lord in return for services such as protection. While in the late sixteenth century some native lords began to feel that they had a right to own the land over which they had influence, as suggested by the 1592 petition to Queen Elizabeth by two of the O'Neill chiefs of Clandeboy for a direct grant to them of all Clandeboy, payment for land on which followers lived was still a token sum.[110] One land grant made by Rowland Savage to Nicholas Fitzsimon in 1571, for example was made 'by the services due and of right accustomed', not an economic rent, and later in the century the inhabitants of Killultagh paid only a

[107] S.R.O., RH15/91/37/1, f 5; *Cal. pat. rolls Ire., Chas. I*, p. 401; SL, 14, no. 243; P.R.O.N.I., T1289/1; T473, f 65. One Gaelic poet noted of Sir Henry O'Neill that his expenditure considerably outstripped his wealth, *Lr. Cl. Aodha Buidhe*, p. 174.

[108] P.R.O.N.I., D552/B/1/1/28, 30, 34; D552/B/3/1/1.

[109] T.C.D., MS, 572, f 8; 'JWH', 'The Anglo-Irish families of Lecale' in *U.J.A.*, 1st ser., i (1853), pp 94-7.

[110] *Cal. pat. rolls Ire., Eliz.*, p. 226.

'token of rent' to Magennis.[111] The new settlers implemented the normal English practice of charging an economic rent for land, although in reality, this was modified by the need to keep rents low to attract tenants. Thus payment for land rose dramatically in many areas settled by English and Scots as a result of the adoption of this concept of an economic rent, and in one case concerning church land the payment quadrupled.[112] Many of the native landlords had problems in adjusting to this new order, mainly because their tenants resisted change. Conn O'Neill, for example, continued to make leases at token rents in the seventeenth century as the 1607 lease of the lands of Castlereagh to 'Moses Hill in perpetuity at five shillings per annum' demonstrates. O'Neill's income was accordingly low and to pay costs determined by the settler market economy he was forced to sell off much of his land and even to break an entail on land reserved for his son.[113]

The problems and complexities involved in the transition from one landholding system to another were difficult to resolve. Sir Hugh Magennis managed to raise the rents on part of his mid-Down lands by making a series of short leases to various tenants and raising the rent on each occasion. As a result he managed to double the rents on some of his property between 1613 and 1630 but in comparison to settler-fixed rents they were still low.[114] On the Savage lands in Lecale more drastic methods had to be used to overcome the resistance of the tenants to change. Patrick Savage, the landlord, was despatched to the Isle of Man, so that tenants could not pressurize him, and his brother-in-law Sir James Montgomery, came in to reorganise the estate. Sir James exploited the main flaw in the gaelic system of land tenure, the absence of leases. He questioned the titles of individual tenants to their holdings, which, in the absence of leases they could not prove, and finding that no title existed in common law, he evicted them. However, immediately after the eviction he obliged them to take new leases 'increasing rents, to be paid in money, besides the usual duties and services'.[115]

---

[111] P.R.O.N.I., D585/1; SP63/277/6, f 2; for the size of these rents see M. Dillon (ed.), 'Ceart Uí Néill' in *Studia Celtica*, i (1966), pp 4-5.

[112] *Cal. S.P. Ire., 1625-32*, p. 538.

[113] P.R.O.N.I., D671/D4/1/1A; D671/D8/1/1-6; S.R.O., GD97/1/364, for examples of native Irish fixed rents. SL, 17, no. 38; D.A. Chart, 'The breakup of the estate of Conn O'Neill' in *R.I.A. Proc.*, xlviii, sect. c (1942-3), pp 119-51.

[114] P.R.O.N.I, D671/D8/1/54.

[115] G.F. Savage-Armstrong, A genealogical history of the Savage family in Ulster (London, 1906), pp 124-5.

IV

By 1640 most settlers had established title to their lands, the majority of property disputes had been resolved, relations with tenants had been stabilised and most estates had become profitable. Admittedly the growing indebtedness of the 1630s was a setback for settlers who had expected rapid returns on their lands, but the problem was not insurmountable. In these circumstances a distinct landed society began to emerge in east Ulster and by 1640 many of the settlers accorded the province priority in their minds over their homeland. The composition of settlers, mainly younger sons and ambitious men that with few or no economic ties to England or Scotland, meant that east Ulster had become their only social, economic and political power base. Any attempt to interfere with that base was strongly resisted. Sir John Clotworthy, son of Sir Hugh, who held an extensive estate around the town of Antrim, attacked the former lord deputy, Thomas Wentworth, in the Westminster parliament of 1641, accusing him of 'some very high actions in his administration of that government [Ireland] in which the lives as well as the fortunes of men have been disposed out of the common road of justice'.[116] Even when sitting in the English parliament Clotworthy's primary interest remained Ireland. In the 1640s he sat on eleven committees of the house, four of which dealt with Ireland, on which he spent most of his time, five with religious affairs, and only two with English matters. Even his thinking on English matters was guided by Irish interests, his membership of the 'peace party' in the English parliament of 1645-8 for example was guided by the need for peace in England before a reconquest of Ireland could be begun.[117] By 1640 the second Viscount Ards was in a similar position. In the early years of the settlement of Down his father, Sir Hugh Montgomery, had retained strong links with Scotland, holding office as burgess of Ayr in 1617 and as Scottish commissioner for the expulsion of Jesuits in 1629 while at the same time he was engaged upon the purchase of land in Wigtonshire. The 1630s saw a weakening of these links as the Scottish land was sold and no new Scottish offices were acquired and in 1641 the family abandoned their Scottish interests to fight for their Irish estate. Indeed, the second Viscount

---

[116] W.D. Macray (ed.), Lord Clarendon, *History of the rebellion*, i (Oxford, 1888), p. 224.

[117] *Commons jn.*, passim; *Cal. S.P. dom., 1641-3*, p. 483; *Cal. S.P. dom., 1644*, pp 59, 229, 309; D. Underdown, *Prides purge* (Oxford, 1971), p. 72. He also aligned himself with the 'city' faction in the parliament of 1640 because of his Londonderry interests, D. Bruton, D. Pennington, *Members of the long parliament* (London, 1954), pp 126-7.

split with his Scottish connections in opposing the covenanting movement while they supported it.[118]

While this emerging 'Anglo-Irish' attitude was predominant among
Ulster settlers by 1640 it was not universal. The earl of Antrim, for example, still retained strong Scottish connections and one of his main
concerns in the early seventeenth century was the restoration of his
family's fortunes in Scotland, which had been eclipsed by the rising
power of the Campbells of Argyll. Thus he wrote to Wentworth in April
1639, 'I must confess I have a natural affection to them [the Scottish
Macdonnells] allied to me by both name and blood and their safety I
shall seek as much as my own' or in a more impassioned moment he
asked the lord deputy 'if your lordship wil not send present relief that all
of my name will be cut off . . . For the love of God my lord let us not
sleep any longer'. Both the first earl and his son made repeated efforts to
recover their Scottish lands from the earl of Argyll. The most concerted
attempt was made in 1635-6 when Antrim attempted to purchase part of
his family lands from Lord Kintyre, son of Argyll, but Argyll used his
influence in the Privy Council to stop the purchases. Repeatedly, using a
number of pretexts, Antrim involved himself in Scottish affairs and in
1639 even volunteered to lead an expedition to Kintyre in return for
which he would be regranted his family lands.[119] Sir Robert Adair of
Kinhilt provides a second example of a man who did not see Ireland as a
permanent base. Although most of his family lands in Wigtonshire had
been sold by 1630 he retained the title laird of Kinhilt and sat as M.P. for
Wigtonshire in the Scottish parliaments of 1639-41 and 1649-50. He was
closely associated with several Scottish movements, especially the
covenanters. Indeed during the Scottish crisis of 1639 he left Ireland and
remained in Scotland throughout the 1640s where he was active in the
presbyterian General Assembly.[120] Both Adair and the earl of Antrim

[118] G.S. Pryde (ed.), *Ayr burgh accounts 1534-1624* (Scottish History Society,
Edinburgh, 1937), pp 258, 261, 262, 265; *Reg. P.C. Scot., 1629-30,* pp 262-3, 321; M.
Perceval Maxwell, 'Strafford, the Ulster Scots and the covenanters' in *I.H.S.*, xviii
(1973), p. 547-8; D. Stevenson, *The Scottish revolution, 1637-44* (Newtown Abbot, 1973),
pp 180, 249.

[119] SL, 19, no. 14; SL, 21, no. 158; *Reg. P.C. Scot., 1633-5,* pp 468, 479, 493; ibid.,
1635-7, p. 38; J. Haig (ed.), *The historical works of Sir James Balfour,* iii (Edinburgh,
1825), p. 70; A. Clarke, 'The earl of Antrim and the first bishop's war' in *Ir. Sword,* vi
(1963-4), pp 108-15; Stevenson, *Scottish revolution,* p. 141.

[120] Balfour, *Historical works,* iii, pp 7, 61, 117, 121, 144, 381; Strafford, *Letters,* ii,
pp 210-20, 226-7, 383; J.S. Reid, *A history of the presbyterian church in Ireland,* i
(Belfast, 1834), pp 293-4, 395.

were untypical of most east Ulster settlers. Adair had arrived in county Antrim late in the settlement and hence had not time to shed his Scottish links by 1640, and the earl of Antrim, being a catholic, was marked off from the rest of the settler community, tending to associate with the Old English of the Pale, marrying his daughters to their sons and leading the Old English group's negotiations on recusancy fines in the 1630s. His connections with the native Irish were less strong, but some did exist.[121]

As the settlers shed many of their contacts in England and Scotland they found it necessary to consolidate their new social positions in east Ulster. In England, an Irish landed estate was not considered as prestigious as English or Scottish land. Whereas in England the mere possession of land was not a road to wealth but rather the evidence that wealth and status had been achieved, the converse was true in Ireland. In 1632 for example the countess of St. Albans refused a financially generous offer by the earl of Antrim for the bethrothal of her daughter to his son because the earl's lands 'so far removed my daughter from all her friends and acquaintance, the uttermost north part of Ireland, and a country so different in condition and breeding'. The predisposition of the court to Ireland was reflected in the attitude of the second earl of Antrim, who had been brought up there, and had 'a mighty contempt of all that is in Ireland'.[122] Thus settlers needed more than land to consolidate their social position, and so they began to seek additional sources of prestige such as titles and royal office in Ireland. Royal office also enabled the settlers to gain access to the sources of patronage which would further enhance them in the eyes of their peers. Lord Cromwell for instance on one occasion pressed Lord Deputy Wentworth for 'some addition of power to pleasure my neighbours and tenants'.[123]

Three main types of office were open to settlers. First, and most importantly, there was membership of the Dublin parliament. This brought individuals into contact with sources of patronage and also enabled them to monitor central government attitudes to the localities more effectively. There was considerable competition for this office and in 1613 both Sir Hugh Montgomery and Sir James Hamilton attempted to secure their election by creating freeholders on their estates and in

---

[121] *Cal. S.P. Ire., 1625-32*, pp 201, 203, 206; P.R.O.N.I., D2977, 1627 'Marriage articles of Lady Sarah Macdonnell'; SL, 1, ff 64, 67; SL, 18, nos 144, 168, 169; *Acts privy council, 1615-16*, p. 261.

[122] Quoted in Stone, *Crisis*, p. 626, Strafford, *Letters*, ii, p. 248.

[123] SL, 14, no. 251.

1640 'diverse sham freeholders' were created in Down as part of an attempt to rig the elections.[124] The second type of office open to settlers was to be appointed to local commissions, such as that on Down shipwrecks in 1637, or to act as county officers, such as sheriffs and justices of the peace.[125] Settlers often undertook these offices even though they were not financially rewarding and one sheriff complained in 1606 that all he had sustained during his period of office was 'loss and hindrance'.[126] A third form of local office which was much sought after was a local military commission. The earl of Antrim, for instance, as 'a person very considerable in regard of his quality', sought an increase in the numbers of horse and foot under his command in 1625 as 'he does so much affect it as a mark of favour'.[127] The dispute between Sir John Clotworthy and Wentworth during the 1630s, provides a further example of the importance attached to commissions since it was, in part, the result of Wentworth's refusal to grant Clotworthy a company of horse, to which he felt entitled because of his social position, that Clotworthy opposed Wentworth so strongly in the 1630s.[128]

While there was considerable concern with acquiring office there was less enthusiasm about exercising it. M.P.s from east Ulster, for example, were relatively inactive in the Dublin parliament: they rarely spoke in parliament, they sat on few committees, and they were frequently fined for non-attendance.[129] The two most active M.P.s were Sir James Hamilton, who was dependent on royal patronage and office for his advancement, having few resources in Scotland, and Sir John Clotworthy, who in the parliament of 1634-5 was closely allied by marriage to the anti-Wentworth faction and hence had a personal reason for attendance. As a result local issues were rarely raised in the Irish House of Commons, in contrast with the Westminster commons which spent the bulk of its time on provincial issues.[130] It was only in the 1640 parliament

---

[124] *Cal. pat. rolls Ire., Jas. I*, p. 397; *Mont. MSS*, pp 305-7.

[125] For example, *Cal. S.P. Ire., 1625-32*, p. 254; *Acts privy council, Jan-Aug. 1627*, pp 458-60; *Acts privy council, Jan. 1623-Mar. 1625*, p. 145.

[126] P.R.O.I., Ferguson MSS, ix, p. 92; cf. *Advertisements for Ire.*, pp 48-9.

[127] *Acts privy council, March 1625-May 1626*, p. 325; Laud, *Works*, vii, p. 188.

[128] Cal. S.P. Ire., 1625-32, pp 366, 452; *Cal. S.P. Ire., 1647-60*, p. 180; H.M.C., *8th Report*, appendix 2, p. 596.

[129] Appendix F.

[130] G.R. Elton, 'Tudor government: the points of contact. 1 Parliament' in *R. Hist. Soc. Trans.*, 5th ser., xxiv (1974), pp 191-6.

that any number of local issues, such as the importation of tobacco at Carrickfergus, were raised, and these as a stick with which to beat Wentworth. Landlords were usually too concerned with building up their own interests at a local level, consolidating their lands and rights and acquiring offices to underpin their new social position, to be concerned with national politics. Their initial interests were estate rather than county or country based.

The consolidation of landlord positions entailed building up a network of relations within east Ulster, mainly through judicious marriages, in order to recreate the closely knit kin structure of English or Scottish lowland society which had been disrupted in the migration. This network oiled the mechanisms of social interaction since families were often the source of loans, as safe mortgagors and as arbitrators in disputes. Robert Adair, for example, in 1636, mortgaged most of his lands to his brother-in-law, and when Patrick Savage was not able to pay an instalment on the dowry of his sister, Maria, to Cahall O'Hara, of county Antrim, it was to his father-in-law, Viscount Ards, that he turned for a substantial loan.[131] Given the reluctance of east Ulster settlers to take business to the central courts, the family often acted as arbiters in disputes. Isobell Edmonston, for instance, arbitrated between her son, Archibald, and her son-in-law, Robert Adair, in November 1629, and on the Savage estate Viscount Ards arbitrated in a number of disputes.[132] Families could also be fruitful recruiting grounds for further settlers such as John Peacock, who succeeded his cousin William Edmonston to a tenancy at Greyabbey when Edmonston moved to Antrim.[133]

Once a family was securely established in east Ulster it could afford to widen its horizon and make contact with influential families in other parts of Ireland which was a noticeable trend of the 1630s. Richard Boyle, first earl of Cork, and his circle were much in demand as a source of marriage partners as they were one of the most influential planter groups in Ireland. Lord Clandeboy attempted to marry his son into the Boyle family in the 1630s but failed due to the stubbornness of Boyle's daughter. Sir John Clotworthy was more successful in his suit for Mary

---

[131] P.R.O.N.I., D929/F1/1A; D552/B/1/1/19, 21, 30, 38; D552/B/3/1/1.

[132] East Suffolk R.O., HA12/A2/1/38; P.R.O.N.I., T829/9; D1430/3; D552/B/f/1 /25.

[133] H.M.C., *Various*, v, p. 131; P.R.O.N.I., T1030/4.

Jones, a daughter of Lord Ranelagh, one of Boyle's main political allies.[134] Contacts with prestigious English or Scottish families were also resurrected by the settlers in order to aid them in their search for recognition of their new place in the social hierarchy. Viscount Ards, for example, discovered a distant family connection with the earl of Eglinton and attempted to revitalise it by drawing up an extraordinary document swearing loyalty to Eglinton.[135]

Not only were family groups a key element in everyday social life but they also provided settlers with the main means of consolidating their long-term hold on land after the first generation through the mechanism of inheritance. Inheritance provided an important strengthening of the settlers legal claim to land for while first generation settlers had to rely on their patents for legal claim to land these second generation colonists relied on inheritance which could not be challenged by a simple possessory action at law but required the more complex writ of right. Many settlers went to considerable lengths to ensure that their lands would pass intact to the next generation with little dispute and Sir Randal Macdonnell even obtained permission to introduce a private bill in parliament to ensure the succession of his lands.[136] Since it was usually the eldest son who inherited the family lands to avoid splitting the power base by dividing the estate, the younger sons had to be provided for in a number of other ways. Many fathers provided their younger sons with a small proportion of land, as did Lord Cromwell who granted his second son enough land for 'sufficient maintenance' on a thousand-year lease.[137] Settlers also resorted to a variety of other means of providing for younger sons who would not inherit the family estate. Thus many were equipped with a good education to fit them for a profession so that they would not contest the succession which would place the future of the lands in jeopardy or become a charge on the estate. The earl of Antrim's sons, for instance, were all sent to travel on the continent

---

[134] For Clandeboy, *Lismore papers,* 1st ser., v, pp 73, 101, 116, 363; ibid., 2nd ser., v, p. 8; on Clotworthy, G.E.C., *The complete peerage,* sub. Masserine; *Lismore papers*, 1st ser., iii, pp 61, 154, 164; N.P. Canny, *The upstart earl* (Cambridge, 1982), pp 101, 107.

[135] H.M.C., *Eglinton,* pp 2, 34.

[136] Bodl., Clarendon, ii, no. 68; *Cal. pat. rolls Ire., Jas. I,* p. 250.

[137] P.R.O.I., D20559; native Irish adopted similar practices, O'Laverty, *Down and Connor,* ii, pp lxi-lxii; P.R.O.N.I., T185, f 3; E.D. Atkinson, *An Ulster parish* (Dublin, 1898), pp 25, 131, 134; P.R.O.I., Thrift MSS, nos 86, 113.

and at least one entered the church, as did one of Sir Arthur Magennis's sons.[138] A good case-study of the fate of younger sons is provided by Sir Hugh Montgomery's sons who were all sent to university in Glasgow, then to an Inn of Court and finally to travel on the continent. Sir Hugh's eldest son inherited the family lands but the second son, Sir James, was given a small portion of land near Greyabbey and was to acknowledge himself well contented and 'never to seek or crave any further of his father's possessions or proceed any way to the prejudice of his father's heir'. He later acted as an agent on his father's estate and became involved in business dealings with Sir David Cunningham, an important Ayrshire landowner and London merchant.[139]

These provisions for younger sons highlight the concern with the consolidation of the landed estate and its preservation through primogeniture. This concern together with the desire to underpin their recent social elevation by the acquisition of royal offices bred a distinctive settler society in east Ulster. Settlers were concerned that their landed rights should not be encroached on by any source, especially by the central government, since it was these rights which formed the base for their newly acquired social status. Such a society, highly conscious of status, was clearly sensitive to the nuances of etiquette and protocol. The earl of Antrim, for example, objected strongly in 1636 to being omitted from a commission on alehouses to which he considered himself to belong by right. Sights on a man's status were taken seriously and the earl of Antrim was involved in at least two major slander cases, one of which went as far as the Dublin court of Castle Chamber.[140] This display of newfound social status also took the form of building monuments to the family to perpetuate the lineage. Sir James Hamilton and Sir Arthur Chichester both demonstrated their social success by constructing magnificent tombs, at Dunlop in Ayrshire and in St. Nicholas's church Carrickfergus, respectively. Chichester spelt out clearly his reasons why a tomb should be erected on the death of his sister in 1614 when he

---

[138] *Cal. S.P. dom., 1623-5,* p. 302; C. Giblin, 'Francis Macdonnell' in *Seanchas Ardmhacha,* viii (1975-6), pp 44-6; D.F. Cregan, 'The social and cultural background of a counter reformation episcopate' in A. Cosgrove, D. McCartney (eds), *Studies in Irish history* (Dublin, 1979), p. 92.

[139] P.R.O.N.I., T1030/3; H.M.C., *Eglinton,* pp 33-4; *Memorials of the dead in Ireland,* ii (1892-4), pp 64-5; ibid., v (1901-3), pp 180-82; H.M.C., *Laing,* i, pp 212, 219.

[140] *Cal. S.P. Ire., 1625-32,* p. 398; *Cal. pat. rolls Ire., Chas. I,* p. 399; B.L., Add 18824, nos 41, 61.

insisted that 'a fair monument to be erected upon her and her husband
when God shall call him [which] will make them memorable to posterity
when other temporary expenses (if they be superfluous) will soon vanish
and be forgotten'.[141] The settlers began to see themselves in their new
social roles as landed gentry for as Sir James Montgomery put it on being offered a military command in 1641, 'I shall acquit myself of this
employment . . . as it becomes a gentleman and a soldier'.[142] The settler
society was not England or Scotland writ small but a combination of
both, which was moulded by other factors distinctively colonial: interaction with a Dublin administration intent on establishing its authority
in a newly settled area, and the economics of acquiring and developing
estates and finding tenants in a new environment.

The settlers were not the only ones adapting their social structures to a
new environment. Gaelic Irish landowners were also attempting to
forge new social arrangements within the colonial context. One way of
examining the Gaelic perception of this adaptation of landed Gaelic
society to the new colonial environment is through the Gaelic poetry of
the period. Since Gaelic poets tended to reflect the ideas and perceptions
of their patrons, as it was the patron who was paying to be praised, the
poetry reflects as much the changing attitudes of the Gaelic nobility as
of the poets themselves. An example of the changes which occurred in
east Ulster is the way in which Fear Flatha Ó Gnímh, the principal
seventeenth-century poet of the O'Neills of Clandeboy, changed the
themes of his poems during the early seventeenth century. On the flight
of the earls in 1607 Ó Gnímh composed a series of poems lamenting and
condemning the changes in Gaelic society as many other poets did, and
yet by the 1630s the self-same poet had taken to praising the English vir-
tues espoused by Sir Henry O'Neill, the chief of the remnants of the
O'Neills of Clandeboy.[143] This was a reflection of the fact that the
Gaelic Irish lords gradually accommodated themselves to and made use
of the ideas imported by the settlers. The advent of English law, for

[141] W. and C. Trevelyan, *Trevelyan Papers*, iii, Camden Society, 1st ser., (London,
1872), p. 127.
[142] Bodl., Carte 2, f 154.
[143] O. Bergin (ed), *Irish bardic poetry*, (Dublin 1970), nos 26, 27; Brian O Cúiv, 'A
poem on the I Neill' in *Celtica*, ii, (1954), pp 245-51. For an analysis of the full corpus of Ó
Gnímh poetry see B. Cunningham, R. Gillespie, 'The east Ulster bardic family of Ó
Gnímh' in *Éigse*, xx(1984), pp 106-114.

example, radically changed the way in which the Gaelic Irish viewed themselves and the way the poets portrayed them. As early as 1617, one poet, Lughaidh Ó hEachuidéin, noted that the peaceful state of lower Clandeboy was no disgrace to its lord, despite the fact that one of the traditionally predominant themes of bardic poetry was warfare and the heroic deeds of the lord. Later Fear Flatha Ó Gnímh said Sir Henry O'Neill did not need to go into battle to prove himself as it was now accepted that recourse to the common law was the better way to resolve disputes and that it was not his military prowess which marked his superiority but his learning, justice, wisdom, and his superiority in reading, and the law.[144]

A direct result of such changes in Gaelic society was the decline of the professional poet, who in the new order was no longer required to uphold his patron's prestige and remember his rights. Ó Gnímh, in a poem addressed to Sir Arthur Magennis noted this decline: kinship and poetry, he said, were no longer important under the new order and the poets were forced to seek other employment.[145] This led to a 'backlash' from some poets who, experiencing falling demand for their product, and from a natural fear of change called for a return to the traditional values of Gaelic society. Several poets urged Sir Henry O'Neill to give up his comforts, to perform heroic deeds, and to seek the leadership of Ulster, and even the highkingship. They contended that since Sir Henry had succeeded to the lands of lower Clandeboy, the O'Neills had been satirised and brought into disrepute. And even later in the seventeenth century. Art O'Neill, Sir Henry's brother, was urged to seek the leadership of Ulster and the highkingship of Tara.[146] Furthermore, poets such as Ó Gnímh who had adapted to the changes in Gaelic society were termed 'file an tsluaigh', poet of the masses, a lesser grade of poet, implying that they had compromised their true professional status.[147]

Gaelic society was not extinguished, merely modified. Poetry in the traditional form continued to be composed for the Gaelic lords. As Ó Gnímh reminded Art O'Neill, it was not, in the poet's view, heroic deeds that won the O'Neills fame but the work of the poets in publicising their

---

144 *Lr Cl. Aodha Buidhe*, pp 166, 170, 261; I am indebted to Bernadette Cunningham, M.A. for her assistance in interpreting this text.

145 Bergin, *Irish bardic poetry*, no 28.

146 *Lr Cl. Aodha Buidhe*, pp 176-8, 220-5.

147 *Lr Cl. Aodha Buidhe*, p. 192.

nobility, and it was not in English, Welsh or classical literary forms but
in the Irish form that their nobility could be perpetuated and understood
by their countrymen.[148] The very existence of the *Leabhar Cloinne
Aodha Buidhe* as a monument to the O'Neills of Clandeboy was
evidence that this view was at least partly accepted by them. The blend-
ing of traditional Gaelic society with the ideas of the settlers is exemplified in the 'poem' written for the marriage of Donal Magennis,
fourth son of Sir Arthur Magennis, which continued the tradition of a
poem composed for recital at a great occasion. The 'poem', however,
was a *Crosántacht*, a mixture of verse and prose, rather than the strict
form of classical Gaelic poetry.[149] This innovation in poetic forms
represents in microcosm the adaptation by Gaelic landed society of its
traditional ideas of status and the social order by adopting such features
of the new regime — English law for instance — as they found useful to
bolster up their influence while retaining a separate identity in the colonial environment of early seventeenth-century east Ulster.

V

At the levels below the landed society described above settlers and
natives were also framing social arrangements to meet the problems of a
colonial society, including the need for strong leadership, for protection
and for coherent units of social organisation. Those at the lower social
levels found three structures especially important to the process of adap-
tion to their new environment: the lordship, the local community, and
the family. These three structures constituted the framework within
which the detailed social arrangements of the lower levels of society
evolved.

The largest unit with which most rural dwellers in the early seventeenth century had contact was their landlord's lordship, the combination of rights and property determined by royal patent.[150] The structures of the lordship were moulded by landlords for their own ends, but
these same structures, seen from a different perspective, were also a vital

---

[148] *Lr Cl. Aodha Buidhe*, p. 227.

[149] A. Harrison, *An chrosántacht*, (Dublin, 1979), pp 43-4.

[150] The term 'lordship' as used here in a seventeenth-century settlement context must
not be confused with the term 'lordship' as applied to the native Irish power blocks of the
sixteenth century and earlier, the authority of which was not derived from a royal patent.

element in tenant society. The structures of the lordship revolved around the relationship between landlord and tenant. Many of the tenants on an estate were bound either to the landlord or to a larger tenant by a lease. In essence, the lease was a contract under which the greater landholder provided land and a number of services to the tenant in return for a rent in cash, or a combination of cash and kind. As a lease of 1632 between Rory Magennis and Donell Magennis explained:

the said Rory for himself of his heirs executors administrators and assigns doeth hereby covenant promise and grant to and with the said Donell . . . that he the said Rory . . . all and singular the premises with the appurtenances unto him the said Donell . . . during the said term, fully and absolutely freed acquitted and discharged of and from all manner of former contracts, bargains, sales, feoffments, jointures, dowers, statutes staples, recognisances and forfeitures whatsoever had made or done of for or concerning the premises or any part thereof. And of and from all manner of troubles eviction or molestation of him the said Rory . . . or any other person or persons whatsoever for or concerning the same, shall warrant acquit and defend the said Donell . . . paying the rents as aforesaid, doing and performing all and whatsoever herein contained which on his . . . part is to be performed and done . . .[151]

In a society where population was low and land abundant, it was necessary for the landlord who wished to increase his income from rent to offer incentives, such as initially low rents or services, to attract tenants to his lands.[152] Services provided by the landlord to his tenants took a number of forms. The manor court, for example, was an important service offered by the landlord to tenants, apart from being a source of profit to himself. This court was used as a forum for settling disputes and provided a meeting point for tenants. Secondly, since the lord's patent gave him undisputed title to his lands it enabled him to protect his tenants, and landlords were acutely conscious of their responsibility in this matter. Thus for example, the earl of Antrim wrote in 1629, during a dispute involving some of his tenants and those of an adjoining estate, 'where I have the power the tenant shall not be wronged'.[153]

The protection offered by a lord to his tenants was twofold, legal and physical. Legal protection was particularly important to the security of

[151] P.R.O.N.I., D671/D8/1/22.

[152] Robert Kinaston, for example, deposed in 1643 that he had lost £40 p.a. from his lands due to the loss of tenants, T.C.D., MS 837 f 8.

[153] H.M.C., *Various*, v, pp 140-41.

a tenant's lands because poor definition of landholding boundaries meant that some measure of security apart from the lease was usually required to ensure the integrity of a holding. The problem is well demonstrated in a chancery case of 1627 over the two townlands of Tullyorier, in the barony of upper Iveagh, which had been granted to Arthur Magennis. Difficulties arose when a neighbour, Gilladuff McBryan, who also possessed of a townland called Tullyorier, claimed possession of both townlands since the divisions were not distinct.[154] Hence, the lease was often not an end in itself and landlords had to promise to provide further legal security if required within a period of time stated in the lease.[155]

As an extension of the idea of securing tenure the landlord also offered the service of securing a tenant 'in peaceable possession' by acting as the tenant's legal agent in disputes.[156] In the sixteenth century, when landlord control was weak, tenants acted for themselves, as in 1579 when the 'gentlemen and freeholders of Lecale' sought their own redress for illegal actions against Peter, lord of Trymlestiston through an agent, Nicholas Fitzsimon.[157] In the seventeenth century redress was more usually sought by the tenants' landlord, as Sir Arthur Magennis did for his tenants who had been 'disturbed and molested' by his neighbour, Art McGlassine Magennis, in 1628. Similarly Thomas Barnwall sued six men in chancery for unlawful impositions on his tenants of church lands in Lecale.[158]

The lord also became responsible for the physical protection of his tenants at a time when raids by kern on small settler villages were common. The author of the *Montgomery Manuscripts* for instance, recorded that on the death of the first Viscount Ards in 1636 the tenantry 'loudly lamented for their loss of him . . . because he had been in general careful to protect them all (within his reach) from injuries'.[159] So normal had this expectation of protection become by 1641 that on the outbreak of rebellion in that year most tenants looked not to their own resources

[154] P.R.O.N.I., T588/1, f 11.

[155] For example, P.R.O.N.I., D104/33/5/1; D778/1A, T1030/3; T185; D207/16/9; T956/21.

[156] For use of this phrase, T.C.D., MS 644, ff 118, 169; P.R.O.N.I., D671/D4/1/2; D671/D7/1/61; D929/F2/3/27.

[157] *Cal. pat. rolls Ire., Eliz.*, pp 25-6, 57.

[158] P.R.O.I., Chancery Bills O 83, G 15.

[159] *Mont. MSS*, p. 144.

but to their landlord for protection. Even after such an event as the 'massacre' at Islandmagee, in east Antrim, the native Irish tenants of Moses Hill, the landlord, did not bind together for defence but went to Carrickfergus in order to ask 'their master' for protection.[160] Turning to the landlord to organise defence in this situation was not unusual since it was he who had organised the mustering system in times of peace. In some areas where he was able to do so, the landlord responded to this demand. Alexander McKay, for example, on the outbreak of rebellion, organised those of his tenants who remained loyal into a relief force to lift the siege on Archibald Stewart's house in Cushendun. Other landowners used more orthodox methods, absorbing their tenants into their regiments, with the result that Viscount Ards's force which lay at Comber in 1641 was composed mainly of his tenants armed with 'scythes, cornforks, staffs and a few pikes'.[161] In most cases the scale of the rebellion was such that local lords were incapable of protecting their tenants adequately and so 'protection groups' grew up to fill the vacuum. At Ardglass, in Lecale, the failure of the local lord to provide protection resulted in a number of men paying one Cormac McGuire for protection, and in the parish of Magheragall, in south-west Antrim, offers of protection by Colonel James Macdonnell were followed by a servant to collect payment.[162]

The lord also provided his tenants with a link with the wider world both nationally and within the county. On a national level the earl of Antrim was the vehicle by which complaints by his tenants about the assessment of the 1634 subsidy were conveyed to the Dublin administration.[163] The number of ways a lord's contacts at a county level could be used for the benefit of the tenantry were probably more important. A tenant appearing before any county official, a justice of the peace for example, would usually enjoy the support of his landlord who could bring his influence to bear on the tenant's behalf. Thus after some of the earl of Antrim's tenants appeared before a justice of the peace in 1630,

[160] T.C.D., MS 838, f 200. Similarly, in Down, Phelim Smith deposed that Redmond Fitzsimmons told him that he 'would not come home safe with his life without a protection or a pass from the Lord Viscount Clandeboy', his landlord, T.C.D., MS 837, f 61.

[161] T.C.D., MS 838, f 35ᵛ; H.M.C., *Eglinton MSS*, p. 489; W. Frazer, *Memorials of the Montgomeries*, i (Edinburgh, 1895), p. 244.

[162] T.C.D., MS 837, ff 89, 91; T.C.D., MS 838, f 237.

[163] SL, 15, no. 215; Tenants also expected to be protected from the ecclesiastical authorities, Strafford *Letters*, ii, p. 219.

Antrim wrote thanking him 'for taking so much pains to do right between my tenants which I will requite if any of your tenants come before
me'.[164] The role of the landlord as communicator was particularly important in a society like east Ulster which was composed of individual
autonomous lordships. If a tenant on one estate wished to make contact
with another tenant elsewhere, the best means of doing so was through
the individual landlords. Tenants could be recommended for advancement by letters between lords, and in the absence of an effective policing
system lords could help tenants to find malefactors through their network of contacts. On one occasion for instance, Viscount Clandeboy,
from north Down, wrote on behalf of one of his tenants to William
Edmonston in south-east Antrim, 'the bearer, Robert Clyd, has two
horses stolen from him which he thinks are carried to that side [Antrim].
I entreat you on his behalf to lay out all means for searching after the
said horses, which he will give you the marks of'. More serious cases
could also be dealt with through landlord contacts as when Clandeboy
sent Margaret Stewart to Edmonston with a letter informing him that
she 'has been informed that some residing under you can give her some
light towards the finding out of those that have lately murdered her
husband'.[165]

While this network was of importance it was the services which the
landlord supplied to regulate the day-to-day working of the estate which
were of more significance to the majority of his tenants. The most important of these was the manor court which provided the tenantry with a
peaceful means of resolving disputes and airing grievances without the
trouble and expense of going to the quarter sessions or assizes. There
were two types of manor court, the court leet and the court baron, which
were originally intended to serve the differing needs of settlers. The
former was a franchisal jurisdiction dealing with criminal offences but
this function was gradually becoming redundant with the rise of the
justice of the peace and the quarter sessions. The latter dealt with small
debts, trespasses and actions up to the value of forty shillings, above
which sum a writ was required. In practice these nice distinctions were
abandoned and the courts tended to be used interchangeably. The earl
of Antrim, for instance, commanded his tenants to commence all small

---

[164] H.M.C., *Various*, v, p. 135.

[165] H.M.C., *Various*, v, pp 124, 136. It was the responsibility of the wronged party to
arrest in most cases. R. Bolton, *Justice of the peace*, bk i, pp 24, 28-9.

actions in 'the court leet or court baron' and similar orders were made in the case of Sir James Hamilton's tenants.

All the east Ulster estates had the right to set up at least one manor court presided over by the landlord or his agent and most availed of this right. The courts on the Conway estates in south-west Antrim seem to have been particularly active since in August 1630 George Rawdon, the agent, wrote that he had just held a court day at which he had settled a large number of disputes among the tenants.[166] The measure of the success of the courts is how few problems they left unresolved to be adjudicated upon by a higher court such as chancery. While chancery suits were long and expensive, the opportunity existed to bring cases there since tenants could sue *in forma pauperis* and were doing so to an increasing extent in England.[167] Some sixty-four pleadings in the Dublin court of chancery relating to the early seventeenth century have survived for east Ulster and of these only seven (6·9 per cent) relate to landlord-tenant disputes and a further eight (12·5 per cent) relate to disputes between tenants. Most of this type of dispute arose in the areas of Lecale and mid-Down where estates were scattered, landlord influence weak and the institutions of the lordship, including the manor courts, poorly developed. The estates of Sir Edward Trevor, for example, were scattered, having been acquired piecemeal and those of Lord Cromwell in Lecale so badly managed during his long absences that the agent had to be dismissed.[168]

Where manor courts were ineffective, customs and social practices were changed to meet the deficiency. Thus the absence of manorial courts in mid-Down at least partly accounts for the differences in inheritance customs in this area. In east Ulster the normal method of passing land between generations, among both natives and settlers, was on the death of a father, when, normally, the eldest son presented himself

---

[166] For examples of courts being held see P.R.O.N.I., T588/1, f 38; S.R.O. GD 154/668; P.R.O.I., Ferguson MSS, xxvii, p. 35; *Cal. S.P. Ire., 1625-32*, p. 563; H.M.C., *Various*, v, p. 128; *Mont. MSS*, p. 120.

[167] E. Kerridge, *Agrarian problems in the sixteenth century and after* (London, 1969), pp 72-3; W. Jones, *The Elizabethan court of chancery* (Oxford, 1967), pp 323-8, 487-8; W.G. Hoskins, *Provincial England* (London, 1963), p. 84. For some indication how Irish chancery worked, P.R.O.I., Ferguson MSS, viii, pp 9-12; xix, pp 18-9; G.J. Hand (ed.), 'Rules and orders to be observed in the proceeding of cause in the high court of chancery in Ireland' in *Ir. Jurist*, n.s. ix (1974), p. 110, n. 2.

[168] SL. 14, no. 251; R.E. Parkinson, *The city of Down* (Belfast, 1927), p. 35.

in the manor court, proved his right to the land, paid a heriot, which was enrolled on the court roll, and then entered into the land. In mid-Down and Lecale where the manor courts could not enforce this system, confusion could arise, as on the death of one Lecale tenant, Dermot Knevin when one Simon Knevin entered his lands. As Dermot Knevin's son, also named Simon, pointed out, he was 'of the same nation of the suppliant but of no alliance in any way'.[169] To resolve this problem the practice grew of granting land to the eldest son before his father's death to ensure a smooth transfer, although in most contracts of this nature the father retained the use of the land until his death or else when the transfer was made his own name was inserted jointly with that of his son as tenant.[170]

It is clear therefore that the influence of the institutions of lordship penetrated deep into rural society, even to its most sacred act, the transmission of property. This meant that the relationship between landlord and tenant became not an economic nexus but a more paternalistic relationship. Tenants came to expect not merely land from their landlord but also these other rights and services, and the failure of a lord to fulfil these expectations often had serious repercussions. The tenants of the earl of Antrim, for example, threatened to leave him if they could not have the right to fish in the Bann, and the threat was repeated in 1627 if the earl would not have the number of soldiers quartered on his lands reduced.[171]

The services of the lordship were only used by the tenantry when required, and the normal outlook of most tenants did not extend even as far as the lordship. The two forces which most shaped the everyday working of rural society were more localized than the lordship: the local community and the family. In the colonial environment of east Ulster where natives and settlers were attempting to establish themselves in a new environment, local issues predominated. As one officer wrote to the earl of Ormonde, his commander, in a state of distraction during the rebellion of the 1640s, 'we could not (by any means) draw them [the settlers] together from their own towns either to assist one another or to oppose the enemy in any other place . . . where their own particular

[169] P.R.O.I., Chancery Bills, A 180.

[170] P.R.O.I., Lodge MSS, Records of the rolls, v, p. 333; P.R.O.N.I., D265/33; *Inq. Ult.,* Antrim, Chas I, no. 43.

[171] SP63/219/13; *Cal. S.P. Ire., 1603-6,* p. 519; *Cal. S.P. Ire., 1625-32,* p. 203.

interests did not evidently press them unto it'.[172] Out of this localism came a number of tight knit communities bound together by bonds of kinship, debt, and the mutual cooperation needed to solve common problems in, what appeared to settlers, a strange land. Coherence was also fostered by a number of institutions which provided regular contact for the members of the local community. The church, for example, provided a regular meeting point for members of the parish and the alehouse provided a profane counterpart where business could be done, gossip exchanged and even in one case a rising planned.[173] These local communities tended to be protective towards their members and in the case of the native population, juries drawn from local groups often refused to present recusants. The strength of these community bonds drew complaint from Lord Deputy Chichester that 'the common law is eluded by the subtlety of these people who will not find a bill of indictment be the evidence never so pregnant'.[174]

The tight community structure had a number of important advantages for its members. The local community provided a mutual support system and encouraged joint action. There were a number of problems, such as the allocation of bog or common land among individuals, which could only be tackled by the local community acting together. In another example of community cooperation, when the weather threatened to destroy the autumn harvest of 1624 in the parish of Bangor, the whole community bonded together and worked continuously until all the corn was gathered.[175] The close-knit community was of most use in the preservation of law and order. In small groups where people were well known to each other, tracing criminals was relatively easy, a fact which Sir Edward Chichester appreciated when, in reporting a prison escape in 1636, he did not need to issue descriptions of the men as the men would be well known in the locality.[176] In such a situation the degree of social control was high and public humiliation was an integral part of the punishment. Thus in 1576 a Captain Lloyd was punished for insulting the mayor of Carrickfergus by being

---

[172] Bodl., Carte 2, f 203.

[173] B.L., Royal MSS, 18A, lxv, f 2ᵛ; T.C.D., MSS 672, f 83, 91ᵛ, 73, 63, 69ᵛ; Blair, *Autobiography*, p. 67; SP63/255/144.

[174] H.M.C., *Egmont*, i, pt 1, pp 50, 53; *Cal. S.P. Ire., 1625-32*, p. 220.

[175] Blair, *Autobiography*, pp 62-3.

[176] SL, 19, no. 92.

'disarmed in the market place as a note of infamy', and stocks existed in most east Ulster towns to publicly humiliate offenders. Even in executions public humiliation preceded death as criminals were first 'to be led to the gallows' through the streets of the county town.[177] The presbyterian communities in Antrim and Down exploited this system to the full by drawing their disciplinarians, the elders, from within the communities and in this they differed from the anglican courts with their paid officials. Robert Blair, the presbyterian minister at Bangor, recorded the story of an adulterer who had escaped ecclesiastical sanction by bribing the bishop's official but was reported to Blair by a local elder.[178] Discipline under the presbyterians was not in a remote court but before the local community. When a case of demon possession was uncovered near Bangor, Blair called on 'one man of the village who was under the reputation of a godly man . . . to him I imparted the whole matter desiring him to convene the people of that village' who assembled in the church to witness the penance of the possessed 'to the great edification of the whole congregation'.[179] The tight community could also identify those whom it considered undesirable and keep a special watch on them. One clear illustration of this occurred at the outbreak of rebellion in north Antrim when the parish constable of one parish was ordered by the parish council to keep a special watch on the house of one Rory Duff McCormick because 'at that time all the parish where he dwelt were very suspicious of him, in regard he had been arraigned at the bar at Derry before for villainy, and also did know him to be a man of very bad carriage'.[180]

These controls, although often effective in limiting disorder did not remove tensions from the local community and many of these boiled over when the breakdown of authority in the 1640s presented the

[177] On stocks, *Mont. MSS*, p. 120; T.C.D., MS 837, f 11ᵛ; S. Miskimmin, *History and antiquities of Carrickfergus* (Belfast, 1909), p. 28; J.F. Ferguson, 'The Ulster roll of gaol delivery' in *U.J.A.*, 1st ser., i (1853), p. 265.

[178] Blair, *Autobiography*, pp 68-9.

[179] Ibid., pp 65-9. For other cases, W.T. Latimer, 'The old session book of Templepatrick presbyterian church' in *R.S.A.I. jn.*, xxv (1895), pp 130-34, xxxi (1901), pp 162-75, 259-72; Thomas Houston, *A brief historical relation of the life of Mr John Livingston* (Edinburgh, 1848), p. 78.

[180] T.C.D., MS 838, ff 41, 79ᵛ; McCormick attacked the constable and broke out of the house. Also in 1615 James McEdmond had deposed that Teige Ó Leonán was 'a bad liver', T.C.D., MS 672, f 73.

opportunity. Cormac McGuire, for example, fled from his home in Lecale at the outbreak of rebellion 'for fear of his life', because of a dispute between himself and a brother of Thomas Dixon of Bishopscourt. His fears were justified for he was murdered by Thomas a fortnight after his return to Ardglass. A similar situation occurred in north Antrim when Margaret Erwin, a servant of Mr Haughton of Aghadowey, was left alone in the house with his children because he had fled to Lisburn for fear of a neighbour, Collo McKnogher, with whom he was in dispute. Other types of tensions also boiled over, such as those behind the accusation that Jeanette Dilson of Ballintoy was a witch and had protected the village against the rebels by witchcraft.[181] Yet the system effectively controlled the eruption of these tensions into violence, for of all those delivered from east Ulster gaols in 1613, few had committed violent crimes near their homes. The social links between criminal and victim were nearly always weak, the attacker usually being a stranger in the place where the assault took place.[182]

A structure of even more importance than the local community in social regulation was the family which was the basis of control, cooperation and regulation in all areas. Unfortunately because of the paucity of sources, it is extremely difficult to gain any real insight into the internal workings of the family as a social unit in east Ulster rural society. However, some light can be shed on it by examining the ways it disposed its most precious resource, land, among its members.[183] Since a will was not recognised at common law in Ireland before 1635 and even then only for certain types of tenures the main means of devising land was by arrangement within the family and these arrangements reveal the nature of family structures.[184] Such arrangements transgressed all cultural boundaries since they were responses to common problems of devising land and the techniques described below were used by both settler and native.

[181] T.C.D., MS 838, f 273; E. Hogan (ed.), *A history of the war in Ireland* (Dublin, 1873), pp 93-4; T.C.D., MS 837, ff 144, 79.

[182] Based on Ferguson, 'Gaol delivery'.

[183] J. Goody, J. Thirsk, E.P. Thompson (eds), *Family and inheritance* (Cambridge, 1978), pp 1-9.

[184] Wills became recognised by the statute of wills, 10 Chas. I, s.2, c.2.(Ir). The church could administer wills before this in the preogative court but this was little used in east Ulster, only four wills being passed. A. Vicars, *Index to the perogative wills of Ireland* (Dublin, 1879), pp 310, 110, 269. The indices of the diocesan courts in P.R.O.I. show only one pre 1641 will for Connor proved there, five for Down and none for Dromore.

Four main patterns of devising land common to both settler and native can be discerned in east Ulster. The first was simple primogeniture, the land being passed on the father's death to his eldest son.[185] This had the disadvantage that sons might have to wait for some time to be able to establish themselves independently as was the case when Richard Fitzharris's father died in February 1630: Richard, who inherited the land, was already thirty years old and married. The second way of devising land was a variant on this, the land being placed in the hands of the eldest son before the father's death.[186] This was frequently done to ensure the succession when there was no other way, such as the safeguard of the manor court, of protecting the rights of the eldest son. A third inheritance custom was that of partible inheritance, by which land was divided unequally among a number of sons, but this was rare in east Ulster, only two cases having been traced.[187] Both of these occurred in the poor land of mid-Down where it was necessary to retain younger sons on the land for their labour, and hence they had to be given a portion of the land to maintain them. A fourth custom involved the devising of land to daughters if there was no son. If the daughters were not married the land was usually divided amongst them equally but if the daughters were married, the inheritance was distributed equally among them and was absorbed by their husbands. Most of the lands of the Boyd family of north Antrim, for example, were acquired by the family through the marriage of Hugh Boyd, the rector of Ramoan parish, to Rose, the only daughter of Hugh McNeill of Duneany.[188]

This evidence from inheritance customs suggests a tightly knit family structure which sought to prevent the alienation of lands outside the immediate family, preferably keeping the holding intact in the hands of the eldest son. This impression is confirmed by examining the problem in other ways such as through the degree of discord within families. There were internal tensions within families, such as those which arose over the allocation of the profits from a land sale between two daughters at Balysport in the Ards, but these were resolved mainly within the framework of the family or through the normal legal procedures and

[185] *Inq. Ult.*, Antrim, Chas I, No. 31; Antrim, Jas. I, nos 7, 13, Chas I, Nos 6, 56.

[186] *Inq. Ult.*, Down, Chas I, nos 52, 56; P.R.O.I., Thrift MSS, no. 79.

[187] P.R.O.I. Chancery Bills, G 411; *Inq. Ult.*, Down, Chas I, no. 89.

[188] O'Laverty, *Down and Connor*, iv, p. 41; P.R.O.I., RC6/2, p. 109; J.C.W. Wylie, *Irish land law* (London, 1975), p. 12.

unlike England there appears to have been little intra-family violence, no cases being recorded on the gaol delivery roll.[189] The cohesion of the family is also illustrated in the low incidence of marital breakdown and infidelity. The seventeenth-century church laid down that marriage was a holy institution sent from God to provide companionship and freedom from fornication and the state reinforced these views with legislation on bigamy, adultery and buggery.[190] Hence marriage could only be dissolved on grounds of adultery or desertion and only one case of formally dissolved marriage is known from east Ulster before 1640.[191] The incidence of sexual misdemeanours was also low; few rape cases for example being recorded in the east Ulster gaol deliveries of 1613-15. Additional evidence for the low level of sexually motivated crime is provided by the presbyterian Antrim meeting session book for the years 1654-58 which recorded sixty-three cases of adultery, of which six were unproved, sixty-seven cases of fornication and ten cases of bigamy, desertion or wrong marriage.[192] By the standards of contemporary England this incidence of adultery and fornication was low, and in statistical terms an east Ulster settler was more likely to commit murder than adultery.[193] Most of the marital offences recorded in the session book were the result of the confusion of the 1640s, spouses wrongfully believing their partner's dead and remarrying. Even sexual misdemeanours were often kept within the family for in six of the proven cases of adultery the partners came from the same family group. George Hunter, for example, committed adultery with his niece and Isobel Atcheson of Ballyclare with her nephew and brother-in-law. All these indicators again point to the cohesion of the family, with considerable emphasis on the eldest son.

[189] For this case, P.R.O.I., RC6/2, p. 109. For comparison with higher rates in England, J.A. Sharpe, 'Domestic homicide in early modern England' in *Hist. Jnl.*, xxiv (1981), pp 29-48.

[190] L. Stone, *Family, sex and marriage in England* (London, 1977), pp 37-8; K. Thomas, 'The puritans and adultery' in D. Pennington, K. Thomas (eds), *Puritans and revolutionaries* (Oxford, 1978), pp 257-77; *Westminster Confession*, ch. XXIV; 10 Chas I, s.2, c.20 (Ir.); ibid., c.21 (Ir.).

[191] D. Campbell, *The clan Campbell*, viii (Edinburgh, 1917), pp 77-8.

[192] P.R.O.N.I., D1759/1A/1.

[193] Stone, *Family*, p. 632; F.G. Emmison, *Elizabethan life: morals and the church courts* (Chelmsford, 1978), p. 6; S.J. Davies, 'The courts and the Scottish legal system, 1600-1747' in V.A.C. Gatrell, B. Lenman, G. Parker, *Crime and the law: the social history of crime in western Europe since 1500* (London, 1980), p. 124.

An integral part of the household, if not the family, were the servants, although a strong dividing line was drawn between master and servant. There is, for example, only one case of fornication between mistress and servant in the Antrim session book.[194] Domestic servants, such as those in Jane Ellis's house in Antrim, were needed to run the house, and others, such as shepherds and cowherds and a ploughman, were also needed on the farm. At peak times in the agricultural cycle additional temporary servants were also hired to help with the harvest.[195] The relationship between master and servant was similar to that between landlord and tenant described above. The bond was a contractual one, although many servants felt justified in disregarding it if the employer did not also provide favourable conditions. The master could provide for his servants in a number of ways, including subletting land to them or keeping them in his own household. However, if they were not treated properly they would leave as the servants of the dowager countess of Antrim threatened to do in 1641 because she would not make their whiskey strong enough.[196] Although such action was a felony it was unlikely that any of the absconding servants would ever be caught because of the lack of an effective, impartial policing system.

The evidence of the position of servants only serves to confirm that the family was tightly knit together and tended to resist outsiders. The master may have had legal responsibility for his servants but there the severely contractual obligation ended. This family structure is what might have been expected in the circumstances. Settlers and natives were both attempting to consolidate their positions and they wanted their lands, whether newly acquired or a venerable patrimony, to remain within the family. Furthermore, even within the family unit, they desired that lands would not be split but would remain concentrated in one person, the eldest son. Apart from ensuring the integrity of the family lands, primogeniture had a second important role in settler society. Most of the first generation settlers lacked the seniority in age that

---

[194] P.R.O.N.I., D1759/1A/1, p. 114.

[195] For examples, T.C.D., MS 837, ff 51, 65, 30, 103, 105; T.C.D., MS 838, ff 51, 85, 126, 161; *Mont. MSS,* pp 64, 135; *Cal. S.P. dom., 1631-3,* p. 263; SL, 24/25, no. 51.

[196] For examples of servants on land, T.C.D., MS 838, f 80ᵛ; P.R.O.N.I., D671/D8/1/19A specified that the land mentioned on that lease was not to be sublet 'except to . . . manual labourers residing in and upon the premises'. For indoor maintenance, P.R.O.N.I., D265/27; T.C.D., MS 838, ff 23ᵛ, 62.

constituted the main bulwark of authority in contemporary England and so heads of families had to depend on their control of land to exert their authority.[197] Primogeniture provided a means whereby a father could exercise control over the actions of his eldest son by the threat of disinheritance which would deprive the son of the economic ability to set up a family of his own. Thus while a father held land he also acted as a powerful agent of social control within the family.

These cohesive familial structures, based on primogeniture, although solving many social problems also created a number of difficulties, especially the provision for widows and younger sons. The family itself provided the solution to many of these problems. A widow, for example, could be taken into her son's household, as was the case with the Thompson household at Glenarme.[198] In other cases the eldest son could provide for his younger brothers by giving each part of his land, as Bryan Magennis did in 1636.[199] Other means were also used to provide for other members of the family. A widow had her marriage portion under the arrangements of the marriage and if the land was freehold she could also claim as a dower one-third of the lands. This could be supplemented by the widow taking a lease of land which could then be sublet to provide an income.[200] Younger sons also fared better than might be supposed, since land was readily available in east Ulster and younger sons could move away from the parental home. The younger sons of George Camack, who in 1610 settled in Ballymoney in north Antrim, for instance, went to England, Dromore, and Dervock to set up for themselves, and by 1641 Manus O'Cahan, a younger son of Gilduff of Dunseverick, had left his father's lands and moved into the town of Dunluce.[201]

The general picture of the lower levels of rural society in east Ulster in

[197] For the age structure, see appendix A, iii; K. Thomas, 'Age and authority in early modern England' in *Brit. Acad. Proc.*, lxii (1976), pp 205-48.

[198] T.C.D., MS 838, f 225; T.C.D., MS 837, f 112.

[199] P.R.O.I. Chancery Bills, N157. The land granted was acquired later than the main block of Bryan's father's land and may have been acquired for the younger son, *Inq. Ult.*, Down, Jas. I, No. 7.

[200] P.R.O.I., Chancery bills, N157, X16; Wylie, *Irish land law*, pp 12, 77, 128; P.R.O.N.I., D265/53, 62, 67; D263/23; *Inq. Ult.*, Antrim, Chas. I, nos 38, 40, 87, 107, 115, 140, 141.

[201] T.C.D., MS 838, ff 155-6; *Inq. Ult.*, Antrim, Chas. I, no. 43; F.O. Fisher, *Memoirs of the Camacks of Co. Down* (Norwich, 1897), p. 75; B.L., Harley 1514, f 68ᵛ.

the early seventeenth century is of small close knit communities bound together through bonds of kinship, geography, and common interest. These communities were composed of cohesive family units concerned to establish themselves in a society where land transfers were rapid. These structures were held together by the lordship, a unit embracing the land, rights and responsibilities of the landlord, which provided a framework of dispute-settling mechanisms, protection, both legal and physical, and a control on social mobility. Initially this society, like that of the landed elite, was heavily influenced from Scotland. Bonds of debt, kinship and landownership still linked many of the settlers to Scotland but by the 1620s these ties were being broken as land was sold in Scotland and debts paid off.[202] The severing of these links is a testimony to the fact that the tenantry in east Ulster, like their landed counteparts, had found a satisfactory way of organising themselves for their activities in the new land.

[202] S.R.O., RH11/45/5; RS12/7, ff 279, 63-4, 484; RS12/3, ff 372, 374, 574, 581; RS 12/4, f 58; RS40/2b, f 30; RS40/4a, f 304; M.H. Sanderson, 'Kilwinning at the time of the reformation' in *Ayrshire archaeological and natural history collections*, 2nd ser., x (1970-72), p. 123; W. Lamont (ed.), *An inventory of the Lamont papers* (Edinburgh, 1914), p. 138; W.J. Fullerton (ed.), T. Pont, *Topographical account of the district of Cunningham* (Glasgow, 1858), p. 209.

VII

URBAN SOCIETY

RURAL SOCIETY WAS ONLY part of the picture of east Ulster in the early seventeenth century, since a similar process of creating structures in which the everyday life of a colonial society could operate was also going on in towns. Towns were clearly delineated from the countryside and some, such as Carrickfergus, Newry, Ardglass and Downpatrick, still had walls, the remnants of their medieval origins. The newer towns, such as Belfast and Bangor, had no walls but their areas of jurisdiction, as defined by the charters, marked them off from the surrounding countryside. Within this area of jurisdiction, which in the case of Belfast was three miles from the edge of the borough, the institutions of the town, the corporation, the town courts and the apprenticeship system, operated. Although these institutions affected only a few — perhaps as little as 10 per cent of the east Ulster population were urban dwellers — in the eyes of early modern commentators the significance of towns in establishing a settlement was considerable. Edmund Spenser, the poet and Munster settler, remarked in 1596:

for nothing doth sooner cause civility in any country than many market towns, by reason that people repairing often thither for their needs will daily see and learn civil manners . . . Besides there is nothing doth more stay and strengthen the country than such corporate towns, as by proof in many rebellions hath been proved . . . And lastly there doth nothing more enrich the country . . . than many towns.[1]

In the later context of the Ulster plantation the central government

---

[1] Spenser, *View*, ed. Renwick (1970), p. 165; Sir John Davies, 'A discovery of the true causes' in H. Morley, *Ireland under Elizabeth and James* (London, 1890), pp 340-1; B.L., Add. 39853, f 7; B.L., Add. 31878, ff 73ᵛ-4.

again considered all these urban functions vital to the success of the settlement.[2] These elements were also in the minds of those administrators who dealt with east Ulster, since when they drew up the patent for a market town at Dundrum in 1629 it was declared that the market was to be

for the public good of the inhabitants residing in or near Dundrum; and with the intention that they may have free trade and commerce among themselves and with other liege subjects, in buying, selling and exchanging commodities and merchandise by which the rude and country people of that region may be led to a more humane and civil mode of life and the more easily procure a provision of all necessities.[3]

As early as 1607 James I had begun to build up an urban base for the settlement with the preparation of a grant of corporations at Belfast, Bangor, Coleraine, and Carrickfergus 'for the better settling and encouraging of the new colonies of English and Scotch which do daily endeavour to make civil plantation within the counties of Down and Antrim', but the grant was not made.[4]

As well as being a necessary precondition of 'civility' towns had a more practical function as military strongpoints in case of rebellion. As early as 1550 it had been stressed that the towns in Antrim and Down were vital as strategic centres so that in 1573 it was natural that the earl of Essex should be keen to erect a corporate town at Belfast because of its importance in guarding the pass between upper and lower Clandeboy.[5] The military significance of towns was underlined during the rebellion of the earl of Tyrone when the towns of east Ulster acted as centres for the supply of food and arms and as bases for troops during the military campaigns. Carrickfergus, for example, was responsible for supplies of food and munitions to Belfast, Masserine, Toome and Inishloughlin, all forts within marching distance of it. Again, during a campaign of 1602 against Brian McArt O'Neill, a rebel leader in Down who had retreated to the Dufferin, supplies for the army were shipped from Carrickfergus to Lecale.[6]

---

[2] *Cal. pat. rolls Ire., Chas. I*, p. 452.

[3] R.J. Hunter, 'Towns in the Ulster plantation' in *Studia Hib.*, xi (1971), pp 40-46.

[4] *Cal. S.P. Ire., 1606-8*, pp 133, 233.

[5] SP61/2/57, 58; *Cal. Carew, 1515-74*, pp 229, 448, 475; Benn, *History*, p. 41, n. 3.

[6] *Cal. Carew, 1589-1600*, pp 216, 271; P.R.O.I., M2441, ff 6, 8, 20-21, 22, 34, 56.

The functions of defence and promotion of 'civility' were the urban roles emphasised by central government but local landowners viewed towns in a somewhat different light. They saw urban centres as important social and trading centres where local gentry could gather and merchants could sell and buy goods. Landowners in east Ulster were also keen to establish market rights for the towns which lay on their estates since markets generated income through tolls and market court revenues. Thus the landlord perspective on urban growth was profit orientated and many of the new towns of the seventeenth century owed their birth to a desire by landowners to maximise profit. This urban growth was not a new phenomenon of the seventeenth century. Ardglass, Dundrum, Strangford, Newry and Carrickfergus had been important medieval trading ports and Dromore and Downpatrick were ecclesiastical centres.[7] However, many of these towns had declined in importance during the sixteenth century. The ports of Ardglass and Strangford had never fully recovered from the effects of the military campaigns of the 1540s in Down and in 1573 Lord Deputy Fitzwilliam complained that Carrickfergus was almost deserted.[8] Despite this decline there was still considerable traffic between towns and the countryside in the sixteenth century. In 1549, for example, Sir Nicholas Bagnall noted that the rebuilt town of Newry had become a centre of marketing for native Irish as far away as Armagh, and in the 1596 negotiations for a cessation in the Nine Years War the earl of Ormond and the archbishop of Cashel, the two representatives of the English forces, promised 'that the English should not encroach upon them [the natives] beyond the boundary, excepting those who were in Carlingford, Carrickfergus and Newry, who were at all times permitted to deal and traffic'. The movement of goods was not exclusively from settler to native for later in 1596 Shane McBrian O'Neill 'made proclamation throughout his country that none of his followers, upon a pain, shall bring any victuall to that town [Carrickfergus]',

---

[7] E.M. Jope (ed.), *An archaeological survey of County Down* (H.M.S.O., 1966), pp 391-2, 405, 430, 435; *Cal. pat. rolls, 1476-85*, pp 20, 39, 160; *Cal. pat. rolls, 1467-77*, pp 161, 193, 583, 596.

[8] R.C. Parkinson, 'Downpatrick, the medieval city' in *Proc. Belfast Nat. Hist. and Phil. Soc.*, viii (1970), pp 32-7; E. McCrum (ed.), S. Miskimmen, *History and antiquities of Carrickfergus* (Belfast, 1909), pp 23, 379, 384; *Cal. S.P. Ire., 1598-9*, pp 25, 70; D.B. Quinn, 'Anglo-Irish Ulster in the early sixteenth century' in *Proc. Belfast Nat. Hist. and Phil. Soc.* (1933-4), pp 60, 62-3.

demonstrating that native Irishmen did market their goods in towns.[9]

This sixteenth-century base provided a foundation for urban expansion in the early seventeenth century. Older functions of towns, as garrisons for instance, began to decline and newer ones emerge. By 1631 Newry and Carrickfergus, the main garrison towns of the sixteenth century were both poorly supplied with arms; Carrickfergus having no arms and Newry only 0·62 per cent of the Irish total. A similar situation existed with gunpowder.[10] This decline in older functions was compensated for by the rise of new urban roles. With the increased involvement of central government in local administration in the early seventeenth century, centres in which royal government could be based were required and, hence, certain towns became important as regional administrative centres. In country Antrim, Carrickfergus and Ballymena were favoured centres, the former in the south of the county and the latter in the north. At these two centres 148 of the 152 Antrim inquisitions carried out in the early seventeenth century were taken and in county Down, Newry, Downpatrick and Dromore, each of which served a distinct part of the county, accounted for 114 of 125 early seventeenth-century Down inquisitions. These towns provided points of contact between central government, local government and the governed where courts could be held and the rudiments of royal policy spelt out through proclamations which were to be read in 'shire towns, county towns, market towns'.[11] As these new urban functions developed, certain towns such as Belfast, Newtownards, Newry and Carrickfergus became increasingly complex in their government, social structure and economy to form an urban elite, while others such as Lisburn and Glenarme, although never achieving the predominance of this first group, became important regional centres. Below these groups of substantial towns there was a myriad of small market towns and villages whose history is unclear. Most is known about the towns of the first rank which had a complex government structure, exemplified by the existence of a corporation established by charter. They acted as regional capitals, and as administrative, trading and residential centres. Given the considerable significance of these towns it is important to understand their history in order to appreciate fully the urban structure of east Ulster.

[9] SP 61/2/39; *A.F.M.*, sub 1596; *Cal. S.P. Ire., 1596-7*, p. 69.
[10] SL, 1, f 36.
[11] Steele, *Tudor & Stuart proclam.*, ii, no. 302.

I

Towns of the first rank in east Ulster grew rapidly in the early seventeenth century. One such town, Bangor, on the north Down coast, had forty-four households, or 226 people, in 1625 but by 1630 the population of the town and its hinterland had increased to 987.[12] A neighbouring town, Holywood, reflects a similar pattern since in 1611 it had twenty households which had increased to thirty-six, or 183 people, by 1625 and at the time of the 1630 muster roll the population of the town and surrounding lands stood at 329. In west Down the Plantation Commissioners recorded in 1611 that Dromore was a small settlement with only a few recently built houses, yet by 1630 it had a population of 184 and was a flourishing market centre. Such rapid expansion was achieved by continuing migration into towns and the absence of plague which, due to poor sanitation and high population density, could decimate a town's population. Of these, immigration was the more important. Although there was some early seventeenth-century movement from the surrounding countryside to apprenticeships in the towns the bulk of the urban population was settler in origin. In the case of Belfast, a 1639 survey of the inhabitants suggests on the basis of surnames, that 43·5 per cent of the town's population were Scots, 41·3 per cent English, 6·5 per cent Irish, the remainder being untraced.[13] It is significant that most of the Scots settlers in towns whose origins can be traced had an urban background and so provided expertise in urban administration. William Montgomery, a burgess of Irvine, for example, settled in Donaghadee and William Barclay, also a burgess of Irvine, moved to Bangor.[14]

This rapid urban expansion was fueled by the opportunity of profitable speculation which it offered landlords. Rental income from towns was much higher than from agricultural lettings because towns had a concentrated number of rent payers on a small area of land, which was often of little agricultural value. A 1575 rental of the Bagnall estate,

---

[12] P.R.O.N.I., T811/3; B.L., Add. 4770, ff 238-45; for the techniques used to derive these figures, see pp
[13] R.M. Young (ed.), *The town book of the corporation of Belfast* (Belfast, 1892), pp 11-12.
[14] W. McLeod (ed.), 'The protocol book of Robert Brown' in *Arch. and hist. coll. relating to Ayrshire and Galloway*, vii (1893), pp 198-201, 139-141; viii (1894), pp 107-11; ix (1895), pp 193-5.

for example, shows that the town of Newry alone accounted for 25 per cent of the total rental.[15] Later in 1630 the incomes from the towns of Belfast and Carrickfergus amounted to about a third of the rental income from all Sir Edward Chichester's extensive lands in east Ulster, the town of Belfast alone being the fifth most productive unit of all the Chichester's Irish property.[16]

Despite this incentive to expansion, the towns of east Ulster remained smaller than their English counterparts. Belfast, when it was enclosed by a rampart in 1642, covered eighty-six acres or one-seventh of a square mile. While this may be due to the relative youth of Belfast in English urban terms even the older towns such as Downpatrick, the largest of the medieval towns in Down were also small, one quarter of a square mile in Downpatrick's case, and Carrickfergus, even after an expansion during the rebuilding of the walls in 1610, was only one-thirty-eighth of a square mile.[17] This cannot be attributed to lack of enthusiasm by landowners but rather to the generally low numbers of settlers in east Ulster from which the urban residents could be drawn.

Despite this problem of low population, landlord enthusiasm and government pressure was such that by 1611 the construction of towns in counties Antrim and Down was well under way. At Belfast artificers were building 'good timber houses with chimneys after the fashion of the English pale' and Bangor, in north Down, and Dunluce, in north Antrim, were both being constructed in a similar way.[18] In the case of Belfast the report of the Plantation Commissioners makes it clear that the landlord, Sir Arthur Chichester, laid out the building plots but it was the responsibility of the tenant to erect the building which was also the case at Bangor and Templepatrick. This device, known as the building lease, was used to minimise the outlay of the landlord by giving a short lease to a tenant which obliged him to build and to maintain the property and clauses were inserted in subsequent leases to keep the property in repair.[19]

[15] Bodl., University College 103, f 142. This is increased to 29 per cent if allowance is made for irregular income such as heriots and for the customs revenue of the town.

[16] P.R.O.N.I., D389/4; T712/5.

[17] Benn, *History*, p. 276; Jope (ed.), *Archaeological survey*, p. 273; P.R.O., MPF 98.

[18] P.R.O.N.I., T811/3.

[19] P.R.O.N.I., T811/3; D929/F2/3/15; on building leases. L. Stone, *Crisis*, pp 357-63; N.L.W., Cross of Shaw Hill MSS, Deeds no. 174.

This type of small, mainly wooden-built, town had a number of serious problems. Fire was a particularly serious threat. Newry, for example, was burnt down in 1600 as a result of an accident while distilling whiskey in a private house, and Bangor almost suffered a similar fate in 1623 but fortunately the fire was controlled.[20] The corporation of Belfast did try to take some preventative measures against fire when in March 1638 they ordered that people who did not replace their wooden chimneys with brick ones should be fined forty shillings.[21] Towns also had to face other natural hazards, such as the experience of Bangor which was partially blown down by wind in 1624 and it was feared that the whole town would be demolished.[22] By far the most serious urban problem was disease which could spread rapidly in densely settled towns with poor sanitation. An example of the devastation which disease could wreck was provided during four months in 1643, when disease swept through the towns of Coleraine, Carrickfergus, Belfast and Lisburn, killing a substantial part of the population.[23] Urban authorities in Belfast did attempt to alleviate the more acute infection problem by fining those who dumped manure and carrion in the streets and river and in 1642 they employed a man to bury carrion.[24]

A town was dominated, architecturally and otherwise, by the local landlord's house. Sir William Brereton for instance, commented that Chichester's house at Carrickfergus was 'very stately . . . or rather like a prince's palace' and, to Brereton, Belfast castle was 'the glory and beauty of that town' though less impressive than the house at Carrickfergus.[25] Such was its influence that the civic and commercial life of most east Ulster towns revolved around the landlord's house. In the case of Belfast the market place was situated beside the castle as was also the case at Newry and Downpatrick while in Carrickfergus the market-place was in its more traditional location, beside the church, because Joymount, Chichester's house, was outside the town.

A second important element in urban topography was the town fields. Since towns were particularly vulnerable when cut off from their rural

20 *Cal. S.P. Ire., 1600*, p. 226; Blair, *Autobiography*, pp 59-60.
21 Young, *Town book*, p. 11.
22 Blair, *Autobiography*, p. 63.
23 D. Harcourt, *The clergies lamentation* (London, 1644), p. 9.
24 Young, *Town book*, pp 16, 23; Benn, *History*, p. 195.
25 Brereton, *Travels*, pp 127, 128.

hinterland an alternative source of food had to be available for years of poor harvests when there was little surplus of food to be sold to townsmen. This problem was alleviated by granting townsmen land near the town on which they could grow some grain and commons on which cattle could be grazed were also provided near some towns. In the case of Carrickfergus Sir Henry Sidney, the lord deputy, noted in 1570 that 'the inhabitants of Carrickfergus have certain corn growing on the ground beside the said town of Carrickfergus which they, and their adherents, have sown to their no small charge'.[26]

The way in which the town fields were managed varied from town to town. At Carrickfergus they were vested, as were the lands of the county of Carrickfergus, in the hands of the corporation by a royal grant of 1601.[27] The corporation granted holdings in fee farm in the town fields to individual inhabitants of the town who were obliged to enclose their land within three years and were also granted grazing and turbary rights.[28] The making of perpetuity leases by the corporation was an attempt to raise money by charging high entry fines in return for long leases but because these leases were so long they led to speculation in the town fields which soon became concentrated in fewer hands. Richard Dowdell, for example, purchased in 1596 some of the lands of Henry Ockford, another burgess, and in 1603 he bought the rest of Ockford's land. Similarly by 1627 Ingrahan Horsham, who held no land in 1603, had bought up the holdings of three individuals. One of these, Thomas Wytter, had been granted one and a half shares in the town fields in 1606 and by 1620 he had added a further two shares to this and finally sold all the lands to Horsham for £104.[29] Such speculation and consolidation was not confined to Carrickfergus because in 1652 Lord Clandeboy complained that at Killileagh:

his father, in his lifetime, had purposely laid off the common belonging to Killileagh for the only benefit of those which had not town acres either for corn or grass, which good intention of his towards them they had become deprived of, since the breaking out of the rebellion, by the richer and abler sort.[30]

[26] Miskimmin, *Carrickfergus*, p. 288.

[27] *Cal. pat. rolls Ire., Eliz.* pp 607-17.

[28] Miskimmin, *Carrickfergus*, pp 296-301; P.R.O.N.I., T686; T1107/1-4; LPC 253; LPC 1246.

[29] P.R.O.N.I., T686/1/1-3; T686/2,4,6; D1905/2/155B.

[30] *Ham. MSS*, app. vii, p. lxxii.

Carrickfergus was unique in east Ulster in having its own lands vested in the corporation since because most of the major towns were the outcome of landlord enterprise the landlord owned and ran the town lands. At Belfast, Chichester allocated the lands of the sixteenth-century castle for the use of the townsmen and at Bangor, Dundonald and Killileagh, Sir James Hamilton set aside lands, designated on Thomas Raven's map as 'parcels laid to the townsmen', for urban dwellers and also commons for their cattle.[31] The usual method of allocating plots in the town fields was to link each tenement in the town to a parcel in the fields.[32] Just as the manor court regulated the lands of a manor so the corporation of a town, acting for the landlord, could sit as a court to regulate the use of the town fields. In 1619, for example, the corporation of Belfast ordered that all those who had not enclosed their holding in the fields be fined the sum of two shillings which was to be used to appoint a surveyor to supervise the erection of fences.[33]

While it is relatively easy to uncover details of the topography of the early seventeenth-century towns of east Ulster it is much more difficult to probe their social and economic structure particularly since only two corporation books and one incomplete set of freemen's rolls have survived. As a result, aspects of urban life such as the occupational structure must remain vague but the urban base was not well enough developed in early seventeenth-century east Ulster to support much occupational specialisation and every man had to be able to do a number of things such as brewing beer for domestic consumption, working the land in the town fields and possibly engaging in two or more other occupations. Much urban employment was seasonal and so many urban dwellers had to have a range of skills to carry them over a full year. Tanning, for example, depended on good drying weather as well as on the supply of skins and so the corporation of Belfast would not permit the sale of leather produced in winter time because it proved inferior.[34] An indication of this diversity of trades is provided in an indenture of apprenticeship made in 1648 when John Rigby, a Belfast tanner, took his

---

[31] Benn, *History*, pp 41-2. The boundaries of the town fields of Belfast are traceable in leases of the late seventeenth century, P.R.O.N.I., T811/1-2; T870.

[32] P.R.O.N.I., T761/3; M.A.K. Garner, 'North Down as displayed in the Clanbrassil lease book' in *Proc. Belfast Nat. Hist. and Phil Soc.,* viii (1970), pp 24-5; Benn, *History,* pp 275, 283-4; P.R.O.N.I., T549/3; LPC 1058; D929/F2/3/15.

[33] Young, *Town book*, p. 7.

[34] Ibid., pp 55-6.

brother, Thomas, as an apprentice 'in the art, craft, mystery and occupation of a tanner and also in all other faculties, labours, works, occasions and businesses of the said John Rigby' which indicates that John
had more than one occupation.[35]

The survival of one set of freemen's rolls for Belfast however makes it
possible to gain some insight into the occupational structure of the
town.[36] The occupations fall into well defined groups reflecting the different functions of the town. The high percentage (12·5 per cent) of
freemen of the town who were gentlemen, indicates the town's importance as a social centre. Patrick Adair, a presbyterian minister, commented in 1649 that Belfast was 'the place where country gentlemen and
officers then most haunted' and the high proportion of wealthy inhabitants was also reflected in a 1643 Belfast assessment for highways in
which 37 per cent of the town's population were assessed above the
mean of four shillings and 10 per cent paid over ten shillings.[37] Much of
the attraction of Belfast lay in its being the Ulster residence of the
Chichester family. The founder of the town, Sir Arthur, was lord deputy from 1605 until 1615, and this conferred prestige on the town and
hence attracted local gentry many of whom had close personal ties with
Sir Arthur. Many gentlemen who were enrolled as freemen of Belfast,
such as Humphry Norton, Sir Moses Hill and Henry le Squire, also had
substantial estates outside the town on which they resided for most of
the year. Other towns also had important gentry contacts and despite
owning considerable estates in Antrim and Down, Sir Fulke Conway,
Hercules Langford and Moses Hill all retained houses in Carrickfergus.[38] Downpatrick, as the county centre for Down, also had a
number of houses belonging to local landowners. A nucleus of gentry in
a town conferred a certain prestige on it and hence attracted other
groups. Newry, for example, was the main centre of merchant activity in
Down even though the town was a bad port and goods had to be landed
at Carlingford and shipped to Newry in small boats. The merchants
chose Newry as their base not for its economic potential but because of
its prestige value as the local assize town and the seat of the major local

[35] Young, *Town book*, pp 59-60.

[36] Appendix G.

[37] W.D. Killen (ed.), P. Adair, *A true narrative of the rise and progress of the
presbyterian church in Ireland* (Belfast, 1866), p. 168; Young, *Town book*, pp 25-7.

[38] P.R.O.N.I., T1107/4; T.C.D., MS 838, f 312; *Cal. S.P. Ire., 1625-32*, p. 437.

landowning family, the Bagnalls.[39] Lord Mountnorris, the comptroller of the king's works, recorded the importance of this phenomenon in the development of Belfast.

When Carrickfergus was constituted a port in this kingdom there was hardly a house in Belfast except Lord Chichester's castle. Afterwards his lordship coming there to live, several British families did come to settle, upon which, for the good of the English interest his lordship did prevail with James of blessed memory who gave it a charter. It had few or no merchants trading beyond the seas. Now by the encouragement of the earl of Donegall . . . and the industry with God's blessing, upon the endeavours of the merchants . . . the trade imported and exported at Belfast is at least seven eighths parts of the whole customs and excise that are taken at the port of Carrickfergus.[40]

The impact of this gentry group on the economy of towns was significant. The assize, for example, could bring considerable wealth to a town by attracting local gentry and its removal could be a source of grievance. Thus when the assize was moved from Newry to Dromore in 1628 Newry was 'much impaired by its removal' and so the summer assize was restored to it.[41] A high proportion of gentry in a town created a heavy demand for consumer goods. Carrickfergus, for example, imported large quantities of luxury goods, such as silks, which were not imported into other east Ulster ports. Imports of wine reveal a similar demand for luxury goods in Carrickfergus which imported £300 worth of customable wine in 1640 while Donaghadee and Bangor, towns with a small gentry population, imported only £11.16s.3d. worth.[42]

Merchants formed the second most important occupational group in early seventeenth-century Belfast comprising a quarter of all admissions to freedom in Befast for the years 1635-9. Belfast had become an important port by the early seventeenth century due to the expansion of its hinterland as far west as Lisburn and the decline of its northern rival, Carrickfergus, in the 1630s. By 1632 Christopher Lowther, a Whitehaven merchant with strong Dublin contacts, felt that Belfast had become sufficiently important to base his partner, Rowland Jackson,

---

[39] B.L., Harley 2138, f 169ᵛ; Gilbert, *Contemp. hist., 1641-52,* i, pp 419, 575.

[40] *Cal. S.P. Ire., 1647-60,* p. 336.

[41] *Cal. pat. rolls Ire., Chas. I,* pp 415, 558.

[42] Leeds City Library, TN/PO7/1/1-4; Syon House, Northumberland MSS, Y.11.26 (N.L.I., p3682/7).

there.[43] Many of these freemen merchants were non-resident and moved about considerably becoming freemen of individual towns solely to establish trading rights there. Robert Barr, for example, who was engaged in the trade between Ireland and Scotland had established himself in Londonderry by 1635, where he also ran the customs until the lord deputy, Thomas Wentworth, regarded him as unsuitable for the position. By 1638 he had moved to Belfast where he was exporting iron until forced by political pressures in 1639 to flee to Scotland where he purchased land in Ayrshire.[44] The case of another Belfast merchant, George Martin, demonstrates greater mobility. In 1633 he was based in Carrickfergus, shipping corn to England, and from there moved to Belfast shipping iron along the coast to Drogheda and Dublin. By 1637 he had moved to Lisburn where he was dealing in tobacco with a local agent, John McDowell, who later became a merchant in his own right at Newtownards. At the time of his death in 1639 Martin had moved back to Belfast, dealing in tobacco and had acquired land at Drumbeg, to the east of the town, by marriage.[45]

Just as merchants tended not to trade from any one single centre neither did they specialise greatly in their cargoes. As their main role was as intermediaries between producer and consumer, they dealt in anything in demand. In 1621, for example, Robert Kile, an Irvine merchant, imported a wide variety of goods into Belfast including ten hogsheads and fourteen barrels of white salt, twelve firkins of soap and two bottles of whiskey and in 1639 the goods of William Clugston, a Belfast merchant comprised eighteen dozen needles, six dozen knives and a firkin of treacle.[46]

The merchants usually played an important role in towns by providing a money transmission service through bills of exchange and as providers of credit. Because of the problems of shortage of specie and absence of high value Irish coin in the early seventeenth century many of the merchants transactions were conducted on credit, as were most

---

[43] D.R. Hainsworth (ed.), *Commercial papers of Sir Christopher Lowther, 1611-44* (Surtees Society, Newcastle-upon-Tyne, 1977), passim.

[44] SL, 15, no. 22; Bodl., Carte 66, f 18; Strafford, *Letters*, ii, p. 227; G. Robertson, *A genealogical account of the principal families of Ayrshire*, ii (Ayr, 1824), pp 302-3.

[45] Bodl., Carte 67, f 7; P.R.O.I., Ferguson MSS, xii, p. 242; B.L., Harley 2138, f 180; P.R.O.N.I., T761/8; P.R.O.I., RC9/1, Chas. I, no. 2.

[46] Young, *Town book*, p. 11; P.R.O.I., RC9/1, p. 37, no. 2.

financial dealings in towns. The will of Robert Boyd of Carrickfergus demonstrates a complex web of debts among the townsmen for work done by him, and a Belfast merchant, Robert Barr, was described by Wentworth as having a large number of debtors.[47] As a result of this web of debt much of an urban merchant's wealth was held in debts, goods and investments in trading projects with little cash in hand for lending to neighbouring landowners. On the death of William Clugston, another Belfast merchant, his estate comprised of £30.11s.8d. in goods, debts of £11, and trading credits of £100. George Martin, also a Belfast merchant, had goods and debts owing to him to the value of £75 and indeed one of the problems of settling Martin's estate on his death was the amount of money tied up in debt.[48]

Various techniques were used to manage this complex network of debt; the most usual being an obligation of debt: a debt acknowledged by the debtor and to be paid at a future date.[49] More complex was the bill of exchange, which laid down a time scale for repayments. The time laid down could be anything from three days to a year and the bills could be discounted at any place which gave a merchant breathing space to sell part of his goods in order to pay debts.[50] Bills of exchange became increasingly popular in the seventeenth century because developments in the law of contract in the sixteenth century had no longer required them to be made under seal and thus made bills easier to obtain. Towns provided an important service for merchants in registering, discounting and enforcing these more easily drawn up bills through the market court and the corporation and many bills were registered in the corporation book of Belfast with a view to providing a formal record of them.[51] Credit could also operate on a simpler level, through the issuing of tokens by merchants themselves. Many traders had shops in Belfast where a wide range of goods such as tobacco and leather could be purchased, but such purchases were too simple to warrant bonds or bills and so, in the absence of small change, merchants struck their own in the form of

---

[47] P.R.O.N.I., T828/4; SL, 19, no. 74.

[48] P.R.O.I., RC9/1, p. 37, no. 2; RC9/1, Chas. I, no. 2; SL, 19, no. 74.

[49] M.S. Shaw (ed.), *Some family papers of the Hunters of Hunterstown* (Scottish Record Society, Edinburgh, 1925), p. 80, nos 8, 9.

[50] Hainsworth (ed.), *Commercial papers*, pp 29, 45; Young, *Town book*, pp 29, 33-4, 57-8.

[51] On changes in the law of contract, A.W.B. Simpson, *A history of contract at common law* (Oxford, 1975), passim.

tokens on discs of copper.[52] In this way, merchants contributed significantly to the development of the east Ulster economy, easing the urban cash problem by building up credit networks instead.

Besides the merchants a number of other, less important, occupations developed in the towns of Antrim and Down. One of the distinctive features of the regional centres, such as Belfast or Carrickfergus, was the evolution of an infrastructure to provide services for local gentry, travellers or visiting government officials. The most important of these was the inn which provided lodging, ale and a meeting point in the towns. As early as 1611 an inn was established at Belfast and by the 1630s most important towns, such as Newry, Carrickfergus, Bangor, Lisburn and Dromore had inns.[53] A second important Belfast industry was clothing, as shoemakers, clothiers, tailors and glove-makers, accounted for about a third of all freemen before 1640. Items such as gloves and shoes were luxuries in early seventeenth-century Ireland and so the gentry influence may be detected here. However there were too many shoemakers in Belfast for them to be catering exclusively for the gentry community and since shoes do not feature among Belfast's exports a substantial number of pairs of shoes must have been sold in the town and surrounding countryside. The high proportion (41·6 per cent) of leather workers in the clothing industry reflects a high degree of integration within the occupational structure of the town since they were linked with two of the other important groups in Belfast, butchers and tanners. Butchers formed the main food processing group in the town and by the 1630s Belfast was sufficiently noted for its meat for Christopher Lowther to send his partner there to purchase beef to be shipped to Bristol.[54] The butchers who produced meat sold the by-products, skins, to the tanners in the area, men such as Thomas Waring who had an extensive business on the outskirts of Belfast.[55] Tanning, in turn, was linked with the iron workings which developed around the town since oak bark, which was left over from the making of charcoal used in iron smelting, was the raw material of tanners. Iron works had

---

[52] For examples of shops, P.R.O.N.I., T671/8; G. Benn, 'Notices of local tokens issued in Ulster', in *U.J.A.*, 1st ser., ii (1854), pp 29-31, 230-2.

[53] P.R.O.N.I., T811/3; T808/12455; P.R.O.I., Chancery bills L46; Brereton, *Travels*, pp 126-9, 132; Blair, *Autobiography*, p. 67.

[54] Hainsworth (ed.), *Commercial papers*, pp 12, 15, 51, 121.

[55] McCracken, *Ir. woods*, p. 83; Benn, *History*, p. 249.

developed near the town at Newforge by 1630 and at Ardoyne and Stranmillis by 1640.[56]

There was little industrial development in Belfast. Two smiths enrolled as freemen by 1640 are the only ones we know of who were engaged in heavy industry, and they were probably linked with the local iron industry outside the town. They also probably provided a service for the surrounding countryside by producing agricultural implements. Tuck mills at Belfast by 1640 and corn mills at Carrickfergus and Newry by 1600, also provided services for the countryside.[57] Shipbuilding developed in Belfast on a small scale and it was in a small ship built at Belfast that a group of presbyterians attempted to leave Bangor for America in 1636.[58]

Thus the occupational structure of Belfast was geared both to the demands of the gentry for luxury items and to the processing of the products of the countryside. As a result it developed, by English or even colonial New England standards, a very restricted occupational structure. An English provincial centre, such as Norwich would have had over a hundred trades in the early seventeenth century and most market towns had between twenty and thirty.[59] Belfast, by comparison, could only muster twenty occupations, and these were mainly service industries. Newry, due perhaps to greater antiquity, could boast a reasonable range of craftsmen engaged in manufacturing activity as well as gentry and merchant communities, but this was still a restricted range when compared with English or colonial American towns.[60] The main aim of those who worked in towns was to invest their profits in land which not only provided them with greatest security but was made doubly attractive by its status value. Since the late sixteenth century the urban inhabitants of east Ulster had been purchasing lands near the towns or speculating in town fields. By 1592, for example, John Lugge of Carrickfergus also

[56] McCracken, *Ir. woods,* app. 3; L.A. Clarkson, 'The leather crafts in England' in *Ag. H.R.*, xiv (1966), pp 29-30, 32, 38; *Cal. S.P. Ire., 1608-10,* p. 89; Benn, *History,* pp 334-5.

[57] H.D. Gribbon, *The history of water power in Ulster* (Newtown Abbot, 1969), pp 39, 55; P.R.O.I., Ferguson MSS, xx, p. 64.

[58] Adair, *True narrative,* p. 42. The development of shipbuilding in Belfast had also been suggested in 1583 by the lord deputy, Sir John Perrott, *Cal. Carew, 1575-88,* p. 370.

[59] P. Clarke, P. Slack, *English towns in transition* (Oxford, 1976), p. 5. Lurgan, a market town in Co. Armagh, had 20 occupational groups in 1622.

[60] T.C.D., MS 837, ff 2, 4, 12.

held four townlands in the Ards but it was usually merchants who managed to accumulate enough capital to purchase land.[61] By 1607 Christopher Fleming, a Newry merchant, had acquired a substantial estate in Monaghan by purchase and a smaller amount in Armagh while Thomas Crelly, another Newry merchant, acquired extensive lands in mid-Down from Sir Arthur Magennis.[62] The availability of land resulting from the breakup of Conn O'Neill's estate in north Down after 1605 allowed a number of townsmen including Moses Hill of Carrickfergus, Michael Whit, a Mayor of Carrickfergus in 1611, and Henry le Squire of Belfast to acquire substantial tracts of land.[63] In this way towns acted as reservoirs for settlers in the early stages of the colonisation and provided a necessary foothold for the settlers migrating to east Ulster and hence this drive for land outside towns was an important impetus for the colonisation of east Ulster. Many of the colonists settled first in the towns because they needed less capital to move to a town than directly to an estate. Moses Hill, for example, acquired most of his lands in county Down while he was resident at Carrickfergus, where he was sheriff in 1594 and mayor in 1603. John Dalway, a south-east Antrim settler, had been Mayor of Carrickfergus in 1592 and 1600, and Sir Fulke Conway, who held land around the town of Antrim, had been Mayor of Carrickfergus in 1608 and 1609 as well as Governor in Sir Arthur Chichester's absence.[64]

The urban economic structure was underpinned by the apprenticeship system which controlled admissions to trades and hence occupational mobility. Under the apprenticeship system the apprentice wishing to learn a trade was bound to a master by indentures by which the apprentice promised to serve his master for seven years, or on some occasions eight. In return the master was to provide for him 'meat, drink, clothes and apparel and all other necessities fitting for an apprentice of profession and faculty'. At the end of the apprenticeship the

---

[61] SP63/167/52.

[62] *Cal. S.P. Ire., 1606-8*, pp 169-71; R.J. Hunter, 'The Ulster plantation in counties Armagh and Cavan' (M.Litt., T.C.D., 1967), p. 34; P.R.O.I., Lodge MSS, Wards and liveries, p. 85; Lodge MSS, Records of the rolls, vi, pp 392-3; *Cal. pat. rolls Ire., Jas. I*, p. 12.

[63] P.R.O.N.I., D671/D4/1/2; SL, 17, no. 38; Benn, *History*, p. 237.

[64] Miskimmin, *Carrickfergus*, pp 411-12, 474-5; A.T. Lee, 'Notes on bawnes' in *U.J.A.*, 1st ser., vi (1858), p. 129; SP63/217/94.

master was to ensure that the apprentice was made a freeman and was expected to assist the apprentice to establish himself with either 'such help of tools' or a sum of money. This provision of capital was important because capital accumulation was difficult during the apprenticeship as wages were low or non-existent. For this reason trades usually ran in families as tools and workshops were passed from one generation to another. One agreement on the estate of John Smith, a Belfast smith, made in 1647 observed that 'half [of the smithy] was given unto him [William Partridge, Smith's son in law] in marriage with his [Smith's] daughter and also all the work tools was likewise given unto him by his said marriage'.[65] Since many probably entered an apprenticeship either as first generation settlers or as a way of achieving social mobility, they had no family to provide them with the necessary tools and premises and therefore the apprenticeship system was vital to establishing themselves when trained. Enforcement of the apprenticeship system was a problem since no system of craft guilds grew up in Antrim or Down during the early seventeenth century. The apprenticeship regulations were supervised by the corporations who enrolled apprenticeship indentures in their records and supervised their execution.[66]

While the economic life of the town was controlled by agreements between individuals, the political structures of these principal towns were underpinned by the royal charter. The charter defined the government and politics of a town by creating a civic elite, the burgesses, and by regulating its relationship with local and national authorities. The charter defined the rights and privileges of the borough and hence was carefully protected. Thus in 1603 the corporation of Carrickfergus provided a chest with three or four locks, 'for the safer and better keeping of the town charter' the keys of which were to be dispersed among four people and were not to be taken out of the liberties of the town. This proved a wise precaution because, in 1638, the corporation was forced

[65] Young, *Town book*, p. 48. Similar provisions were made in England, D. Paliser, *Tudor York* (Oxford, 1979), pp 86, 150. For examples of fathers taking sons into apprenticeship, P.R.O.N.I., T707, ff 32, 41; Young, *Town book*, pp 59-60.

[66] P.R.O.N.I., T707, ff 37-41. Some guilds appeared in the later part of the century; for example in Carrickfergus the Tailors and Glovers Guild (1680) and Shoemakers (1674), *Mun. corp. Ire., rep., app. II*, pp 316-17. The absence of guilds was probably due to the small number of occupational groups and high population mobility in the towns.

by central administration to exhibit its charter before claiming its privileges.[67]

In the sixteenth century the privileges of the corporation of Carrickfergus had grown to such an extent that by the latter part of the century the central government were becoming alarmed by its powers. This concern was voiced by Sir Geoffrey Fenton in 1581 when he remarked to Lord Burleigh that more care should be taken in manipulating the Carrickfergus corporation.[68] As a result of this growth of power, it became clear that the central administration would have to exercise more control over local authorities by modifying patents. The Carrickfergus charter of 1402, modelled on that of Drogheda, was invalidated in 1578 by the lord deputy, Sir Henry Sidney, by the simple expedient of its seizure. It was replaced by a charter which modified considerably the town's rights in the collection of customs and increased the Queen's rent from the town.[69] New charters were issued to most of the east Ulster towns in the early seventeenth century before the elections for the parliament of 1613-15. These charters standardised the government of towns so that each was to be governed by twelve burgesses and a sovereign, who was known in some towns as a provost. This group constituted the corporation and was charged with the running of the towns.

The charter created the machinery of government but the recruitment of men to serve as part of the system and the establishment of authority by the corporation proved to be two major problems in its implementation. The problem of recruiting men of sufficient standing who were prepared to serve as burgesses and other officers of the corporation was a serious one. In England, town government was frequently controlled by a small merchant oligarchy but in east Ulster the merchant community was smaller than its English counterpart and much more mobile. Many merchants only became freemen to avail of trading rights and others were interested in profit rather than political involvement.[70] Many offices in urban government were expensive and troublesome and hence there was considerable reluctance by residents to accept them. In

[67] P.R.O.N.I., T707, f 37; P.R.O.I., Ferguson MSS, xxvi, p. 110.

[68] Miskimmin, *Carrickfergus*, pp 377-8, 385-6; P.R.O.N.I., D162/1.

[69] SP63/81/41; O'Laverty, *Down and Connor*, iii, pp 29, 44; *Cal. pat. rolls Ire., Eliz.*, pp 607-11.

[70] Clark, Slack, *English towns*, pp 129-30.

1627 Belfast corporation was forced to pass a bye-law which imposed a fine of £5 on any person who refused the office of sovereign, suggesting that refusal of the office was becoming an all too frequent occurrence.[71] The selection of office holders in a town was also considerably affected by the degree of landlord control there. The charters of 1612-13 named the first twelve burgesses of a town from lists sent by landlords but subsequently the burgesses elected men to their own ranks and the sovereign was chosen annually by the landlord from a list submitted to him by the burgesses.[72] As a result of this landlord influence the officers of the town were often drawn from a relatively small pool of men approved by him. Thus the sovereign, already a powerful figure since he was a justice of the peace, clerk of the market, and escheator for the town, could also become the landlord's personal representative in the town. In the case of Belfast, the early seventeenth-century sovereigns were all connected with the Chichester family who controlled the town. Henry le Squire, for example, was Sir Edward Chichester's land agent and on his death left £10 worth of plate to Sir Edward. Chichester was also a pall bearer at the funeral of William Leathes who was sovereign in 1638.[73] The loyalty of Thomas Theaker, sovereign in 1643, to Chichester was demonstrated when he was faced with a petition from the commonalty of Belfast for the free election of burgesses and for the Covenant to be made compulsory in the town. He seized the petition, left the town and fled to Chichester, who was at Dublin.[74] Thus it is not surprising that in Belfast and Carrickfergus the sovereigns were drawn from a small number of families approved by Chichester and that men were 'imported' from the surrounding countryside to make up the required number of burgesses. In Belfast the first twelve burgesses included Moses Hill, Thomas Hibbots, Sir Fulke Conway and Humphry Norton, all of whom lived outside the town and were closely linked to Chichester. This situation was troublesome since burgesses were not in the town to deal with problems as they arose and the corporation only met infrequently. This problem of a shortage of working burgesses was partly solved in Belfast by creating a new body which was referred to in a bye-law of 1635 as the 'grand jury representative of the commonality of

---

[71] Young, *Town book*, p. 8.
[72] Bodl., Carte 62, ff 157, 207, 216.
[73] Benn, *History,* pp 239, 243.
[74] T.C.D., MS 838, ff 1-2.

the said corporation' which acted as a sort of substitute corporation to deal with day-to-day problems in the town.[75]

In other towns, where landlord control was less strong, there was more danger from competing political factions since there was little landlord supervision of the government of the town. In the 1630s at least one major dispute occurred in Downpatrick where the landlord, Lord Cromwell, was an absentee, and even in strictly controlled towns the absence of the landlord could lead to serious disputes as in 1607 when an election for the mayorality of Carrickfergus degenerated into a riot in the absence of Sir Arthur Chichester.[76]

The main function of the corporation, apart from returning two M.P.s, was to represent the freemen in matters affecting the common good of the town. The corporation also acted for the town in the distribution of town fields, in regulating social practices, such as meting out punishment to scolds, and controlling the abuses of ale houses.[77] All this was done by making bye-laws as when the freemen of Carrickfergus came to the burgesses in May 1576 and 'made humble request for certain good orders to be set down to the advancement of a common weal, which for that they were commodious were granted accordingly'.[78] These bye-laws were enforced by the corporation sitting as a court as was the case in 1630 when two Belfast men, Ralph Dyson and Thomas Donnington, were disenfranchised and fined twenty-five and twenty shillings respectively for refusing to obey the 'customs of the town' as laid down by the corporation.[79]

Two of the most serious problems with which this machinery of urban government had to deal were violence and poverty. In the towns of east Ulster street brawls were frequent. In 1642, for example, one Mr. Porters 'was fearfully beaten by the wives of Belfast' and in 1646 John Stewart, a merchant, used 'scandalous words' and physical violence in public against Mr. Hannington, a burgess of Belfast.[80] More serious

[75] *Mun. corp. Ire., app. II*, p. 235. This body had no basis in law.

[76] SL, 15, no. 303; the Carrickfergus case is examined in R. Gillespie, 'Urban oligarchies and popular protest in the early seventeenth century: two Ulster examples' in *Retrospect* (1982), pp 54-7.

[77] P.R.O.N.I., T707, ff 1, 7, 9.

[78] P.R.O.N.I., T707, f 13.

[79] Young, *Town book*, pp 4-5.

[80] P.R.O.N.I., T1547/17; Young, *Town book*, pp 43-4; P.R.O.I., Ferguson MSS, ix, p. 103.

than simple street brawls were acts of violence or contempt directed against officials of the corporation while they were executing their official duties. On 1 March 1644 the corporation of Belfast ordered:

That if any person or persons whatsoever shall at any time or times hereafter be refractory or disobedient to any lawful good and honest law order or decree which shall be ordered decreed made and established for the good and peaceable government of this corporation and for the necessary affairs thereof or shall wittingly or willingly by act or deed or by any malignant or contemptuous words abuse and disobey the sovereign or burgesses or any of them or any other person or persons which shall be lawfully put in authority or in any place or office for the affairs of this town shall suffer imprisonment until they submit themselves by humble petition unto the bench and shall forthwith pay such fine and further imprisonment as by the sovereign and burgesses shall be legally ordered.[81]

This indicates that the situation had become so disorderly that it merited a special order. Between 1569 and 1640 the corporation book of Carrickfergus recorded nineteen cases of violence, all of which, save one, involved a member of the corporation. In Carrickfergus during these years the Mayor was most likely to be attacked physically but was rarely slandered while other officers were attacked both physically and verbally. The problem of disrespect for the corporation and its officers was therefore a severe one.

The second major problem was that of poverty. In early seventeenth-century England a combination of the official poor law and local poverty relief schemes, such as those at London, Bristol, Norwich and York, ameliorated this problem.[82] In Ulster no such schemes existed and corporations attempted to solve the problem by punitive measures to keep the poor out of towns. In one case the corporation of Belfast decreed in June 1620 that 'no burgess or free commoner within this corportion shall take into their houses any sub-tenant or inmate without leave of the sovereign . . . under pain of ten shillings for every such default'.[83] The lack of official local schemes meant that the initiative on poor relief was left to individuals through bequests and donations such as those of George Carlton of Carrickfergus in 1590, who left £30 to provide for 'poor sailors', and Edward Holmes in Belfast in 1631, who left £40 to

[81] Young, *Town book*, p. 28.

[82] J. Pound, *Poverty and vagrancy in Tudor England* (London, 1971), ch. 5.

[83] Young, *Town book*, pp 7-8; the Carrickfergus corporation did this in 1625, P.R.O.N.I., T707, f 51.

the poor of the town.[84] Holmes's bequest was to be administered by the corporation who failed to use it for its intended purpose but speculated with it instead. Their investments were less than prudent as in November 1647 they had to threaten legal action against those they had loaned it to in order to obtain the interest and security for the loan.[85]

The problems of violence and poverty illustrate the two main limitations on the actions of the towns in east Ulster during the early seventeenth century. The first limitation was the scale of the problems which they faced and the limited manpower available to tackle them. Only one man, the constable, was employed to enforce the corporation's byelaws so in many cases responsibility for carrying out the decisions of the corporation was farmed out to groups. An example of this was provided in 1600 when defence arrangements were being made in Carrickfergus and aldermen from each ward had to supervise progress in his own ward rather than participate in a general supervision. Similarly, the construction of the Carrickfergus town wall in 1577 demonstrated a lack of general supervision since money was given to each householder who held lands butting on to the wall and each was required to build a section of wall on his land.[86]

The second major limitation on urban government was that of finance. The English corporate town could draw up to half its income from its lands but the town lands in east Ulster, with the exception of Carrickfergus, were in the hands of local landlords, which considerably impoverished the towns.[87] In the case of the one exception, Carrickfergus, the lands had been let out on long leases at low rents and hence there was little chance of raising rents as prices rose. Towns were also deprived of other sources of income because, since they were landlord owned, the corporation received neither rents nor the profits from the market courts. Furthermore the courts of the merchant staple never effectively operated in Antrim or Down, thus eliminating another

[84] *Mun. corp. Ire., rep., app. II*, p. 325. R.M. Strain, *Belfast and its charitable society* (Oxford, 1961), pp 5-6.

[85] Young, *Town book*, pp 73-4; Strain, *Charitable society*, pp 6-9.

[86] P.R.O.N.I., T707, ff 16, 26.

[87] W.T. McCaffrey, *Exeter, 1540-1640* (Harvard, 1975), pp 58-9; W.G. Hoskins, 'An Elizabethan provincial town: Leicester' in J.H. Plumb (ed.), *Studies in social history* (London, 1955), p. 50; R.J. Hunter, 'Towns in the Ulster plantation' in *Studia Hib.*, xi (1971), pp 50-51. Most other Irish towns had corporate land, Peter Gale, *An inquiry into the ancient corporate system of Ireland* (London, 1834), ch. 3.

source of revenue. Yet the corporations had to provide not only the salaries of their officers but also had to maintain the facilities of the towns, such as roads. In some cases *ad hoc* taxation was resorted to but this proved inadequate, and as a result many towns fell into debt.[88] By 1625 the corporation of Carrickfergus was imposing severe economies on its officers which resulted in the sheriff's entertainment allowance, the town clerk's expenses and the grant of one-third of the customs to the Mayor being discontinued. At the same time the machinery for collecting the town's debts was reviewed and overhauled and new debt collectors were appointed. The impact of these economies was limited and the corporation remained in debt and in 1637 it was forced to sell its customs rights to the crown. Another concerted attempt was made by the corporation in 1640 to recover Carrickfergus's debts and raise revenue but again this was ineffective and the town was still severely in debt in 1644.[89]

By 1640 therefore these corporate towns found themselves with considerable problems. Despite rapid growth their small size failed to fulfil the settlers' expectations for rapid profit, their economic structures had failed to diversity due to the social composition of urban populations. They had only a limited income and had severe law and order problems to resolve. Most seriously, no town had developed a stable merchant community which would generate trade, capital and, hence, investment. In contrast the experience of the towns of the second rank was a happier one.

II

Towns of the second rank lacked charters and thus had no complex corporations and their influence was felt in a more restricted geographical area. These non-corporate towns lacked the organs of government which the charter established in the corporate towns and so they were forced to develop their own forms of government. They utilized whatever institutions were available locally, such as the market court which was set up by patent granted to a landlord authorising him to hold a market or fair and to hold courts to control the legal aspects of marketing. These courts were usually run by the landlord-appointed

[88] P.R.O.N.I., T707, f 51; Young, *town book*, pp 11-12, 19-20.
[89] P.R.O.N.I., T707, ff 54-61, 62-3.

clerk of the markets, who in the corporate towns was usually the sovereign. In the non-corporate towns the market courts could be used as a forum from which the town could be governed although they had little power to enforce their decisions.[90] In the larger towns the sovereign was automatically a justice of the peace, but the bailiff of the market court had few formal sanctions. In the case of Donaghadee, because of its importance as a port of entry, it was ordered that the clerk of the market, who was Sir Hugh Montgomery's seneschall, should also be a justice of the peace.[91] In practice the landlord on whose land the town was established often made his own arrangements for urban government as in Ballymena where the landlord, William Adair, obliged most of his urban tenants to look after various aspects of town government by including appropriate clauses in their leases.[92] This meant that in many of these non-corporate towns landlord power was considerable. In Dromore, for example, the bishop's power over the town was so great that on the outbreak of rebellion in 1641 all the inhabitants, save one merchant, left when the bishop left and refused to return until he did so.[93] The landlord could even go as far as to organise aspects of economic life of the town, as was the case in Lisburn, a landlord-planned town, which acted as an inland centre for Belfast merchants. Here, in 1630, the landlord suggested that he might purchase all the goods the tenants had for sale and subsequently offer them to merchants. Merchants would thus be guaranteed a substantial market in goods at Lisburn and would visit the town regularly.[94]

The main role of these towns was economic. They acted principally as trading centres, most having patents for weekly markets for regular transactions and also seasonal fairs for the sale of surplus agricultural produce. They became local distribution and collection points for merchandise and were frequented by merchants and smaller traders. As a customs surveyor reported in 1636 'the merchants and pedlars discharge at Glenarme . . . and fill the county full of commodities . . . The pedlars out of Scotland take advantage of such unguarded creeks and swarm

---

[90] For example, P.R.O.I., Ferguson MSS, ix, p. 82.

[91] Bodl., Carte 62, f 384ᵛ. Manor courts could also be used presided over by the agent of the estate who was usually a J.P.

[92] For example, P.R.O.N.I., D929/F2/3/15, 31.

[93] Cambridge, U.L., Add. 4352, ff 29-30; Brereton, *Travels*, p. 129.

[94] P.R.O.N.I., T343; *Cal. S.P. Ire., 1625-32*, pp 497, 515-16.

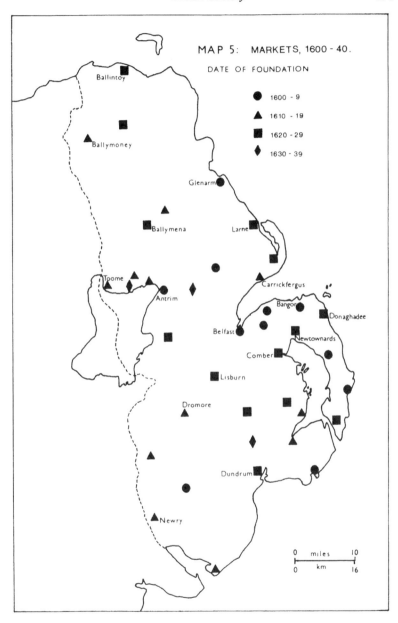

MAP 5: MARKETS, 1600 - 40.

DATE OF FOUNDATION

● 1600 - 9
▲ 1610 - 19
■ 1620 - 29
◆ 1630 - 39

Ballintoy

Ballymoney

Glenarm

Ballymena

Larne

Toome

Antrim

Carrickfergus

Bangor

Donaghadee

Belfast

Newtownards

Comber

Lisburn

Dromore

Dundrum

Newry

0   miles   10
0   km   16

about the country in great numbers, and sell all manner of wares'.[95] Dunluce even had a resident merchant, William Kidd, a burgess of Irvine. The best example of this group of towns is Donaghadee regarding which Charles Monck, the customs surveyor, commented that it had been 'raised for the most part by cattle that are brought from other parts by reason of the aptness of transportation'. The geographical importance of Donaghadee, was enhanced by the building of a pier there in 1616 and by its appointment in the same year as the official port for the movement of men and goods from Ulster to Scotland.[96] From the mid 1630s its importance was increased by attempts to improve the harbour at Portpatrick, the usual Scottish destination from Donaghadee, by building a pier there.[97] The occupational structure of these towns is unclear but in the case of Dunluce one inhabitant, William Boyd, held a considerable amount of land outside the town as well as some salmon fishings, which suggests he may have been a farmer who lived in the town.[98] This phenomenon was probably widespread and in these smaller centres the dichotomy between town and countryside was less rigid than in the larger towns, illustrating their closer economic and social integration with the rural world on which the success of the smaller towns ultimately rested.

III

Below this group of second-grade towns with no corporate status there also existed small, local market centres. Many of these may have been of medieval origin as in the case of Muckamore, in south-west Antrim, where the first formal grant of a market and annual fair had been made in 1430.[99] The number of these marketing centres grew rapidly during the early years of the settlement, especially in the second and third decades of the seventeenth century and by 1640 there were forty-one weekly markets and thirty-one annual fairs in east Ulster.[100] The

---

[95] B.L., Harley 2138, f 180.

[96] Perceval Maxwell, *Scottish migration*, pp 246-7; Bodl., Carte 62, f 384.

[97] S.R.O., GD 214/503-4; SL, 15, no. 270.

[98] Hill, *Macdonnells*, app. III.

[99] L. McKeown, 'The abbey of Muckamore' in *Down and Connor Hist. Soc. Jn.*, ix (1938), p. 57.

[100] See map 5 for markets.

distribution of these markets was determined mainly by agricultural activity. Grain was costly and difficult to transport and hence many landlords were reluctant to take grain surplus as rent. It therefore had to be marketed locally and as a result markets were most dense in important grain areas. Cattle, on the other hand, were mobile and could be walked to the local town for sale to butchers or merchants. Thus landlords in grain growing areas developed villages on their estates to serve as marketing centres. They took out patents for markets so that they could hold a market court to regulate weights and measures and thus provide a legal framework for marketing which increased trade and consequently encouraged increased agricultural output. Sir James Montgomery for example, developed Portaferry from 'some fishermen's cabins and an old Irish castle' for his brother in law, Patrick Savage, by beginning a market there.[101]

Below this group of small marketing towns were villages. A settlement at Dundrum, for example, had twelve cottages outside the castle in 1601 and a similar settlement near the town of Antrim had, in 1641, thirteen houses, a church, a mill with a number of associated buildings, a kiln and at least four barns. One occupant of the village, Throgmorton Totesbury, possessed £10 worth of plate, three trunks of clothes, some bedding and 'an abundance of household goods'.[102] Most of these settlements were probably sixteenth century in origin, growing up around castles or abbeys.

By 1640 it was clear that most of the corporate towns in east Ulster were experiencing severe problems with finance, personnel and their economic structure but other forms of urban life were flourishing. A chain of non-corporate marketing centres had developed in the countryside as the central government had hoped. These developed on a firm sixteenth-century foundation of small, periodic market centres which the settlers regularised through royal grants of market rights which placed the trading system in a formal legal framework. In this respect the settlement created a new urban society bound together by links of debt, trade and legal obligations. Even if the corporate towns were experiencing difficulties in the 1640s they, and the smaller urban centres, had made a fundamental contribution to the success of the east Ulster

[101] Steele, *Tudor & Stuart proclam.*, nos 249, 251, 278; *Mont. MSS*, p. 304.

[102] O'Laverty, *Down and Connor*, i, pt i, p. 68; E. Berwick (ed.), *Rawdon letters* (London, 1819), pp 87-8; SP63/30/90.

settlement by creating a foothold in east Ulster for the early settlers, establishing marketing centres and creating social bonds among the inhabitants.

VIII

ANTRIM, DOWN AND THE WIDER WORLD

LOCAL STUDIES SUCH AS this have both their merits and their drawbacks. On the one hand, the historian is permitted to see events from the bottom up rather than relying on the perspective of the central administration. On the other hand there is a danger that the limited geographical area studied may deviate excessively from the wider national trend, and so it is important to measure the extent to which the patterns of any one study can be imposed on a more general Irish picture. It is a truism to say that society in early modern Ireland was regional in its outlook, yet it is crucial to appreciate this regional perspective in the early seventeenth century. There were, for example, wide variations in dress, language and customs throughout Ireland. If anything the settlements of the seventeenth century emphasised regional differences. Munster became closely linked with south-west England and adopted many ideas from there whereas Ulster became an extension of south-west Scotland as demonstrated by its religious and trading contacts. The various regions were bound together after 1603 by the expansion of Dublin as a centre of government, law, the army and social and economic organisation.[1] Smaller regional centres, such as Cork, Galway and Limerick, also served to bind regions together internally and also create interdependence. Despite this, men's minds and experiences were rarely lifted from local affairs and it was only when controversial decisions of the central government were enforced in the localities through the use of Dublin officials or the army that a national

---

[1] On dress, H.F. McClintock, *Handbook on the traditional old Irish dress* (Dundalk, 1958), pp 2-12; on language, T.F. O'Rahilly, *Irish dialects past and present* (Dublin, 1976), ch. 20; for a poetic expression of this regionalism, L. McKenna (ed.), *Iomarbhágh na bhfhileadh* (Ir. Texts Soc., London, 1918).

perspective imposed itself on local experiences. This was especially true in the interrelated areas of land and religion, as illustrated by the local reactions to the plantation of the Byrne's country in 1615, the attempted plantation of Galway in 1639, and the persecution of the Ulster presbyterians in 1638-40.

Within the localities society was knit together by a delicate series of bonds and alliances. Richard Bellings, a secretary to the supreme council of the Confederation of Kilkenny and Old English in origin, recognised the crucial role of these bonds in providing social cohesion and regulation when he noted 'the colonies . . . were as perfectly incorporated, and as firmly knit together as frequent marriages, daily ties of hospitality and the mutual bond between lord and tenant could unite any people'.[2] The nature of the social bonds, and of the checks and balances which regulated social, economic and political activity in the localities, varied considerably according to the character of settlement in different parts of Ireland. Some areas, such as most of Ulster, counties Leitrim, Longford and the province of Munster, were subjected to formal plantation schemes and therefore had basic guidelines for their social structure laid down by the various rules for the plantations. Other areas, such as counties Antrim, Down, Monaghan and Sligo, were subjected to a more informal process of colonisation as new settlers purchased land from natives and slowly infiltrated these counties. These areas exhibited a wide variation in types of landholding and in the character of the settlement and the landlord's control over his lands depended on how scattered or consolidated they were. These first two processes were by no means discrete and the midlands, for example, were subjected to extensive colonisation before the formal plantation occurred. Still other areas experienced little settlement and were left to adapt to the new order as best they could. The earls of Clanrickard and Thomond provide excellent examples of men who made the transition from Gaelic to English organisation with relatively little settlement on their lands. Finally, the counties of the pale were a unit of social organisation with a different historical experience and economic structure and had greater involvement with the Dublin administration than the rest of Ireland so that the families of the pale evolved over a long

---

[2] Gilbert, *Ir. confed.*, i, p. 2. For Chichester's views on the social bonds SP63/226/44.

period to form reasonably cohesive dynastic groups.[3]

The aim of this chapter is to measure the extent to which the society which evolved in east Ulster during the early seventeenth century was peculiar to that region or whether the conclusions of this analysis have a wider application. It is intended to do this by examining in a wider context three of the themes crucial to the understanding of east Ulster society, landed society, the landlord's relations with the Dublin administration and his relations with his tenants.

I

Landed society in early seventeenth century Ireland was composed of three cultural elements: the settlers, the Old English, and the remains of the native landowning group. The backgrounds of each group considerably influenced their behaviour. In the case of the settlers, the forces at work prompting emigration from England or Scotland were socially selective and thus most migrants tended to be drawn from the socially downwardly mobile who wanted to reverse their fortunes, or from small landholders wanting to rise in the world. Sir Arthur Chichester explained in 1610 to Lord Salisbury, the principal English secretary of state, that the settlers for the Ulster plantation were disappointing, 'those from England are, for the most part, plain country gentlemen . . . If they have any money they keep it close; for hitherto they have disbursed but little . . . The Scottish come with greater part and better accompanied, but it may be with less money in their purses'. Chichester's impressions were confirmed by a survey of the wealth of the undertakers finally chosen. None of them had an income of more than £2,000 per annum and less than a fifth of those who provided income figures had over £1,000 per annum.[4] This was not an uncommon situation as similar pictures could be drawn for Sir Nicholas Malby's attempted settlement in Roscommon in the 1580s, where the settlers were 'the scum of their countries', and for Mathew de Renzi's settlement of

[3] L.M. Cullen, *The emergence of modern Ireland* (London, 1981), p. 204; R. Frame, *English lordship in Ireland, 1318-61* (Oxford, 1982), pp 36-7; D. Jackson, *Intermarriage in Ireland 1560-1650* (Montreal, 1970); A. Clarke, 'Colonial identity in early seventeenth century Ireland' in T.W. Moody (ed.), *Nationality and the pursuit of national independence: Historical studies*, xi (Belfast, 1978), pp 57-71.

[4] SP63/229/135, 150.

the 1620s in the midlands.[5] Most settlers in Ireland were younger sons, who had little hope of advancement at home, or were among those interested in speculation or social advancement, or were imbued with the taste for colonisation. One settler, an apothecary and alderman of Canterbury, described his reasons for migrating in the 1630s as 'his hopes are that Ireland may be better to him than England'.[6] At the close of the Nine Years War, Lord Cecil, principal secretary of state in England, received many petitions for Irish lands from speculators, younger sons, colonisers; a typical one being that of Lord Audley, later a prominent planter in Armagh and Tyrone, who wanted 'to advance the ruin . . . of an old and decayed house'.[7] There were those settlers who fled from ruin in England, such as Mathew de Renzi, a German cloth merchant, whose business in England had collapsed during the slump of 1603.[8] Younger sons with no inheritance in England or Scotland also play a significant part in the colonisation of Ireland. Beckingham Butler from Nottinghamshire, for example, even went as far as to mortgage part of his own estate to send his younger brother, Stephen, to Ulster as an undertaker at Belturbet, county Cavan.[9] Also among the migrants to Ireland were those inveterate colonisers who invested in most plantation schemes for speculation, adventure or for ideological reasons to promote 'civility'. Some 12 per cent of those who considered investing in the plantations of Londonderry and Munster also held shares in other colonial enterprises.[10] Individual examples of this phenomenon include Cecil Calvert, later Lord Baltimore, who held land in Longford as well as America, and the founder of the Nova Scotia colony in Canada, Sir William Alexander, earl of Stirling, who also held land in Armagh and Donegal. Perhaps the best example of the 'lust for adventure' motive was Captain Ennis who, in 1636, wanted to see

[5] SP63/77/60; B. McCuarta, 'Newcomers in the Irish midlands, 1540-1640' (M.A., U.C.G., 1980), p. 47.
[6] SL, 16, no. 132; for speculation SP63/254/117; Moody, *Londonderry plantation*, p. 327.
[7] H.M.C., *Salisbury*, xvi, p. 52; ibid., xv, p. 110; ibid., vi, p. 394; ibid., xi, p. 547.
[8] H.M.C., *Salisbury*, xviii, pp 10, 24, 239, 323.
[9] B.L., Add. 18824, no. 63; Hill, *Plantation*, pp 281, 465-6; J. Thirsk, 'Younger sons in the seventeenth century' in *History*, liv (1969), pp 358-61, 368; D. Laing (ed.), *Royal letters, charters and tracts relating to the colonisation of New Scotland* (Bannatyne Club, Edinburgh, 1867), p. 42.
[10] T.K. Rabb, *Enterprise and empire* (Harvard, 1967), pp 118, 156-7.

Ireland because he had already seen Jerusalem, Constantinople and Cairo and wanted a new challenge![11]

Conditions in early seventeenth century Ireland favoured an expansion of settlement. Most native landholders were in financial trouble as a result of the Nine Years War and were willing to sell land and after 1603 new regions were opened up for settlement as English control extended over the whole country. Many pale families took advantage of this situation and expanded into previously uncolonized areas such as Wicklow, the midlands, and Connacht.[12] The backgrounds of these families were little more auspicious than those of the immigrants, for many pale families were also suffering from dwindling finances. The acts of supremacy and uniformity cut many of them off from the profits of office and the Nine Years War had disrupted the normal trading activities of the pale ports, Dublin, Dundalk and Drogheda. Increasing population in the pale also imposed a strain on resources, leading to increased pauperisation for many social groups there.[13]

The social origins of most settlers, whether migrant or immigrant, meant that many experienced the problem of finding enough initial capital to establish themselves. Building up an estate was an expensive business as one Munster settler, Sir Philip Perceval discovered when during the 1630s he spent over £14,000 in acquiring mortgages to build up a landed estate. Sir Philip was fortunate in being able to raise most of this either as loans from Dublin merchants or through the profits from his office as clerk of the court of wards.[14] Others were less fortunate and as a result of heavy demands on limited resources, in their early years in Ireland, most men had problems in establishing themselves in their newly acquired lands. Some, such as John Baxter, an Elizabethan soldier who acquired lands in Sligo, failed to raise enough money to establish a viable estate and were finally forced to sell it off. Even corporate bodies such as the London companies in Londonderry had considerable difficulty in raising enough cash to develop their lands, losing, they

[11] Strafford, *Letters*, i, pp 179-80; Hill, *Plantation*, pp 507-8, 562-3; SL, 16, no. 73.

[12] SP63/99/37; SP63/223/65; M. O'Dowd, 'Landownership in Sligo, 1580-1641' (Ph.D., U.C.D., 1980), pp 403-4; McCuarta, 'Newcomers' pp 12-15; *Cal. S.P. Ire., 1606-8*, pp 93, 449; *Cal. S.P. Ire., 1611-14*, p. 266; L.J. Arnold, 'The restoration land settlement in Dublin and Wicklow' (Ph.D., T.C.D., 1967), chs. 2, 3.

[13] N.P. Canny, 'Early modern Ireland' in *Ir. ec. and social hist.*, iv (1977), p. 62.

[14] B.L., Add. 47036; Add. 46923, ff 37, 49, 76, 101, 113, 150, 165.

estimated, £40,500 by this failure.[15]

These financial problems were not unique to settlers and many native Irish and Old English experienced similar problems of insufficient capital to consolidate and develop their estates. The native Irish were especially badly hit because their ideas of estate management were radically different from the new ideas of the settlers. One of the main features of the Irish system of land tenure was that the land was not parcelled out into large estates but was held by freeholders who owed loyalty but not rent to a lord. In return for protection and other services, such as legal judgements, they paid to the lord a small historically immutable 'ceart' or 'cheifry'. These small sums were badly hit by the growing predominance of a market economy geared to the idea of an economic rent in sixteenth-century Ireland. By 1588 the right paid by O'Sullivan to McCarthy Mór in Kerry was regarded as 'but little worth nowadays', and indeed the whole revenues from the extensive McCarthy Mór lordship were only £266.5s.10d. in 1598.[16] As English influence grew in early seventeenth-century Ireland so did the market economy but most native Irish lords failed to make the necessary adjustments and hence fell into debt since their nominal income could not support them in a market orientated world. By 1616, for example, many of the native landholders in Sligo were in severe financial straits and as a result of similar problems many native landholders, such as those of Monaghan, were forced to sell out to settlers by 1641.[17] The pattern of increasing indebtedness among the older inhabitants is clearly shown in the case of the Barry family of county Cork. In 1632 James and his son Michael Barry owed Sir Philip Perceval £2,573 but a year later this had increased to £3,500 and by 1638 their indebtedness to Perceval had risen to £13,600. After legal proceedings in 1641 they were forced to mortgage all their lands to Perceval for £8,000 in an effort to reduce their debt.[18]

[15] P.R.O.I. Chancery Bills AA III; Moody, *Londonderry plantation*, pp 335, 339; McCuarta, 'Newcomers', pp 128-9, 131-2, 152; J. Ainsworth, 'Reports of documents in private hands' in *Anal. Hib.*, xx (1958), pp 59, 67, 70.

[16] Butler, *Gleanings*, pp 14, 34 n.19; *Inchiquin MSS*, no. 1321; A.S. Green, 'Irish land in the sixteenth century' in *Eriu*, iii (1907), p. 178.

[17] O'Dowd, 'Landownership', pp 238-40; 244-56, 337-8; for other areas McCuarta, 'Newcomers', p. 125; *Inchiquin MSS*, nos 1418, 1301; P.J. Duffy, 'The territorial organization of Gaelic landownership and its transformation in county Monaghan 1591-1640' in *Ir. geog.* xiv (1981), pp 1-20.

[18] B.L., Add. 470, ff 5ᵛ-6; Add. 47046, ff 6, 8, 19, 39; Add. 47045, ff 2-2ᵛ.

Similarly, by 1635 Dermot McCarthy of county Cork had been forced to mortgage over 70 per cent of his lands to cover his debts.[19]

Some sixteenth century lords, such as the earls of Clanrickard and Thomond, did manage to make the transition to the new economic order although as late as 1637 Clanrickard's rents were described as the lowest in Ireland.[20] The transition may have been easier for those of Anglo-Irish origin, such as Clanrickard or the McWilliam Burkes in Mayo, because they had never fully adopted native systems of land tenure. The *Seanchas Burcach*, a sixteenth-century compilation of poetry, genealogy and land rights, recorded that 'it is on the land that MacWilliam's [Burke] rent is derived' and not on followers and that land was devised 'according to the testimony of stewards and of the charters' not by tradition as in Gaelic polity.[21] Others who made the transition to the new order were small sixteenth century landholders who rose to prominence with the collapse of the older lords. These men had neither respectable ancestry nor a well defined place in the native Irish social hierarchy and hence were much satirised by the poets who were the bastions of Gaelic tradition.[22] The transition to a new economic order also caused problems for settlers who acquired land already occupied by native Irish tenants whom they found difficult to remove. The bishop of Clonfert and Kilmacduagh, for example, recorded in the 1630s that the natives on the church lands would not pay an economic rent for their land but 'only a bare cheefe' and when he pressed the point the tenants ignored him and paid their 'cheefery' to the local secular landlord, the earl of Clanrickard, instead.[23]

If the initial economic problems of landlords were not exclusive to

---

[19] B.L., Add. 46920, f. 26.

[20] B. Cunningham, 'Political and social change in the lordships of Clanricard and Thomond, 1569-1641' (M.A., U.C.G., 1979), pp 233-4.

[21] T. O'Raghallaigh (ed.), 'Seanchas Burcach' in *Galway Arch. Soc. Jn.*, xiii (1925-8), pp 111, 117; the Anglo Irish may have been reorganizing their land tenure system in the late sixteenth century, L. Price, 'The Byrnes country in county Wicklow in the sixteenth century' in *R.S.A.I.Jn.*, lxvi (1936), pp 58-9.

[22] N.J.A. Williams (ed.), *Pairlement chloinne Tomáis* (Dublin, 1981), pp 22-3, 83; N.J.A. Williams (ed.), *Dánta Mhuiris Mhic Dhaíbhí Dhuibh Mhic Gearailt* (Dublin, 1971), p. 51; A. de Blácam, *Gaelic Literature surveyed*, 2nd ed. (Dublin, 1973), pp 149-51; P. de Brun, B. Ó Buachalla, T. Ó Concheanainn (eds.), *Nua dhuanaire*, i, (Dublin, 1975), p. 18; D.F. Gleeson, *The last lords of Ormond*, (London, 1938), p. 130.

[23] *Cal. S.P. Ire., 1625-32*, pp 548, 668.

east Ulster neither was their sequel. After an initial uneasy period in the early years of the seventeenth century, Irish landed finances seem to have been healthy until the 1630s when a crisis developed, similar to that described for Antrim and Down. In Cavan, Charles Lambert was forced to mortgage his estate for £4,000 and in the Pale, Richard Nugent, the newly created earl of Westmeath, feared that this new dignity could bankrupt him, so perilous were his finances.[24] This crisis hit hardest at those whose political or other activities had entailed high expenditure. The finances of Richard Boyle, earl of Cork, were showing strain by the 1630s because of his political activities and the earl of Clanrickard, who spent most of his life at the English court, was in debt by £25,000 in 1637. Even the Irish lord chancellor, Adam Loftus, was complaining of the excessive strain which political activity was putting on his purse.[25] Political activity, however, was not the only cause of indebtedness as taxation in Ireland was felt to be high in comparison with England and by 1640 it was complained that many of the nobility were leaving the country because of this high taxation.[26] The fundamental cause of chronic debt problems in Ireland generally, as in east Ulster, was related to the availability of credit to finance development in a cash starved economy. As early as 1629, when the earl of Desmond's land was show-ing signs of financial strain, it was shown that he was not insolvent but rather had liquidity problems.[27] The key to this problem lay in the lack of credit facilities and most landowners were keen to stress their credit-worthiness. The earl of Clanrickard showed special concern for his land titles both before and after the attempted plantation of Connacht because he feared an unsound title would affect his credit, and Andrew Stewart, an east Tyrone planter, pleaded with Wentworth in 1637 for cash as his credit was at stake.[28] Even if credit could be obtained the price was usually very high, usury was common and the rate of interest ranged as high as 30-40 per cent. This was partly due to the shortage of

[24] SL, 15, no. 26; SL, 14, f 286.

[25] T. Ranger, 'The career of Richard Boyle, first earl of Cork, in Ireland' (D. Phil., Oxford, 1959), pp 253, 388; SL, 16, nos 70, 143; SL, 17, no. 125; Cunningham, 'Political and social change', p. 239; H.M.C., *9th Report*, appendix 2, p. 294.

[26] B.L., Sloan 29, f. 2.

[27] B.L., Add. 18824, no. 8; *Cal. S.P. Ire., 1633-47*, pp 8, 85.

[28] SL, 17, no. 34; SL, 18, no. 1; SL, 19, nos 61, 62; even the government had con-siderable problems in borrowing, *Cal. S.P. Ire., 1611-14*, p. 166-7; *Cal. S.P. Ire., 1615-25*, p. 20.

money in Ireland but also since the backgrounds of many of the settlers were dubious, lending to them was risky and so the high risk had to be compensated for by a high return on the money lent. There were several attempts to control the level of interest rates in early seventeenth-century Ireland, including a statute of 1634 which attempted to fix the interest rate at 10 per cent, but these had little effect.[29]

Landlords attempted to resolve this cash crisis in two main ways. Following a period of sluggishness they began to raise rents in the 1630s as in counties Londonderry, Tyrone, Armagh, the province of Munster and the pale, where rents rose rapidly.[30] This process proved counter-productive for it resulted in increased poverty among tenants and, ultimately, in falling estate revenues because tenants could not pay the higher rents. In some areas the poorer sections of the tenantry were even forced to sell corn while it was still in the ground.[31] Borrowing by tenants also increased. The numbers of those borrowing money from the Munster settler, Sir Philip Perceval, tripled in the five years before 1641 but even on this estate arrears of rent mounted so that by 1641 they amounted to £242, some of which went back three years.[32]

The second main way landlords attempted to cope with this cash shortage was to look for ways of turning fixed capital into liquid assets and they resorted to mortgaging as a way of doing this. The result was a simplification of the mortgaging process with the introduction of the deed of rentcharge to replace the older customs.[33] By the late 1630s the deed of rentcharge was prevalent in Ulster and Connacht, although in the pale and Munster the older form survived longer, mainly due to the accessibility of the staple courts at Dublin, Drogheda and Cork, which

[29] *Advertisements for Ire.*, p. 25; *Cal. S.P. Ire., 1608-10*, p. 243; *Cal. S.P. Ire., 1611-14*, p. 250; *Cal. S.P. Ire., 1615-25*, p. 169; Moody, *Londonderry plantation*, p. 352. B.L., Add. 29975, f 11; *Herbert corresp.*, no. 127.

[30] Moody, *Londonderry plantation*, p. 332; R.J. Hunter, 'The Ulster plantation in Armagh and Cavan' (M. Litt., T.C.D., 1969), pp 280, 343, 400-1; *Cal. Carew, 1603-24*, p. 410; *Herbert corresp.*, nos 118, 119, 163; *Ormonde MSS*, n.s., i, pp 20-21; H.M.C., *9th Report*, appendix 2, p. 294; P. Dwyer, *The Diocese of Killaloe from the reformation . . .* (Dublin, 1878), pp 133-8 suggests rents from church land rose between four and ten fold in the 1630s.

[31] *Herbert corresp.*, nos 157, 161; Moody, *Londonderry plantation*, p. 352; SL, 16, f. 39.

[32] B.L., Add. 46925, f. 174.

[33] For older forms, P.R.O.I., Chancery Bill BB 149; RC9/1 p. 276.

were vital to operating the old form of mortgaging.[34] Richard Boyle, the earl of Cork, clearly appreciated the key role which cash flow had to play in early seventeenth-century debt management and he organized his estate so that rents were collected on four occasions during the year rather than the usual two. Secondly, he developed a complex credit system of bills of exchange based on his personal contacts in Ireland and England and he also used his ironworks to generate credit for trading purposes.[35]

Within this economic climate, landlord attitudes to Ireland varied considerably. Many settlers felt unstable and insecure in their new environment since most had risen rapidly from relatively low status in England or Scotland and had to adjust to a position of new-found wealth which was, in the eyes of many of their former neighbours, vulgar and ostentatious.[36] The erection of a lavish tomb in St. Patrick's cathedral, Dublin, by the earl of Cork, formerly a penniless younger son, for example, was regarded by Wentworth as a symptom of his 'vanity and insolent novelties' characteristic of the *noveau riches*.[37] Since wealth alone could not in the eyes of their peers secure these men a new position in the social hierarchy most settlers craved after local and national office, as many east Ulster settlers did, and they concerned themselves with the trappings of their new-found social positions.[38] Treatises began to appear on protocol and the precedence of the Irish nobility, and in the Dublin parliament questions of precedence and status were hotly debated.[39] By the 1630s many of the native Irish

[34] W. O'Sullivan (ed.), *The Strafford inquisition of County Mayo* (I.M.C., 1958), passim; B.L., Add. 19843; J. Ainsworth, 'Survey of documents in private keeping' in *Anal. Hib.*, xxiv (1967), pp 151-2.

[35] Ranger, 'Richard Boyle', pp 163-6; I am indebted to Michael McCarthy Morrogh for a discussion on Boyle's activities.

[36] T. Ranger, 'Strafford in Ireland: a revaluation' in *Past and Present*, xix (1961), pp 26-45; N.P. Canny, *The upstart earl* (Cambridge, 1982), examines this phenomenon in the case of Richard Boyle, first earl of Cork.

[37] SL, 6, f 34; SL, 8, ff 59-60.

[38] McCuarta, 'Newcomers', p. 30; many settlers felt divorced from civility, P.R.O.I., Chancery Bills, A145, B48, G 206.

[39] Bodl., Rawlinson C.921; R.D. Edwards (ed.), 'The letter book of Sir Arthur Chichester' in *Anal. Hib.*, viii (1938), p. 172; *Lords jn. Ire.*, i, pp 21-2; There was also considerable debate as to their position in relation to the English nobility, S.M. Reynolds (ed.), *The table talk of John Selden* (Oxford, 1892), pp 106-7.

landholders were also attempting to consolidate their place in the new social order by enrolling funeral certificates, which described their genealogy and heraldic arms, in the office of arms in Dublin. Also in an attempt to fix themselves in the new social order they emulated the attempts of the settlers to display their new-found wealth by, for example, building impressive tombs so that about a fifth of sculptured tombs erected in early seventeenth-century Ireland were built by natives, the same quantity by Old English and the remainder by settlers.[40]

These attitudes were not uniform among the Irish landed gentry but varied considerably according to local circumstances. In areas like Sligo where no coherent group of landlords developed, because estates were widely scattered, there was little concern with such matters as precedence and the enrolment of funeral certificates.[41] In areas where a coherent landed society did develop, concerns with social position began to emerge in the 1620s when most of the initial land speculation had ceased and when the remaining landowners began to adjust themselves to their new position.[42] Finally in areas such as east Ulster, parts of Munster and Connacht, which enjoyed compact estates and a high degree of continuity of ownership after 1603, these attitudes tended to emerge earlier since the gentry community had more cohesion.

The experience in the pale was rather different to that described above. The Old English group there regarded themselves as a colonial elite with their own lineages which bound them into well defined families and social groups. They had been settled in Ireland since medieval times, had adjusted to the environment and tended to be more 'Irish orientated' that the new English settlers who were preoccupied with profit and advancement. Sir Richard Shee, a Kilkenny landowner, for instance, demonstrated his concern with issues other than personal ones when, in 1603, he recorded in his will that Marcus, his son, was to be sent to an Inn of Court 'in hope that he may be the better member of the commonwealth'.[43] A similar attitude was expressed in some clauses

[40] R. Loeber, 'Sculptured monuments to the dead in early seventeenth century Ireland' in *R.I.A. Proc.*, sect. C, lxxxi (1981), pp 267-93.

[41] O'Dowd, 'Landownership', p. 183.

[42] McCuarta, 'Newcomers', p. 141; Perceval Maxwell, *Scottish migration*, appendix I, II; *New Hist. Ire.*, iii, p. 205.

[43] J. Ainsworth, 'Survey of documents in private keeping' in *Anal. Hib.*, xx (1958), pp 228, 232.

in Old English demands of the 1620s, the Graces, which demanded improvements in the government of Ireland for their own sake rather than for private profit. All these forms of landed society reflected differing attitudes to the main preoccupation of the age, the local landlord's concern with his rights and privileges in an era of growing centralisation.

II

The relationship between local lords and the central administration was the real determinant of the amount of power and influence which could be exercised by any one local magnate. Royal policy in the sixteenth century had stressed the selective expansion of local power to create trustworthy, powerful magnates in key areas of Ireland who could act as centres of loyalty and stability in a fluctuating political climate. In 1575, for example, the earl of Essex had been granted a strategically important area of Monaghan, the barony of Farney, with considerable powers to control it and the earl of Kildare's position in Leinster had been strengthened by a series of regrants of his lands each with wider powers.[44] This policy was continued into the early seventeenth century as James I attempted to establish stability in Ireland and also reward followers.[45] By 1605 it was already becoming clear that this policy had its drawbacks since it did not promote the 'commonwealth' attitude desired by central government. Sir Francis Bacon, for example, considered it detrimental because 'the bane of plantation is when the . . . planters make such haste to a little mechanical present profit, as disturbeth the whole frame and nobleness of the work for times to come'. Such a view was strongly endorsed by key New English administrators such as Sir Arthur Chichester, the lord deputy, Sir John Davies, the attorney general, and Sir John Dunham, the chief justice of king's bench.[46] As a result by 1610 government attitude towards these power blocks began to change but not before a substantial number had

---

[44] SP63/54/33; *Ormond deeds, 1584-1603*, pp 26-8; *Ormonde MSS* n.s. i, p. 2; O'Dowd, 'Landownership', pp 114-15.

[45] SP63/215/111.

[46] J. Spedding (ed.), *The life and letters of Francis Bacon*, vi (London, 1872), p. 206; J. Davies, 'A discovery of the true causes' in H. Morley (ed.), *Ireland under Elizabeth and James I* (London, 1890), pp 276, 281, SP63/233/25; *Cal. S.P. Ire., 1603-6*, p. 378; *Cal. S.P. Ire., 1608-10*, p. 521.

been created. Policy began to shift more towards maintaining order by creating a balance of power in the localities as an alternative to having a dominant authority in an area. This approach was reflected in Lord Deputy Wentworth's observations in July 1639 that 'it had been the constant endeavour of this state to break the dependancies which great lords draw to themselves of followers, tenants and neighbours' whether the lords were gaelic Irish or New English.[47] This was to be effected in a number of ways. First the powers of the lords were to be limited by the enforcement of the common law which regulated the relationship between lord and tenant so that lords could not build up followers who might act as a threat to the local influence of central government. Secondly, the Dublin administration attempted to impose tighter controls on land grants to prevent too much property accumulating in any one man's hands. As a result the escheator system was remodelled and the escheator general replaced by four regional officials. The 1606 Commission on Defective Titles was an attempt to enforce these new measures but it backfired and was used by those such as Richard Boyle, who had built up substantial estates in the sixteenth century and who wished to have their titles confirmed.[48] Thirdly, the Dublin administration began assaults on any power block which it considered a threat. The medieval palatinate jurisdiction of Tipperary, for example, was attacked as were the powers of the Munster towns which had refused to accept religious conformity in defiance of Dublin's instructions in 1603. By the second decade of the century the presidency courts of Munster and Connacht were being slowly phased out, as business was being centralised in the Dublin courts.[49] Such moves were not welcomed by any landlord grouping in Ireland. The natives and Old English, whose right to land was unclear in English law, feared increased monitoring of their activities which could result in the weaknesses of their title being exploited

---

[47] SL, 21, no. 199; B.L., Harley 3292, f 278; Add. 34313, ff 49-50; Add. 4784, f 113; Bodl., Rawl. D.922, f 49.

[48] Ranger, 'Richard Boyle', pp 64-5; other reforms, such as the abolition of 'books' of land, *Cal. S.P. Ire., 1603-6*, pp 299-300 and reform of escheator, *Cal. S.P. Ire., 1606-8*, pp 75, 98; *Cal. Carew 1603-24*, p. 101.

[49] V.H.T. Delaney, 'The palatinate court of the liberty of Tipperary' in *Am. jnl of legal history*, v (1961), pp 102-3; O'Dowd, 'Landownership', p. 122; D.J. Kennedy, 'The presidency of Munster under Elizabeth and James I' (M.A., U.C.C., 1973), chs 8, 9; *Cal. S.P. Ire., 1600*, pp 402-3; *Acts privy council, 1599-1600*, p. 45; *Cal. S.P. Ire., 1615-25*, p. 17.

by a government anxious to expand its authority. Settlers were also uneasy about increased controls on their activities since they desired a *laissez faire* environment in which they could develop their own lands to achieve their twin desires of profit and upward social mobility. As Wentworth expressed it, the settlers were 'private men . . . whose sole ends and aims have been their own enriching and such who have had no hand here in public affairs have only been prosperous for themselves and compassed much wealth'.[50] Given this attitude it is not surprising that most landlords resented government interference, the earl of Cork complaining in 1624 of 'the troublesomeness of the times wherein every action is narrowly looked into'. Many settlers refused to admit government officials onto their land. Because of this sheriffs could not collect M.P.'s wages in 1614 and in an instance in 1625 a riot erupted over the right of a sheriff to enter lands in Donegal.[51]

The ability of individual landlords, however, to resist the growing influence of central government varied considerably throughout Ireland. In east Ulster, settlers with large, compact estates succeeded in retaining a large measure of autonomy as did men in other parts of Ireland. The earl of Clanrickard, for example, was so successful in consolidating his power base that he was accused in 1639 of being a 'count palatine' because, as well as a large estate, he had also absorbed into his own hands the presidency of Connacht and even when he resigned that office in 1616 he secured the office of governor of Galway for himself thus ensuring that his lands would remain free from government influence.[52] His neighbour, the earl of Thomond, pursued a similar end even more vigorously. Since the late sixteenth century Thomond had been resisting the right of sheriffs to enter his lands, a tactic he continued into the seventeenth century, so that by 1628 it was complained that his lands had become a refuge for the lawless because of Thomond's effectiveness in excluding royal authority. Like Clanrickard he attempted to manipulate the office of the presidency, in his case that of Munster, and having secured that office arranged to have his estate removed

[50] SL, 21, no. 79, f 11; SL, 8, f 11; Ranger 'Richard Boyle', pp 265-70.

[51] *Lismore papers*, 2nd ser., iii, pp 120-25; *Commons' jn. Ire.,* i, pp 69, 73, 81, 82; B.L., Sloan 3827, f 62; SP63/274/30.

[52] SL, 21, no. 199; Cunningham, 'Political and social change', pp 54-5, 57-8, 62-3, 210-12; SP63/219/157; O'Dowd, 'Landownership', pp 119-21.

from its jurisdiction in 1616.[53]

Even in areas where the government had sanctions against the building up of such power blocks, as for example the various conditions for plantation, consolidation still went on. In Ulster, the earl of Abercorn, chief undertaker for the barony of Strabane, introduced his blood-relatives as planters, thus using ties of kinship to consolidate his influence and when an attempt was made to stop this in 1610 he complained to the King that men of whom he did not approve were allowed to settle in that barony. In 1617 the administration recognised his power there and he was put in sole charge of the plantation in that barony.[54] The earl of Cork used similar techniques to build up his sphere of influence in Munster and both Sir Arthur Chichester and the earl of Ormond attempted to use this method but were stopped by the central administration.[55] In some other planted areas the problem was less acute since the largely absentee landlord population of the midland plantations cared more about revenues than rights and hence never properly consolidated their estates or their influence there. In Sligo, absenteeism and the scattered disposition of settler estates meant that it was too difficult to consolidate effectively and so the problem of power blocks never arose. In addition many Sligo landowners were Galway merchants who simply wanted grazing land, others were New English speculators whose aim was profit rather than power, and many of the Old English settlers had a power base in the pale and sought mainly profit for their Sligo lands.[56]

The break-up of such power blocks as existed in the early seventeenth century was seen to be essential for effective government. Soon after 1603 the central administration began to tackle the problem but their efforts tended to be piecemeal and relatively ineffective as, for example,

---

[53] Cunningham, 'Political and social change', pp 49-53, 118-19; *Cal. S.P. Ire., 1615-25*, pp 118-19; *Cal. S.P. Ire., 1625-32*, p. 64; SP63/219/99, 101; for complaints of similar activity in the palatinate of Tipperary in the sixteenth century see Spenser, *View*, ed. Renwick, p. 30.

[54] N.L.S., Denmilne MSS, iii, no. 45; B.L., Add. 39853, f 101; Perceval Maxwell, *Scottish migration*, p. 369.

[55] Ormond MSS, n.s., i, p. 26; Ranger 'Richard Boyle', pp 118, 352; *Tanner letters*, pp 63-4; *Cal. S.P. Ire., 1606-8*, p. 617.

[56] In the midlands a significant exception was Mathew de Renzi who introduced settlers, McCuarta, 'Newcomers', pp 26-7, 29, 46, 48, 50-51, 57, 133; O'Dowd, 'Landownership', p. 347.

Antrim, Down & the Wider World

the commissions of 1610 and 1616 in Sligo which had investigated land titles there but failed to ensure the effective working of local government. Similar moves had been attempted in Munster but these proved unsuccessful because many of the settlers had become so deeply entrenched during the sixteenth century. The problem, however, was not as simple as mere resistance from local lords since the central administration was hampered by other difficulties such as poor communications and incomplete knowledge of administrative and landowning boundaries, especially relating to those lands which continued to be held by the native Irish.[57] Written evidence was often scant and on one occasion Chichester complained that the earl of Tyrone had granted the barony of Strabane, county Tyrone, to Turlough O'Neill 'by what deed I know not but I think by word rather than writing'.[58] This situation however improved dramatically during the early seventeenth century. Rising land values encouraged landlords to define and consolidate their property rights and specify their boundaries more clearly, a process which was aided by government pressure to establish well defined administrative units. Government, however, often neglected to keep track of these developments. Record keeping was poor, most current records being scattered in private houses in Dublin and hence open to falsification or theft and it was not until the 1630s that any serious attempt was made to centralise record keeping. As a result the Dublin administration often lacked detailed factual information on individual areas and thus found it difficult to determine and hence exploit its rights in relation to wardships, liveries and other quasi-feudal dues.[59]

Part of the reason for this lack of intelligence from the localities stemmed from the considerable problems with the functioning of local government in the counties, the chief difficulty being the lack of adequate personnel. Since the settler population was thinly and unevenly distributed, there were rarely enough settlers in any area to make up a jury, the institution on which much of the common law process

[57] O'Dowd, 'Landownership', pp 99, 125-33, 163-4, 403.

[58] J.H. Andrews, 'Geography and government in Elizabethan Ireland' in *Ir. geog. studies*, pp 178-91; *New Hist. Ire.*, iii, p. 167; *Advertisements for Ire.*, p. 33-4; Bodl., Carte 61, f 44; H.M.C., *Salisbury*, xxi, p. 121.

[59] *P.R.O.I. guide*, pp viii-xi; P.R.O.I. Ferguson MSS, x, pp 78, 151; xi, p. 69; xiii, p. 2; SP63/127/13; SP63/172/31.

depended.[60] It was equally difficult to find enough men to undertake effectively royal offices in the localities. In Leitrim, eight men from seven families held the office of sheriff between 1605 and 1641, in Clare twelve men from ten families held the office, and in Cork which was better, although still unevenly, supplied with settlers, nineteen men from fifteen families were sheriffs in forty years.[61] The office of justice of the peace was also affected and in 1633 there were not enough Clare justices of the peace to form a quorum.[62] The central administration had little alternative but to appoint the few local men available to royal office regardless of quality. In Londonderry for example, one man, Richard Kirby, was sheriff four times despite grave breaches of the law and procedure by him while sheriff.[63]

In contrast to the normal machinery of local government the central administration was more effective with irregular methods of controlling landlords. Initially, many of these methods, such as the court of wards, had been run by landowners in their capacity as royal officials and had manipulated them for their own ends but during the 1620s this began to change as these institutions were reformed.[64] The court of wards was reorganised and by the mid 1620s new escheators were operating in most parts of Ireland collecting alienation fines and investigating wardships. The expansion of the role of the court of wards was assisted by the promise in the graces to the Old English of equitable treatment which persuaded both the old English and native Irish to enrol alienations and liveries in the court.[65] This process of reformation of institutions and growth of central government influence in the counties reached its zenith under Lord Deputy Wentworth who exploited already existing

[60] SL, 10, f 49; SL, 16, no. 23; *Cal. S.P. Ire., 1611-14,* pp 373-4, 378, 418-19; *Cal. S.P. Ire., 1615-25,* pp 270, 588; *Cal. S.P. Ire., 1625-32,* pp 59, 220; Dwyer, *Diocese of Killaloe,* p. 143; B.L., Add. 39853, f7ᵛ.

[61] J. Meehan, 'List of high sheriffs of Leitrim, 1605-1800' in *R.S.A.I. jn.,* xxxviii (1908), p. 386; H.F. Berry, 'Sheriffs of County Cork' in ibid., xxxv (1905), pp 47-8; T.J. Westropp, 'Notes on the sheriffs of County Clare' in ibid., xxi (1890), pp 70-71.

[62] SL, 13, no. 90; figures were low for most counties, T.C.D., MS 672.

[63] Moody, *Londonderry plantation,* pp 282, 286-7, appendix F.

[64] T. Ranger, 'Richard Boyle and the making of an Irish fortune' in *I.H.S.,* x (1957-8), pp 257-97; V. Treadwell, 'The Irish court of wards under James I' in *I.H.S.,* xii (1960-61), pp 1-27.

[65] Kearney, *Strafford in Ire.,* pp 76-7; J. Ainsworth, 'Report of documents in private keeping' in *Anal. Hib.,* xx (1958), p. 61.

institutions, such as the court of wards, against the greater landowners with considerable success. By 1636 his Commission on Defective Titles had forced over one hundred landowners to take out new patents with increased crown rent and, occasionally, reduced jurisdictions.[66] The culmination of this policy was to be an attack on the earl of Clanrickard by a proposed plantation of Galway but it failed and with it Wentworth's scheme for the increase of royal authority in the localities.[67]

In reality there was little that the central administration could do to clip the wings of the great landlords who grew up in some areas, including east Ulster. The real threat to these landowners was that posed by the relationship with the tenants on their own estates. If the tenantry refused to assist with the process of estate consolidation trouble could ensue, as happened to the earl of Thomond who was plagued by disputes with his own tenants. This could well result in a breakdown in landlord-tenant relations, as in part happened to the earl of Cork in the late 1630s. Such an eventuality was potentially dangerous because it opened rifts in the lord's power base which could be expoited by royal officials, which had earlier played a part in the fall of the earl of Tyrone.[68] Thus the lord's relationship with his tenants was crucial not only from an economic but also a political perspective and for this reason many groups including the central government attempted to influence it.

III

The government scheme for landlord-tenant relations rested on the common law idea of a contractual bond between lord and tenant, the lease. Placing relations on a contractual basis would limit landlord influence since a tenant would have a legal remedy if the landlord became too powerful or despotic. Such a remedy became a reality in 1591 for Nicholas Elcock, the mayor of Drogheda, who found himself charged by one of his tenants, Walter Chevers, of 'divers intolerable exactions'.[69] A lease also bound a tenant to his land for a fixed term, hence

---

[66] Kearney, *Strafford in Ire.,* appendix 3; *Herbert corresp.,* no. 121.

[67] Cunningham, 'Political and social change', ch. 6.

[68] For Thomond, P.R.O.I., Chancery Bills BB162, AA186, G208; N.P. Canny, 'Hugh O'Neill and the changing face of Gaelic Ulster' in *Stud. Hib.,* x (1970), pp 23-4; Cunningham, 'Political and social change', pp 278-9.

[69] P.R.O.I., Chancery Bills A 47.

reducing mobility which the government felt was dangerous and it also gave the landlord a degree of responsibility for the control of potential malefactors living on their lands. As late as 1625 Donegal landowners were ordered to deliver the names of their tenants, for whom they would remain legally responsible, to the sheriff.[70] What actually developed between landlord and tenant was not a standard relationship but a patchwork of agreements which were the varying response to socio-economic conditions over various areas. In the pale, tenants were plentiful and the tradition of a contractual agreement well established but there was little estate consolidation in the seventeenth century and hence little concern to keep a tight rein on tenants. Pale lands were leased, usually for a cash rent and few labour services and since there was no shortage of tenants landlords did not have to provide additional services for those who worked their land. Manor courts, for example, functioned only irregularly and unlike east Ulster there was no legal protection for pale tenants who were left to fight their own legal battles.[71] In the pale competition was for tenancies rather than tenants and landowners could even insist on the type of tenant which they wanted. The bishop of Leighlin for instance complained in 1615 that catholicism only survived in his diocese because certain landowners would only take catholic tenants. The result was that landlords had considerable control over their tenants as the bishop of Leighlin appreciated when, in 1615, he did not go directly to tenants about a problem concerning them but approached the landlord instead.[72]

In most other parts of the country tenants were scarce as Robert, earl of Essex, soon discovered on his Monaghan lands and he complained that 'good land which should be well planted by his [majesty's] subjects is only grazed on by sheep'.[73] The problem of low population was

[70] B.L., Sloan 3827, f 62; Bodl., Rawlinson A237, ff 115-16; B.L., Royal 18A, lvi, f 18ᵛ; Edwards (ed.), 'Letter book', p. 161.

[71] This is based on H.M.C., *9th Report*, appendix 2, pp 306-11; A.J. Otway-Ruthven, C. McNeill (eds), *Dowdall deeds* (I.M.C., 1960); *Ormonde deeds*, iv-vi; C.A. Empey, 'The Butler lordship in Ireland, 1185-1515' (Ph.D., T.C.D., 1970), pp 492-3; P.R.O.I., Ferguson MSS xiii, p. 82; In 1594 grievances among tenants on the earl of Ormond's estate were so considerable that a special commission had to be appointed to deal with them, *Ormonde deeds* vi, pp 8-9.

[72] *Second report from commissioners on the public records of Ireland* (1812) (Dublin, 1815), p. 264.

[73] SL, 17, no. 2.

compounded by the socially selective nature of the migration to Ireland which meant that good tenants were even harder to find. Landlords tried to vet tenants as best they could in order to obtain reliable ones who would not exploit their land but develop it.[74] The process of vetting could be carried out when potential tenants applied to a lord with a bid for a tenancy which the lord accepted or rejected. The criteria used to judge the bid were often economic as in Fermanagh, where the bids of the native Irish were usually accepted because the rent offered was higher than that of the settlers.[75] To persuade tenants of sufficient quality to apply for land which was plentiful, landlords offered extra inducements. The earl of Cork offered loans at little or no interest to make his tenants dependent on him and in Tyrone, Sir George Hamilton provided houses to attract tenants. To encourage tenants to improve some landlords offered compensation to tenants for any improvements made during the term of the lease and most landlords allowed tenants to sell their leases but only after giving the landlord first refusal. In some areas the custom grew up whereby the landlord offered the sitting tenant the first right of renewal when the lease expired if the tenant had been satisfactory: the 'tenant right' of the late seventeenth-century Ulster commentators. The lord also provided services, such as legal protection, as was the case in the countess of Kildare's attempt to stop recusancy fines being levied on her tenants.[76]

Thus bonds grew up between landlord and tenants which were neither economic nor legal. The consequences of such bonds were experienced by Francis Lloyd, a servant on Lord Herbert's estate in county Kerry, who complained of the loyalty of tenants on disputed land to the other claimant, Lord Baltinglass, and in Monaghan Thomas Petre, a

---

[74] *Ormond MSS*, n.s., i, pp 20-21; on shortage of tenants, SP46/91, f 10ᵛ; SP63/164/26, 39.

[75] *Herbert corresp.*, no. 161; *Ormond MSS*, n.s., i, pp 22, 24; P. O'Gallachair, 'A Fermanagh survey' in *Clogher Record*, ii (1957-9), pp 296, 310; Cunningham, 'Political and social change', p. 232.

[76] Ranger, 'Richard Boyle', pp 114, 181; H.M.C., *Hastings*, iv, p. 171; Bodl., Rawlinson C 439, n.f., n.d., Lord Deputy Falkland to countess of Kildare. In 1624 when three of Boyle's tenants were involved in a Star Chamber case he paid their expenses and gave them the use of his Dublin house for the duration of the trial, *Lismore papers* 1st. ser. ii, p. 129. W.H. Crawford, 'Landlord tenant relations in Ulster 1609-1820' in *Ir. Econ. and Social Hist.* ii (1975) pp 6-12; H.F. Hore, 'The archaeology of Irish tenant right' in *U.J.A.* 1st ser. vi (1858) p 121-3; R.J. Hunter, 'The Ulster plantation in the counties of Armagh and Cavan' (M.Litt., T.C.D., 1969), pp 423-4, 523-4.

Dubliner who purchased land there, complained that not only would his tenants not pay rent but they would not 'acknowledge him for their landlord' because their loyalty was to the previous owner.[77] Tenants expected 'good lordship' from their landlord and failure to exercise this by not providing facilities for them or behaving in a tyrannical manner meant that they could leave him.[78] Conversely, a good lord would receive the loyalty of his tenants and fulsome praise from them. The settlers on the Grocers' proportion in county Londonderry, for instance, said of the Grocers' agent, Robert Harrington, that 'so kindly and so uprightly has he dealt with us that we cannot but much desire we may never change him for any other whatsoever'.[79]

The low population levels in most of the settled areas of Ireland combined with the landlords' desire to obtain a tight hold over their tenants for political reasons meant that the sort of quasi-legal, paternal relationship described above, sprang up in many areas. Even in areas where landholding was scattered and a paternal relationship was difficult to establish because the authority of the lord was weak, it still took root to some extent. In other areas where population was thinly scattered and agriculture was mainly pastoral, boundaries were rarely disputed so that there was little need for such services as manor courts and thus no such relationship between lord and tenant evolved.

The reaction of the central administration to this landlord-tenant relationship was hostile since it resembled the lord-follower situation which, it was held, had caused many sixteenth-century rebellions because the lord could count on the loyalty of his followers in rebellion. Oliver Cromwell condemned the relationship as injustice, tyranny and oppression of landlords because it did not conform to English legal principles and in county Londonderry, allegations were made during the inquiry of 1631 that the companies had subjected their tenants to a tyranny unsurpassed by even that of the Inquisition.[80] The tenants' reactions to the system were very different and many exploited it for their own ends. Patrick Groome O'Dufferin, for example, realised that there was

---

[77] *Herbert corresp.*, no. 127; N.L.I., 'Reports on special collections', no. 142, p. 1326.

[78] Moody, *Londonderry plantation*, pp 325-6; O'Gallachair, 'Fermanagh survey', p. 302.

[79] Moody, *Londonderry plantation*, p. 324.

[80] W. Abbott (ed.), *The writings and speeches of Oliver Cromwell* (Cambridge, Mass., 1939), ii, pp 186-7; Moody, *Londonderry plantation*, p. 263.

a lack of suitable tenants on Sir Claud Hamilton's estate in Tyrone and so accumulated all of it into his own hands within three years and subsequently sublet it. In other areas, such as the Herbert estate in Kerry, substantial middlemen played on this lack of suitable tenants to engross more land into their hands and many small Connacht landowners likewise took the opportunity to enlarge their holdings by becoming middlemen.[81] This was a risky development for the landlord since it could result in some tenants becoming sufficiently powerful to present a challenge to their authority and so some, such as the earls of Clanrickard and Thomond, monitored the activities of their tenants carefully to ensure that none of them would become too powerful.[82]

IV

The economic base on which all these social arrangements rested varied considerably throughout Ireland. There was considerable variation in natural resources, social practices and the sixteenth-century basis for agricultural practice throughout the country. Munster, for example, specialised mainly in cattle and sheep during the early seventeenth century. The pale grew more corn and in the areas around the major towns of Dublin, Cork and Galway, agriculture tended to be more commercialised in order to supply the towns with food but in all areas the pace of agricultural change was slow.[83] The main engine of change, population, grew unevenly and the total population of Ireland was still small in 1641. One commentator complained 'that there are not enough [men] therein [Ireland] to maintain agriculture or manufacture'. While the evidence is very patchy it is probable that in the country as a whole labourer's wages remained relatively stable in the early seventeenth century suggesting that the population increase resulting from immigration had little effect on the labour market. This is not surprising given the considerable amounts of land available for settlement on easy terms allowing most settlers to acquire their own land rather than work for others. Indeed,

---

[81] Edinburgh Univ. Lib., Laing MSS II, no. 5; *Herbert corresp.*, no. 161; J. Graham, 'Rural society in Connacht' in *Ir. geog. studies*, pp 200-01.

[82] Cunningham, 'Political and social change', pp 200-7.

[83] N.L.W., Powis Castle, Deeds and documents, nos 14611, 15290; J. O'Donovan, *An economic history of livestock in Ireland* (Cork, 1940), p. 35.

one of the main reasons why the proposed plantation of Connacht in the late 1630s failed was a lack of settlers. Labour was scarce and settlers had considerable problems in obtaining household and agricultural servants.[84] There was even some pirating of apprentices from Middlesex in 1615 when Richard Lightfoot of High Holborn, London, was accused of enticing apprentices from their masters to go to Ireland.[85] The shortage of labour was dramatically demonstrated in the early weeks of the 1641 rising where the depositions show the rebels taking considerable care of skilled labourers and making them work for them. Nevertheless the population did expand, possibly even doubling between 1600 and 1641, and by the 1620s Munster even had sufficient surplus population to supply migrants to America. This increased population caused modification of agricultural activity, especially in field systems as previously scattered strips were consolidated to provide for more labour intensive and efficient farming. In some western areas this was paralleled by a move towards primogeniture and the breakdown of the older gavelkind system as the population of Connacht rose significantly in the early seventeenth century as a result of migration from the pale and England.[86]

The role of the landlord in agricultural change is difficult to assess. Most landowners in early seventeenth century Ireland made some attempt to improve their estates, especially if like the earl of Clanrickard they had been in contact with English society. Clanrickard introduced improving clauses in his leases, as did many landlords, but it was difficult to enforce them. In county Cavan, for instance, many tenants simply ignored such clauses and eviction was difficult since it was hard to find new tenants.[87] In Munster Richard Boyle, earl of Cork also

---

[84] B.L., Egerton 2533, f 121ᵛ; *New hist. Ire.*, iii, p. 263; McCuarta, 'Newcomers', pp 32, 42-3; P.R.O.I., Chancery Bills AA 56; B.L., Cotton Titus B, xii, f. 120.

[85] W.H. Hardy (ed.), *Calendar of the session records (Middlesex), 1612-18*, n.s., iii (London, 1941), pp 175-6.

[86] SP63/164/39; SP63/158/22; SP63/145/32; SP63/189/48; G. MacNiocaill (ed.), 'Seven documents from the Inchiquin archive' in *Anal. Hib.*, xxvi (1970), pp 48, 55; Cunningham, 'Political and social change', p. 158; O'Dowd, 'Landownership', pp 484-5, 523-9.

[87] Cunningham, 'Political and social change', p. 234; *Cal. S.P. Ire., 1633-47*, p. 3; R.J. Hunter, 'English undertakers in the plantation of Ulster' in *Breifne*, iv (1973-5), p. 483; on this point in an English context, M. Havinden, 'Lime as a means of agricultural improvement: a Devon example' in C.W. Chalkin, M.A. Havinden (eds), *Rural change and urban growth, 1550-1800* (London, 1974), pp 126-9.

conducted an intensive campaign of agricultural improvement including orchard planting, enclosing and building which had a considerable impact on the area although Boyle's efforts may have been
motivated as much by social emulation of his English contemporaries as
by economic motives. Boyle's task was eased by the relatively high
population level and sixteenth-century background of plantation in
Munster and the efficient way in which his estates were managed. His
task was also made easier by the close trading links between parts of
Munster and south-west England and by Boyle's wide range of personal
contacts in England which made borrowing and obtaining bills of exchange easier than in many other parts of the country. As a result
Munster towns escaped many of the urban problems experienced in
other parts of the country arising from unstable merchant communities
and inability to obtain credit. In the midlands and county Sligo landowners also introduced new agricultural techniques such as liming and
marling and brought in new breeds of sheep and cattle. In general
however there was little real incentive to introduce agricultural innova-
tions into early seventeenth-century Ireland.[88] Population remained
low and, at least until the 1620s, the food supply from traditional forms
of agriculture was sufficient. Rents were still low and land abundant so
there was little pressure to increase production in order to raise income
to meet rising rents. Such innovation as there was spread slowly and
many sixteenth century agricultural practices such as ploughing by
horse's tail and pulling wool off sheep's backs remained, mainly
because they were well adapted to the environment. In the case of
ploughing by tail some contemporaries argued that it was superior to
using normal horse tackle since an English horse collar actually impeded
ploughing because the soil was so heavy.[89]

In one area of improvement, that of exploitation of mineral
resources, east Ulster fell behind other regions. The earl of Cork, for example, developed the iron deposits on his Munster lands and in other
areas of Munster searches were made for gold, copper and silver.
Searches were also begun in other places for minerals, such as alum,
iron, coal and copper. As a result of this, industries such as iron working

[88] McCuarta, 'Newcomers', pp 160-61; O'Dowd, 'Landownership', pp 542-3; Ranger
'Richard Boyle', pp 97-8, 118. K. Thomas, *Man and the Natural World* (London, 1983)
pp 204-10 for the 'social' aspect of tree planting.
[89] Bodl., Clarendon MSS ii, nos 61, 62, 80, 99; *Cal. S.P. Ire., 1611-14*, p. 432.

and glass-making developed in the midlands and soap-making was begun in county Londonderry. In general processing industries for agricultural products were little developed and most material such as wool, was exported in its raw state.[90] Some areas excelled in certain types of manufactures. To judge from the exports of the 1620s Ulster's strength was in linen yarn, tallow and, to a lesser extent, hides. Munster, on the other hand, was strongest in timber exported in the form of pipe and barrel staves. Connacht provided large quantities of hides, tallow and barrelled beef. On balance however east Ulster probably fared little worse than most areas in economic development. Nevertheless there were major problems. Throughout the country most landlords did not have capital to invest and the failure of towns to expand in many areas during the early seventeenth century together with the lack of stable merchant communities for trading and investment purposes stunted the development of agriculture. As a result by 1623 there were even complaints that the food supply of Ireland was not keeping pace with the rapid population growth but as that growth was already beginning to tail off the situation never reached crisis proportions. Agriculture was not the only area to be badly hit and there were also complaints that tradesmen were adversely affected by their inability to borrow money. Indeed in 1622 the Mayor and citizens of Londonderry informed the Commissioners for Irish Causes that they had repeatedly petitioned the controling body of the Londonderry plantation, the Irish Society, to send over money 'to lie in bank where tradesmen, for a reasonable consideration upon good security, might get money and keep themselves in employment'.[91]

V

It is tempting to compare east Ulster with other colonial areas such as the contemporary American settlements but such a comparison would not

[90] Ranger 'Richard Boyle', ch. 5; *Cal. S.P. Ire., 1633-47*, pp 5, 85; Moody, *Londonderry plantation*, p. 344; *Advertisements for Ire.*, p. 8, 31-2; Cullen, *Emergence of modern Ireland*, p. 112; N.P. Canny, *The Elizabethan conquest of Ireland* (Hassocks, 1976), pp 6-7; for the spread of the glass industry, E.S. Godfrey, *The development of English Glassmaking* (Oxford, 1975), pp 86, 121, 127-8, 156, 169-70, 192; D. Westropp (M. Boydell ed.) *Irish Glass*, (Dublin, 1978), pp 20-32.
[91] *New hist. Ire.*, iii, pp 175-6; *Commons' jn. Ire.*, i, p. 32; R.J. Hunter, 'Ulster plantation towns, 1609-41' in D. Harkness, M. O'Dowd (eds), *The town in Ireland: Historical*

have been approved of by contemporaries. While they saw Ireland as part of a general colonial spread they rarely made more detailed comparisons between their colonies.[92] Sir Francis Bacon, for example, considered the settlement of Virginia as 'an enterprise in my opinion differing as much from this [the settlement of Ireland] as *Amadis de Gaul* differs from Caesar's *Commentaries'*.[93] Occasionally comparisons were made which highlighted the differences between the two settlements. Richard Hakluyt, the Tudor explorer and colonizer, for example, differentiated strongly between Ireland, which he felt would be difficult to colonize because of its 'warlike' inhabitants, and America, which he felt would be easy to settle.[94] Even those who had settled in Ireland and later played a part in the colonization of the New World seem not to have applied Irish lessons to their later experience. The settlement of Newfoundland in the 1620s for instance involved a number of those who had Irish experience — Sir George Calvert and Lord Falkland, for example — yet rarely did they refer to their Irish experience in the framing of the plans for the new colony.[95] This is not to argue that Ireland and America were kept totally separate in the minds of contemporaries. Both were colonial ventures and many men, fired with the spirit of adventure, were involved in both projects.[96] Furthermore many problems were common to settlers in both east Ulster and America, in particular, the problem of the definition of property boundaries, the low level of population and the problem of dealing with the indigenous inhabitants. Reactions to the new environments were sometimes similar and some American settlers bound themselves into tight communities with rigid social codes as did the east Ulster settlers.[97]

Studies, xiii, (Belfast, 1981), pp 67-78; O'Sullivan, *Econ. hist. Cork city*, ch. 5; *Advertisements for Ire.*, p. 33. D.A. Chart (ed.), *Londonderry and the London Companies, 1609-29* (HMSO, 1928) p. 57.

[92] W.J. Smyth, 'The western isle of Ireland and the eastern seaboard of America' in *Ir. geog.*, xi (1978), p. 1.

[93] Spedding, *Life and letters*, iv, p. 123.

[94] D.B. Quinn, A. Quinn (eds), *The Virginia voyages of Hakluyt* (Oxford, 1973), p. 92.

[95] See G.T. Cell (ed.), *Newfoundland discovered: English attempts at colonization 1610-1630* (London, 1982).

[96] For examples of links, Quinn, *Elizabethans & Irish*, ch. ix.

[97] D.F. Konig, 'Community, custom and the common law: social change and the development of land boundaries in seventeenth century Massachusetts' in *Am. jnl legal hist.*, xviii (1976), pp 133-77.

However, these resemblances can be misleading since the structure of the two settlements was very different due to diversity of opportunity and environment.[98] While east Ulster became an extension of west Scotland, America remained isolated with few contacts with the homeland and ties of landownership, kinship and debt were irrevocably broken by the traumatic Atlantic crossing. Ultimately, the American colonist's solution to his problems differed from that of his counterpart in east Ulster. He was not constrained, except in Baltimore, by a manorial structure nor was he hemmed in by the presence of royal officials such as sheriffs or escheators. The colonists in New England, for example, were allowed to frame their own law codes and work within them.[99] The problems with natives are also dissimilar since the Indian was an unknown entity to the American settlers while the natives of east Ulster had been well known to the English and Scots for four hundred years and there had been considerable trade with them in the sixteenth century. Moreover New England settlements had a degree of cohesion which the Irish settlements never attained. The puritan ideology which inspired some of those who settled in the New World together with their desire to build a godly society was much less common among the settlers in Ireland. There is, for example, no Irish parallel of the church or town covenants which became an integral part of early New England life. While this attitude was to break down among the second generation of New England settlers it did form an important stabilising influence in the early years of the settlement.[100] Nor does the settlement in Virginia, which was almost exactly contemporary with that in Ulster, provide any closer parallel with the Irish situation. Before the governorship of Sir William Berkeley the administration of the Virginia settlement can best be described as chaotic. Attempts to establish a coherent system of local government broke up in disorder and the drive for profit among the settlers was left unconstrained. Any attempt to establish a stable pattern of settlement, which included urban settlement, was doomed to failure as settlers pressed inland in search of rapid profits from tobacco. Perhaps

98 Smyth, 'Western isle', pp 2-3, 10-14; J.T. Lemon, 'Early Americans and their social environment' in *Jnl Historical Geography*, vi (1980), pp 115-31.

99 W.M. Billings, 'The transfer of English law to Virginia' in K.R. Andrews, N.P. Canny, P.E.H. Hair (eds), *The westward enterprise* (Liverpool, 1978), pp 215-44.

100 R. Gillespie, 'The evolution of an Ulster urban network, 1600-41' in *I.H.S.*, xxiv, (1984), pp 15-29.

the most significant differences between the Virginian settlement and that of Ireland was the almost total lack of a 'gentry' group in Virginia which would have given cohesion to the settlement and acted as broker between the tenant settlers and the Virginia Company by assuming local offices. It was not until the 1650s when the settlement had already been established forty years that the problem was tackled by Governor Berkeley when he created a crude system of local government and separated out an elite to man the administration, men who were to become the 'gentry' of Virginia.[101]

In many ways these differences reflected the fact that the American experience was complementary to the Irish one. The American situation was the result of a migration of considerable distance as against a short move, a different demographic and economic structure to that of Ireland, a new world as opposed to one known to the English since the twelfth century and an ineffective system of local government compared with one which was tightening its hold on the Irish localities in the early seventeenth century.[102]

What east Ulster represents is neither early seventeenth-century Ireland nor America in microcosm. There were no 'laws' for plantation, simply the adjustment of settlers to a new environment and the consequent building of a social, economic and political structure to suit it. Inevitably east Ulster shared many of the problems of the rest of colonial Ireland and adopted similar solutions but, as has been suggested above, it had its own distinctive features arising out of its own problems. It is only through a series of studies of different areas, in social, economic and political terms, and relating these to the activities of the central administration that a balanced picture of early modern Irish society will emerge.

---

[101] This is based on K.A. Lockridge, *Settlement and unsettlement in early America* (Cambridge, 1981), ch. 2, especially pp 71-9; E.S. Morgan, *American slavery, American freedom: the ordeal of colonial Virginia,* (Norton, 1975).

[102] N.P. Canny, 'The Anglo-American colonial experience' in *Hist. jnl,* xxiv (1981), p. 489.

EPILOGUE

THE AIM OF THIS analysis has been to demonstrate that in east Ulster, and to a lesser extent in Ireland generally, a special type of social organization developed in the early seventeenth century. The society described was characterised by a period of consolidation of landed, political and economic interests in the early years of the seventeenth century as both settler and native attempted to adjust to a changed political situation in the aftermath of the military conquest of 1603 which had brought all Ireland under the control of the Dublin administration. Initially this process was supported by the central administration, which was prepared to grant considerable privileges to local landowners in return for the cheap and rapid establishment of stability and order. By the end of the first decade of the century this policy had been reversed, but the large power blocks already created remained in the countryside. Settler landlords, most of whom had been driven to Ireland by ambition or a chance of financial gain, were unwilling to give up their new found power bases. Conflict was inevitable as the central government attempted to tighten its hold on the localities in the 1620s and 1630s, especially under Lord Deputy Wentworth. These political tensions coincided with a series of social and economic crises in the 1630s, which resulted from the unstable economic foundation of the Antrim and Down settlement. Low population, insufficient development of the economic base, and a scarcity of investment capital among the landed elite, were indicative of the problems inherent in the economic structure of the settlement which sharpened the detrimental impact of the harvest failures of the late 1630s. The coincidence of a political crisis in the 1630s — the Black Oath and the Covenanter disturbances — with an economic one; shortage of labour and cash, increasing landlord debt, and poor harvests, posed a serious problem for the structure of society in east Ulster. However these crises were subsumed in a more general one precipitated by the outbreak of rebellion in 1641, which proved to be a major catalyst in restructuring Irish society.

By the later seventeenth century, society in east Ulster was radically different from its pre-1641 counterpart. Both the size of the population and the dynamics of growth had altered appreciably by 1660 since most of the pre-1641 setttlers had left to be replaced with new colonists. The structures of local government were overhauled by the Cromwellian administration and the effects of the Cromwellian and Restoration land settlements undermined the confidence of the Ulster landlords. As a result of the rebellion and the heavy taxation of the Cromwellian era, which placed a heavy strain on already shaky finances, most landlords were in a weak financial position in the 1660s. Old settlers sold out, and new landlords such as George Rawdon, William Waring and John Magill, took their place. Other settler families, previously of minor importance, such as the Wards of Castleward in Lecale, were poised to take advantage of these circumstances and rose to prominence with the decline of the older families. It was the task of these new men to shape a different society within the legal, social, economic, and political parameters of their own age.

APPENDIX A: VITAL STATISTICS

A:i Age and marital status of heirs on father's death in east Ulster
     Source: *Inq. Ult.*

Age group	Antrim		Down	
	married	single	married	single
0-15	0	9	0	3
16-19	0	4	0	2
20-4	1	2	2	1
25-9	1	0	1	0
30-4	0	0	6	0
35-9	1	0	0	0
40-4	1	0	0	0
45	1	0	1	0
Total	5	15	10	6

A:ii Letters of denization sued for east Ulster settlers, 1605-35
      Source: W.A. Shaw, *Letters of denization and acts of naturalization,*
      (Huguenot Society, Lymington, 1911)

1605- 9	4
1610-14	9
1615-19	104
1620-24	26
1625- 9	22
1630-35	24

A:iii '1641 ages' of east Ulster deponents
       Sources: T.C.D., MSS 837, 838

age group	number of deponents
20-4	5
25-9	8
30-4	16
35-9	6
40-4	16
45-9	5
50-4	9
55-9	4
60-4	6
65+	2
Total	77

A:iv   Distribution of Irish forces during the Nine Years War
      Sources: (a) *Cal. Carew, 1589-1600*, p. 73
              (b) *Cal. Carew, 1589-1600*, p. 287
              (c) *Cal. S.P. Ire., 1599-1600*, p. 73
              (d) *Cal. Carew, 1589-1600*, p. 199

Lordship	1592 (a) h.	f.	1598 (b) h.	f.	1599 (c) h.	f.	1599 (d) h.	f.
Killultagh	20	100	–	–	–	–	–	–
Kilwarlin	10	120	–	–	140	1000	10	60
Iveagh	122	610	80				40	300
Upper Clandeboy	80	400	120	300	120	800	50	80
Lower Clandeboy	116	760					20	100
Route	90	700	60	600	140	800	100	100
Glynnes	–	200					–	–

A:v   Distribution of pardons, 1590-1625
      Sources: *Fiants Eliz.*; *Cal. pat. rolls Ire., Jas. I*

Antrim		*Down*	
North Antrim	224	Ards	144
Mid Antrim	176	Iveagh	305
South Antrim	128	Kilwarlin	20
Killultagh	37	Lecale and Dufferin	151
		West Down	32

APPENDIX B: AGRICULTURAL ACTIVITY

B:i Values of stock on farms in east Ulster, 1641

Sources: T.C.D., MS 837, f 80; TCD, MS 836, ff 1-15; E. Berwick, *Rawdon letters*, n.p., 1819, pp 87-8; P.R.O.I., RC9/1, p. 41; P.R.O.N.I., T284, D1905/2/155B.

Where numbers of stock are given, they have been converted to cash equivalents using the valuations in T.C.D., MS 837, f 14.

Name	Location	Cattle	Horses	Sheep	Pigs	Poultry	Corn
		£	£	£	£	£	£
Down							
Christopher Crow	Drumbashelane	20	3	2.17.0		–	18
George Hodgkison		7	7	–		–	–
Christopher Jessen	Newry	9	–	–		–	–
Arthur Magennis	Ballinlary	total agricultural losses £125					
Henry Smith	Aghaderick	180	28	30	6.13.4	4	125
Robert Kinaston	Saul	–	–	–	–	–	6
Antrim							
Hugh Cunningham	Townburgh	20	8	–	–	–	185
Throgmorton Totesbury	Antrim	√[1]	√	√	–	–	800
John Temple	Tullycranagh	400	14	–	–	–	√[3]
Josiah Welsh	Templepatrick	90	–	–	–	–	√[2]
John Mitchell	Letticeland	1340	18.10.0	–	–	–	–
John McMyre	Creeverny	490	9	–	–	–	√[4]

[1] Cattle, etc., known to be present but no value given.
[2] 8 Barrels oats, 2 barrels barley, 1 peck barley.
[3] 13 barrels wheat, 4 stacks wheat.
[4] 13 barrels wheat, 4 stacks wheat.

(227)

B:ii *Stock on Agnew estate c. 1645*

Source: S.R.O., GD 154/514.

Tenant	farm size (acres)	corn (bolls)	barley (pecks)	horses	cows	heifers	bullocks	pigs	sheep
William McCayley	5	2	6	1	4	–	–	6	–
Alexander Dunlop	33	8	10	15	6	4	2	–	40
John Knox	20	2	6	1	5	–	–	–	10
Patrick Agnew	25	7	4	1	4	–	–	–	6
Alexander Russel	30	4	4	1	6	–	–	–	4
Thomas McCoy	7	7	3	2	3	–	–	–	12
John Archbold	15	3	2	–	2	–	–	–	4
Thomas Sillsman	1	1	–	–	–	–	–	–	–
John Mitchell	16	4	4	2	4	1	–	–	14
John Andrew	15	2·5	3	1	1(2)[1]	–	–	–	–
John Barnett	15	2·5	3	1	2(1)	–	–	–	3
Alexander Leech	30	6	6	2	3(1)	–	–	–	6
Adam Bottoun	33	8	10	4	2	4	–	–	40
William Cun	15	3	4	2	2	2	1	–	6
John Cumbill	10	2	2	1	4	–	–	–	–
William Tampson	30	6	5	2	6	–	–	–	10
Caun Mure	10	2	1	1	–	–	–	–	–
Hugh Perbelly	15	2·5	3	1	7	–	–	–	11
John Munopense	18	4·5	3	2	1	–	–	–	12
Total	343	77	79	40	64	11	3	6	178

[1] The figures in brackets indicate how many cows on the lands when the survey was made.

APPENDIX C: THE BUSINESS OF THE
COURT OF WARDS

Sources: T.C.D., MSS 643, 644, 645, 648; P.R.O.I., Lodge MSS, Wards and Liveries 1.

	Antrim			Down		
	wards	liveries	alienations	wards	liveries	alienations
1605-6	–	–	–	1	–	3
1607-8	–	–	–	–	1	1
1609-10	–	–	–	–	–	4
1611-12	–	–	–	1	–	–
1613-14	1	–	–	–	–	–
1615-16	–	–	–	–	–	–
1617-18	–	–	–	–	1	2
1619-20	–	–	–	–	–	–
1621-2	–	–	1	–	–	–
1623-4	–	–	1	–	1	3
1625-6	–	–	–	–	–	–
1627-8	–	–	1	2	2	2
1629-30	–	–	1	–	1	1
1631-2	–	–	2	–	2	9
1633-4	–	1	5	–	4	5
1635-6	–	8	6	2	–	12
1637-8	2	5	6	1	1	5
1639-40	–	1	8	–	–	3
1641	–	–	–	–	1	3

APPENDIX D: STATUS AND LITERACY IN RURAL SOCIETY

D:i *Status and rent level on the earl of Antrim's estate, c. 1635*

Sources: P.R.O.N.I., D 265; D2977; T549/3; LPC 1031; LPC 1059; D282/1; LPC 263; D1835/56A/85; D556/10; D828/2A-C; T1531/1/1.

Rent (in £)	Irish gent.	yeo.	Scots gent.	yeo.	Eng. gent.	yeo.
0-4	5	3	1	0	0	2
5-9	6	5	1	1	2	0
10-14	6	5	7	1	1	2
15-19	2	3	2	1	0	0
20-24	2	2	5	0	4	0
25-9	3	2	1	0	1	0
30-34	0	1	5	0	2	0
35-9	0	0	0	0	0	0
40 +	3	1	3	0	1	0
Total	27	22	25	3	11	4

D:ii *Status and literacy on the earl of Antrim's estate, c. 1635*

Sources: As D: i

	Irish gent.	yeo.	Scots gent.	yeo.	Eng. gent.	yeo.
sign	12	5	20	0	10	2
mark	8	17	4	3	1	2
Total	20[1]	22	24	3	11	4

[1] The discrepancy between these totals and those of D:i is due to seven leases being torn or worn at the bottom.

D:iii *Literacy and sex in east Ulster, c. 1640*

Sources: T.C.D., MSS 837, 838

		Irish m.	f.	Scots m.	f.	Eng. m.	f.	Total
Antrim	sign	15	0	6	0	4	1	26
	mark	32	9	8	6	5	1	61
	total	47	9	14	6	9	2	87
Down	sign	11	0	7	0	12	0	30
	mark	13	2	10	0	14	1	40
	total	24	2	17	0	26	1	70

D:iv *Arms on estates c. 1630*

Landholder	no arms	type of arms												total
		sword	sword & pike	sword & hus-ker	sword & snap-hance	sword & hal-bert	sword & tar-get	pike	halbert	target	snap-hance	musket	culiver	
Earl of Antrim	506	374	4	0	0	0	1	4	1	0	1	1	0	892
Adair	45	44	32	2	14	1	3	8	0	0	4	2	1	156
Clotworthy	229	0	0	0	0	0	0	0	0	0	0	0	0	229
Dalway	38	0	0	0	0	0	0	0	0	0	0	0	0	38
Edmondston	46	21	31	0	1	0	0	23	0	1	2	0	0	125
Hill	11	0	0	0	0	0	0	0	0	0	0	0	0	11
Redding	17	0	0	0	0	0	0	0	0	0	0	0	0	17
Upton	88	0	2	0	0	0	0	2	0	0	0	0	0	92
Montgomery	559	339	0	113	0	1	0	0	0	0	0	0	0	1012
Hamilton	0	0	611	212	67	0	0	38	0	0	0	0	0	928
Kildare	48	76	1	0	0	0	0	0	0	0	0	0	0	125
Cromwell [1]	170	239	9	0	3	1	0	80	1	0	1	1	0	504
Melville	34	12	3	0	0	0	0	1	0	0	0	0	0	50
Bishop of Down and Savage	48	14	9	0	1	2	0	0	0	0	2	0	0	76

[1] Not including the force at his ironworks. Source: BL. Add., 4770.

APPENDIX E: ESTIMATES OF LANDED WEALTH c. 1635

| | Subsidy Payable | | Wealth | | |
	In land	In goods	In land	In goods	Total
Earl of Antrim	2000	400	10000	3077	13077
Hugh, Visc. Montgomery	400	80	2000	615	2615
James, Visc. Clandeboy	750	150	3750	1154	4904
Thomas Visc. Lecale	400	80	2000	615	2615
Edward Chichester	1500	300	7500	2308	9808
Edward Visc. Conway	400	80	2000	615	2615
Lady Magennis	75	15	375	115	490
Hugh, Visc. Magennis	200	40	1000	308	2308

Source: SL 24/25 no. 152.   All amounts in £ sterling

APPENDIX F: THE ACTIVITIES OF EAST ULSTER M.P.s, 1613-35

Numbers of committees sat on
Source: *Commons' jn. Ire.* i

1613-14	sess. 1	sess. 2
Sir F. Conway	2	0
Moses Hill	2	0
Thos Hibbots	0	0
Humphry Johnston	0	0
J. Blennerhasset	1	0
George Trevilian	0	0
Sir J. Hamilton	4	5
Sir H. Montgomery	3	1
Richard Wingfield	0	0
Richard West	0	0
Arthur Basset	1	0
John Leigh	0	0
Edward Brabason	0	0
John Dalway	0	1
Edward Trevor	1	0
John Hamilton	0	0
George Cunningham	0	0
James Cathcart	0	0

1634-5	sess. 1	sess. 2	sess. 3	sess. 4
Hugh Montgomery	4	4	0	0
Sir Edward Trevor	3	3	4	4
Arthur Chichester	1	0	0	0
Sir John Clotworthy	0	5	6	1
Henry Upton	0	0	1	1
Sir Thomas Hibbots	0	0	0	0
Charles Price	0	0	0	0
Thomas Bramston	0	0	0	0
James Hamilton	0	0	0	0
Edward Kinaston	0	0	0	0
William Billingsly	0	0	0	0
Robert Loftus	0	0	0	0
Sir A. Terringham	3	0	1	2
Sir Arthur Basset	0	2	1	0
Mathew Brabazon	0	0	1	0
Walter White	0	0	0	0
Paul Reynolds	0	0	0	0
Sir Thos Meredith	1	0	0	0

APPENDIX G: OCCUPATIONS OF BELFAST FREEMEN, 1635-44

Source: R.M. Young, *The town book of the Corporation of Belfast,* Belfast, 1892.

Occupation	1635-9	1640-44
Gentleman	5	11
Merchant	10	10
Shoe maker	4	1
Carpenter	1	0
Joiner	2	0
Clothier	4	0
Weaver	1	0
Tailor	2	1
Glove maker	1	0
Felter	1	0
Tanner	0	2
Wheelwright	1	0
Smith	2	0
Brazier	0	2
Candlemaker	0	1
Glazier	1	0
Chandler	1	0
Inn keeper	0	1
Butcher	2	0
Husbandman	1	1
Servant	2	1
Soldier	0	5
Unknown	11	47
Total	52	83

BIBLIOGRAPHY

This bibliography is, of necessity, select. I have not included works cited in J.G. Simms, 'Bibliography' in *New hist. Ire.*, iii, since full bibliographical references to standard works will be found there. In the case of manuscripts where a title to a collection exists it has been given. Since it is not possible to describe accurately volumes of miscellaneous papers I have preferred to identify them by number alone.

Arrangement

      I   Manuscript sources
     II   Contemporary pamphlets
   III Printed sources
   IV Secondary works

I MANUSCRIPT SOURCES

A *Bodleian Library, Oxford*
      Carte MSS
      Clarendon MSS
      Corpus Christi College MS 297
      Laud MSS
      Rawlinson MSS
      University College MS 103 Rental of the Bagnall estate, 1575

B *British Library, London*

Additional		
	4756	Report of 1622 commission
	4770	Muster roll of Ulster *c.* 1630
	4787	Ware MSS
	4820	Funeral entries, 1634-1729
	11033	Letter book of Lord Deputy Falkland, 1620-33
	11328	
	18824	Letter book of Lord Deputy Falkland, April 1628-July 1629
	19837-42	Chancery recognisances, 1570-1634
	19843-4	Register of the statute staple, 1638-62

	19848	
	34313	
	39853	Cornwallis MSS
	40815-7	Yelverton MSS
	41613	
	46920	Perceval papers
Cotton	Titus B X	
	Titus B XII	
	Titus B XIII	
	Augustus I	
Egerton	212	Observations on the Irish records by Dr. Ledwich
	2333	
Harley	430	Lord deputy Wentworth's petition book, July 1637-March 1638
	2099	Letters patent to the earl of Antrim
	2138	Charles Monck's survey of the customs *c.* 1637
	2183	
	3292	Letters patent to the earl of Antrim
	4297	Commission on ecclesiastical affairs, 1633-4
	5938	
Lansdowne	156	
Royal 18A	LIII	Tracts relating to Ulster
18A	LXV	Ibid.
Sloane	29	Observations of the government, state and condition of the people of Ireland, April 1640
	1856	
	3827	

C *Cambridge University Library, Cambridge*
  Additional 4352
  KK.a. 1.5   Sixteenth century state papers re Ireland

D *Devon County Record Office, Exeter*
  1262M   Chichester MSS

E *East Suffolk Record Office, Ipswich*
  HA 12   Adair MSS

F *Edinburgh University Library, Edinburgh*
  Laing MSS

G *Leeds City Library, Leeds*
    TN/P07   Papers relating to Irish customs, 1612-15

H *Marsh's Library, Dublin*
    Z1.1.13
    Z3.2.5
    Z3.2.6

I *National Library of Ireland, Dublin*
    MSS 8013-15 Rich MSS
    MS 8792   Hamilton MSS
    MS 15584   Copy of patent to Lord Viscount Ards, 1638
    Harris's 'Collectanea de rebus Hibernicis'

J *National Library of Scotland, Edinburgh*
    Delmilne MSS

K *National Library of Wales, Aberystwyth*
    Cross of Shaw Hill MSS
    Powis Castle, Deeds

L *Public Record Office, London*
    C.   Chancery Bills
    SP46   State papers, misc.
    SP62, SP63 State papers, Ireland
    CO 388/85/A15 Irish exports, 1628
    MPF 35   Sixteenth century maps of Ulster
          67   (full descriptions contained in P.R.O.
          77   *Maps and plans*, below)
          86
          87
          88
          89
          92
          93
          98

M *Public Record Office of Ireland, Dublin*
    C562   Hamilton patents
    C564   Hamilton patents
    D20559   Cromwell deeds
    Papers relating to the Colville family: C3446-7, C3450,
      D15237-40
    M2445   Letter book of Lord Deputy Falkland, 1629-33
    M13856   Victualling rolls for army, 1600-3

R.C.   Records of the Record Commissioners
Chancery pleadings
Ferguson MSS
Lodge MSS
Thrift MSS

N *Public Record Office of Northern Ireland, Belfast*

Papers relating to the Adair family:
    D929
    D1430
    D828

Papers relating to the earl of Antrim:
D265	LPC 1246
D282	LPC 1333
D350	LPC 1339
D1835	T473
D2171	T549
D2977	T1531
LPC 253	T2490
LPC 1058	

Papers relating to the Chichester family:
D389	T666
D778	T712
D811	T956
D1905	T1009

Papers relating to the Clotworthy family:
D207	T472
D562	T966
D685	T1139

Papers relating to the Conway family:
    T268
    T343
    T744

Papers relating to the Cromwell family:
D546	LPC 1633
D1556	T646
LPC 137	

Papers relating to the Edmonston family:
D1255
T815
T1030

Papers relating to the Hamilton family:

D1071B	T893
T761	T1065
T776	T1128
T808/2758	T1878
T870	

Papers relating to the Hill family:
D671

Papers relating to the Magennis family:
T185
T588

Papers relating to the Montgomery family:

D556	T1030
D646	T1089

Papers relating to the O'Neill family:
T1287
T1289

Papers relating to the Savage family:
D558
D585

Papers relating to the Trevor family:
D778
D1255

Papers relating to towns:

(a) Newry	T618	
(b) Carrickfergus	T668	T707
	T686	T1107

Papers relating to the church:

D104	T975
T284	D1759
T808/15309	T1275

Other material relating to east Ulster:

D302	T835
D765	T1110

T695	T1180
T765	T2171
T811	Mic 1/3
T2860/13	

O *Scottish Record Office, Edinburgh*

CC9	Ayrshire wills
GD8	Boyd MSS
GD10	
GD25	Ailsa Muniments
GD26	
GD27	Dalquaharran writs
GD39	Glencairn Muniments
GD86	
GD90	Yule papers
GD97	Dunreath Muniments
GD103	Society of Antiquaries, Scotland papers
GD109	Bargany papers
GD138	Galloway charters
GD149	
GD154	Agnew papers
GD180	Cathcart of Greenock MSS
GD214	
GD219	Murray of Murraythwaite papers
GD237	
RH9	
RH11	Deed book of Kilwinning
RH15/39	Haddington papers
RH15/91	Maxwell of Orchardtown papers
RS	Registers of sasines

Acts and decrees of the Lords of Session

P *Sheffield City Library, Sheffield*
    Wentworth Woodhouse Muniments

Q *Syon House, Northumberland*
    MSS Y.11.26 (N.L.I., microfilm p. 3682)

R *Trinity Collge, Dublin*
    MS 570
    MS 572
    MS 664
    MS 672
    MS 743

MS 804
MS 837   1641 Depositions, Co. Down
MS 838   1641 Depositions, Co. Antrim
MS 1059
MS 2512   Index to fines in the court of common pleas,
           1603-84
Mun. P.   College muniments

II CONTEMPORARY PAMPHLETS

W. Basil. *Two letters of William Basil.* London, 1649.
R. Bolton. *A justice of the peace for Ireland.* Dublin, 1638.
A declaration by the presbytery of Bangor in Ireland, July 7 1649. N.p., 1649.
R. Eburn. *A plain pathway to plantations.* London, 1624.
A glorious victory obtained by the Scots against rebels in Ireland. London, 1642.
D. Harcourt. *The clergies lamentation.* London, 1644.
The humble petition of the protestant inhabitants of the counties of Antrim, Down, Tyrone . . . concerning the bishops. London, 1641.
H. Leslie. *A treatise of the authority of the church.* Dublin, 1637.
_____ *A full confutation of the covenant lately sworn.* London, 1639.
News from Ireland concerning the proceedings of the presbytery in the county of Antrim in Ireland. London, 1650.
R. Pike. *A true description of the Scots and English in the north of Ireland.* London, 1642.
A true relation of the proceedings of the Scottish army now in Ireland by three letters. London, 1642.

III PRINTED SOURCES

J. Ainsworth. 'Reports of documents in private hands.' In *Anal. Hib.*, xx (1958).
_____ 'Survey of documents in private keeping'. In *Anal. Hib.*, xxv (1967).
L. Alston (ed.). *De republica Anglorum.* Cambridge, 1906.
Anon. 'Bodley's visit to Lecale'. In *U.J.A.*, 1st ser., ii (1854).
_____ 'Marshall Bagnall's description of Ulster'. In *U.J.A.*, 1st ser., ii (1854).
O. Bergin (ed.). *Irish bardic poetry.* Dublin, 1970.
J. Bliss, W. Scott (eds). *The works of the most reverend father in God William Laud.* 7 vols. Oxford, 1847-60.

J. Cameron (ed.). *The letters of John Johnston and Robert Howie.* Edinburgh, 1963.

N. Canny (ed.), 'Rowland White's "Discourse of Ireland" '. In *I.H.S.*, xx (1976-7).

G.T. Cell (ed.). *Newfoundland discovered: English attempts at colonisation, 1610-30.* London, 1982.

J.P. Cooper, J. Thirsk (eds). *Seventeenth century economic documents.* Oxford, 1972.

P. de Brun, B. Ó Buachalla, T. Ó Concheanainn (eds). *Nua dhuanaire,* i. Dublin, 1975.

J.F. Ferguson (ed.). 'The Ulster roll of gaol delivery'. In *U.J.A.* 1st ser., i (1853).

W.J. Fullerton (ed.). T. Pont, *Topographical account of the district of Cunningham.* Glasgow, 1858.

J. Haig (ed.). *The historical works of Sir James Balfour.* 4 vols. Edinburgh, 1824-5.

D.R. Hainsworth (ed.). *The commercial papers of Sir Christopher Lowther.* Surtees Society, Newcastle upon Tyne, 1977.

G.J. Hand (ed.). 'Rules and orders to be observed in the proceeding of causes in the high court of chancery in Ireland'. In *Ir. Jurist,* n.s., ix (1974).

W.H. Hardy (ed.). *Calendar of the assize records (Middlesex), 1612-18.* n.s., 3 vols, London, 1941.

Historical Manuscripts Commission, Reports:

4th Report
5th Report
6th Report
7th Report
8th Report
9th Report
15th Report
Denbeigh MSS
Egmont MSS
Eglinton MSS
Franciscan MSS
Hastings MSS
Laing MSS
L'Isle and Dudley MSS
Mar MSS
Various MSS, iii
Various MSS, v
Various MSS, viii
Salisbury MSS

E. Hogan (ed.). *A history of the war in Ireland*. Dublin, 1873.

_____ *A description of Ireland, c. 1598*. Dublin, 1878.

T. Houston (ed.). *A brief relation of the life of Mr. John Livingston*. Edinburgh, 1845.

Inquisitionum ad capellam domini regis returnatorum quae in publicis archivis Scotia. 3 vols. London, 1851-6.

D. Laing (ed.). *Royal letters, charters and tracts relating to the colonisation of New Scotland*. Bannatyne Club, Edinburgh, 1867.

W. Lamont (ed.). *An inventory of Lamont papers*. Edinburgh, 1914.

M. Lenihan (ed.). 'The fee book of a seventeenth century physician'. In *R.S.A.I. Jn.*, ix (1867).

J.R. Lumby (ed.). *Bacon's history of the reign of Henry VII*. Cambridge, 1902.

T. McCrie (ed.). *The life of Robert Blair*. Edinburgh, 1848.

W. McLeod (ed.). 'The protocol book of Robert Brown'. In *Arch. and hist. collections relating to Ayr and Galloway*, vii-ix (1894-5).

J.R.S. McPhail (ed.). *Highland papers*. 3 vols. Scottish History Society, Edinburgh, 1914-20.

H.F. McGeagh (ed.). *Register of admissions to the honourable society of the Middle Temple*. 3 vols. London, 1949.

W.D. Macray (ed.). E. Hyde, earl of Clarendon, *History of the rebellion*. 6 vols. Oxford, 1888.

J.P. Mahaffy (ed.). *The particular book of Trinity College, Dublin*. London, 1904.

J.R. Maidment (ed.). *Letters and papers relative to Irish matters from the Balfour MSS*. Abbotsfort Club, Edinburgh, 1837.

_____ *Letters and state papers during the reign of King James VI*. Abbotsfort Club, Edinburgh, 1838.

W. Mure (ed.). *Selections from the family papers preserved at Caldwell*. Maitland Club, Glasgow, 1856.

W. Notestein (ed.). *The journal of Simon d'Ewes*. Yale, 1923.

P. O'Gallachair (ed.). 'A Fermanagh survey'. In *Clogher Record*, ii (1957-9).

T. O'Raghallaigh (ed.). 'Seanchus Burcach'. In *Galway Arch. Soc. Jnl.*, xiii (1925-8).

Parliamentary papers:

    First report of the comissioners appointed to inquire into the municipal corporations in Ireland (with appendices),

        H.C. 1835 (23, 24, 26), xxvii.

        H.C. 1835 (28), xxviii.

        H.C. 1836 (29), xxiv.

Report from the select committee on manor courts, Ireland,
   H.C. 1837 (494), xv.
   H.C. 1837-8 (648), xvii.
*Report of the commissioners appointed to enquire into the state of fairs
   and markets in Ireland*
   H.C. 1852-3 (1674), lxi.
   H.C. 1854-5 (1910), xix.
Public Record Office. *Maps and Plans in the Public Record Office, i,
   British Isles.* London, 1967.
G.S. Pryne (ed.). *Ayr burgh accounts.* Scottish History Society,
   Edinburgh, 1937.
D.B. Quinn, A. Quinn (eds.). *The Virginia voyages of Hakluyt.* Oxford,
   1973.
G.F. Renehan (ed.). *Collections on Irish church history,* i. Dublin, 1861.
*Reports of the commissioners appointed . . . respecting the public records of
   Ireland.* 3 vols. London, 1815-25.
S.M. Reynolds (ed.). *The tabletalk of John Seldon.* Oxford, 1892.
H.S. Shaw (ed.). *Some family papers of the Hunters of Hunterstown.*
   Scottish Record Society, Edinburgh, 1925.
W.A. Shaw (ed.). *Letters of denization and naturalization.* Huguenot
   Society, Lymington, 1911.
J. Spedding (ed.). *The life and letters of Francis Bacon.* 14 vols.
   London, 1857-74.
State of the parishes, c. 1625. Maitland Club, Glasgow, 1836.
R.S. Terry (ed.). Sir Thomas Craig, *De unione regnum Britanniae tractus.*
   Scottish History Society, Edinburgh, 1909.
V. Treadwell (ed.). 'The plantation of Donegal'. In *Donegal Annual,*
   ii (1951-4).
_____. 'The survey of Armagh and Tyrone'. In *U.J.A.,* 3rd ser., xxiii
   (1960); xxvii (1964).
W. and C. Trevelyan (eds.). *Trevelyan papers.* 3 vols. Camden Society,
   1st ser., London, 1856-72.
R. Van Agnew (ed.). 'Letters by John, fifth earl of Cassills'. In *Arch. and
   hist. collections relating to Ayr, and Galloway,* 1st ser., v (1885).
P. Walsh (ed.). 'Worth and virtue unrequited: an Irish poet and the
   English'. In *I.E.R.,* 5th series, xxxi (1928).
T. Westcote. *A view of Devonshire in 1630.* London, 1848.
N.J.A. Williams (ed.). *Dánta Mhuiris Mhic Dháibhí Dhuibh Mhic
   Gearailt.* Dublin, 1979.
_____ *Pairlement Chloinne Tomáis.* Dublin, 1981.

IV SECONDARY WORKS

A. Agnew. *The hereditary sheriffs of Galloway.* Edinburgh, 1893.

W.A. Aiken, B.D. Henning (eds). *Conflict in Stuart England.* London, 1960.

J.H. Andrews. 'Road planning before the railway age'. In *Ir. geog.*, v (1964-8).

K.R. Andrews, N. Canny, P.E.H. Hair (eds). *The westward enter prise.* Liverpool, 1978.

Anon. 'High sheriffs of the country of Antrim'. In *U.J.A.*, 2nd ser., xi (1905).

E.D. Atkinson. *An Ulster parish.* Dublin, 1898.

———— 'The Magennises of Clanconnell'. In *U.J.A.,* 2nd ser., i (1894).

———— *Dromore: an Ulster diocese.* Dundalk, 1925.

G.E. Aylmer. 'The last years of purveyance'. In *Econ. Hist. Rev.*, 2nd ser., x (1957-8).

P.H. Bagenal. *Vicissitudes of an Anglo Irish family.* London, 1925.

T.G. Barnes. *Somerset 1620-40: a county government under the personal rule.* Oxford, 1961.

M. Beckett. *Sir George Rawdon.* Belfast, 1935.

H.E. Bell. *An introduction to the history and records of the court of wards and liveries.* Cambridge, 1953.

G. Benn. 'Notices of local tokens issued in Ulster'. In *U.J.A.*, 1st ser., ii (1854).

———— *A history of the town of Belfast.* Belfast, 1877.

H.F. Berry. 'Sheriffs of County Cork'. In *R.S.A.I. Jn.*, xxxv (1905).

W. Billings. 'The transfer of English law to Virginia'. In Andrews, Canny, Hair.

G.F. Black. *The surnames of Scotland.* New York, 1946.

W.J. Blake. 'Hooker's synopsis chorographical of Devonshire'. In *Reports and Trans. of Devonshire Assoc.*, xlvii (1913).

I.D. Brown, M. Dolley. *A bibliography of coin hoards of Great Britain and Ireland.* London, 1976.

R.D. Brown. 'Devonians and the New England settlement'. In *Reports and Trans of Devonshire Assoc.*, xcv (1963).

D. Bruton, D. Pennington. *The members of the Long Parliament.* London, 1954.

D. Campbell. *The clan Campbell.* Edinburgh, 1917.

M. Campbell. *The English yeoman under Elizabeth and the early Stuarts.* Yale, 1942.

———— 'Of people either too many or too few'. In Aiken and Henning.

N.P. Canny. *The Elizabethan conquest of Ireland.* Harvester, 1976.

_____ 'Early modern Ireland'. In *Ir. econ. and social hist.*, iv (1977).

_____ 'Dominant minorities: English settlers in Ireland and Virginia, 1550-1650.' In Hepburn.

_____ 'The permissive frontier: social control in English settlements in Ireland and Virginia, 1550-1650.' In Andrews, Canny and Hair.

_____ 'The Anglo-American colonial experience'. In *Hist. jn.*, xxiv (1981).

_____ *The upstart earl: a study of the social and mental world of Richard Boyle, first earl of Cork, 1566-1643.* Cambridge, 1982.

C.W. Chalkin, M.A. Havinden (eds). *Rural change and urban growth, 1550-1800.* London, 1974.

D.A. Chart. 'The break-up of the estate of Conn O'Neill'. In *R.I.A. Proc.*, xlviii (1942-3), sect. C.

A. Clarke. 'Colonial identity in early seventeenth century Ireland'. In Moody, *Nationality*.

_____ 'The genesis of the Ulster rising of 1641'. In Roebuck, *Plantation*.

M.J. St J. Clarke. *Thirty centuries in south-east Antrim.* Belfast, 1938.

P. Clarke. *English provincial society from the reformation to the revolution.* Harvester, 1977.

_____ and P. Slack (eds). *Crisis and order in English towns, 1500-1700.* London, 1972.

_____ , _____ *English towns in transition.* Oxford, 1976.

L.A. Clarkson. 'The leather crafts in England'. In *Ag. Hist. Rev.*, xiv (1966).

_____ and J.M. Goldstrom (eds). *Irish population, economy and society.* Oxford, 1981.

Lord Clermont. *A history of the family of Fortescue.* London, 1869.

G.E. Cockayne. *The complete peerage.* 2nd ed., 14 vols. London, 1910-59.

J.S. Cockburn. *A history of English assizes.* Cambridge, 1972.

D.C. Coleman. 'Labour in the English economy in the seventeenth century'. In *Econ. Hist. Rev.*, 2nd ser., viii (1955).

A. Cormack. *Teinds and agriculture.* Oxford, 1930.

A. Cosgrove, D. McCartney (eds). *Studies in Irish history.* Dublin, 1979.

E.J. Cowan. 'Clan, kinship and the Campbell acquisition of Islay'. In *S.H.R.*, lviii (1979).

I.B. Cowan, D. Shaw. *The renaissance and reformation in Scotland.* Edinburgh, 1983.

W.H. Crawford. 'Landlord tenant relations in Ulster 1609-1820'. In *Ir. Econ. and Social Hist.*, ii (1975).

D.F. Cregan. 'An Irish cavalier: Daniel O'Neill'. In *Studia Hib.*, iii (1963); iv (1964).

_____ 'The social and cultural background of a counter-reformation episcopate'. In Cosgrove and McCartney.

J. Crofts. *Packhorse, wagon and post.* London, 1967.

D.W. Crossley. 'The management of a sixteenth century ironworks'. In *Econ. Hist. Rev.*, 2nd ser., xix (1966).

C.G. Cruickshank. *Elizabeth's army.* 2nd ed., Oxford, 1966.

L.M. Cullen. *The emergence of modern Ireland.* London, 1981.

E. Curtis. 'The Macquillan or Mandeville lords of the Route'. In *R.I.A. Proc.,* xliv (1937-8), sect. C.

B. Cunningham. 'Political and social change in the lordships of Clanricard and Thomond, 1569-1641'. M.A. U.C.G., 1979.

_____, R. Gillespie. 'The east Ulster bardic family of Ó Gnímh', in *Éigse,* xx (1984).

K.G. Davies. *The north Atlantic world in the seventeenth century.* Oxford, 1974.

S.J. Davies. 'The courts and the Scottish legal system'. In Gattrell, Lenman and Parker.

Aodh de Blacam. *Gaelic literature surveyed.* 2nd ed., Dublin, 1973.

V.H.T. Delaney. 'The palatinate court of the liberty of Tipperary. In *Am. jn. legal hist.*, v (1961).

J. Demos. *A little commonwealth: family life in Plymouth colony.* New York, 1970.

T. Devine, S.G.E. Lythe. 'The economy of Scotland under James VI'. In *S.H.R.*, 1 (1971).

T. Devine, D. Dickson (eds.). *Ireland and Scotland 1600-1850.* Edinburgh, 1983.

J.S. Dobie. 'The church of Dunlop'. In *Arch. and hist. collections relating to Ayr and Galloway,* 1st ser., iv (1884).

R.A. Dodgshon. 'Landownership foundations of the open-field system'. In *Past and Present,* lxvii (1975).

_____ *Land and society in early Scotland.* Oxford, 1981.

_____ 'Agricultural change and its social consequences in the southern uplands'. In Devine, Dickson.

A.H. Dodd. 'North Wales and the Essex revolt'. In *E.H.R.*, lix (1944).

_____ *Studies in Stuart Wales.* Cardiff, 1971.

A.G. Donaldson. *Scotland: James V-VII.* Edinburgh, 1965.

P.J. Duffy. 'Patterns of landownership in Gaelic Monaghan in the late sixteenth century'. In *Clogher Record,* x, (1981).

_____ 'The territorial organisation of Gaelic landownership and its transformation in County Monaghan'. In *Ir. Geog.* xiv (1981).

P. Dwyer. *The diocese of Killaloe from the reformation to the close of the eighteenth century.* Dublin, 1878.

G.R. Elton. 'Tudor government: the points of contact. Parliament'. In *R. Hist. Soc. Trans.*, 5th ser., xxiv (1974).

_____ *Studies in Tudor and Stuart politics and government.* 2 vols. Cambridge, 1974.

F.G. Emmison. *Elizabethan life: morals and the church courts.* Chelmsford, 1979.

C.A. Empey. 'The Butler lordship in Ireland, 1185-1515'. Ph.D., T.C.D., 1978.

E.E. Evans. *Mourne country.* Dundalk, 1967.

_____ 'Some problems of Irish ethnology: the case of ploughing by tail'. In Ó Danachair.

A.M. Everitt. *Change in the provinces.* Leicester, 1969.

_____ 'Country, county and town: patterns of regional evolution in England'. In *R. Hist. Soc. Trans* 5th ser., xxix (1979).

M.E. Finch. *The wealth of five Northamptonshire families.* Northhamptonshire Rec. Soc., Oxford, 1956.

F.J. Fisher (ed.). *Essays in the economic and social history of Tudor and Stuart England.* Cambridge, 1961.

F.O. Fisher. *Memoirs of the Camacs of County Down.* Norwich, 1887.

M.W. Flinn. *Scottish population history.* Cambridge, 1977.

A.C. Forbes. 'Some legendary and historical refereces to Irish lords and their historical significance'. In *R.I.A. Proc.,* xli (1932-4) sect. 3.

R. Frame. 'The judicial powers of the medieval keeper of the peace'. In *Ir. jurist*, n.s., ii (1967).

_____ *English lordship in Ireland, 1318-1361.* Oxford, 1982.

W. Frazer. *Memorials of the Montgomeries, earls of Eglinton.* 2 vols. Edinburgh, 1859.

J.T. Fulton. 'The roads of County Down, 1600-1800'. Ph.D., Q.U.B., 1972.

Peter Gale. *An inquiry into the ancient corporate system of Ireland.* London, 1834.

M.K. Garner. 'North Down as displayed in the Clanbrassil lease book'. In *Belfast Natur. Hist. Soc. Proc.,* viii (1970).

V.A.C. Gatrell, B. Lenman, G. Parker (eds). *Crime and the law: the social history of crime in western Europe since 1500.* London, 1980.

P.J. Greven. *Four generations: population, land and family in colonial Andover.* Cornell, 1970.

C. Giblin. 'Francis Macdonnell'. In *Seanchas Ardmacha*, viii (1975-7).

J.T. Gilbert. *A history of the city of Dublin.* 3 vols. Dublin, 1859.

C. Gill. *The rise of the Irish linen industry.* Oxford, 1925.

R. Gillespie. *Ulster plantation maps, a guide for teachers.* Belfast, 1977.

_____ 'Thomas Raven and the mapping of the Clandeboy estate *c.* 1625. In *Bangor Hist. Soc. Jnl,* i (1981).

_____ 'Urban oligarchies and popular protest in the early seventeenth century: two Ulster examples'. In *Retrospect,* n.s., ii (1982).

_____ 'Harvest crises in early seventeenth century Ireland' in *Ir. Econ. and Social Hist.,* xi (1984).

_____ 'The evolution of an Ulster urban network, 1600-1641'. In *I.H.S.* xxiv (1984-5).

E.S. Godfrey. *The development of English glassmaking.* Oxford, 1975.

J. Goody (ed.). *Literacy in traditional societies.* Cambridge, 1968.

_____, J. Thirsk, E.P. Thompson (eds). *Family and inheritance.* Cambridge, 1978.

A.S. Green. 'Irish land in the sixteenth century'. In *Eriu,* iii (1907).

H.D. Gribbon. *The history of water power in Ulster.* Newtown Abbot, 1969.

J.W.H. 'The Anglo-Irish families of Lecale'. In *U.J.A.,* 1st ser., i (1853).

G. Hammersley. 'The revival of forest laws under Charles I'. In *History,* xlv (1960).

D.W. Harkness, M. O'Dowd (eds). *The town in Ireland. Historical studies, xiii,* Belfast, 1981.

F.W. Harris. 'The state of the realm: English political and diplomatic reactions to the flight of the earls'. In *Ir. Sword,* xiv (1980).

_____ 'The rebellion of Sir Cahir O'Doherty and its legal aftermath'. In *Ir. jurist,* n.s., xv (1980).

W. Harris. *The ancient and present state of County Down.* Dublin, 1747.

A. Harrison. *An chrosántacht.* Dublin, 1979.

M.A. Havinden. 'Lime as a means of agricultural improvement: a Devon example'. In Chalkin and Havinden.

T. Healy. *Stolen waters.* London, 1913.

M. Hechter. *Internal colonialism.* London, 1975.

A.C. Hepburn. *Minorities in history. Historical studies,* xii, London, 1978.

D. Hey. *Packmen, carriers and packhorse roads.* Leicester, 1980.

G. Hill. 'Gleanings in the family history of the Antrim coast'. In *U.J.A.,* 1st ser., viii (1860).

_____ 'The Macquillans of the Route'. In *U.J.A.,* 1st ser., ix (1861-2).

_____ *The Stewarts of Ballintoy.* Ballycastle, 1976 (reprint).

J. Hogan. 'The tricha cét and related land measures'. In *R.I.A. Proc.,* xxxviii (1928-9), sect. C.

B.A. Holderness. 'Credit in English rural society before the nineteenth century'. In *Ag. Hist. Rev.,* xxiv (1976).

E. Hopkins.   'The releasing of the Ellesmere estate'.   In *Ag. Hist. Rev.*,
x (1962).

W.F. Hore.   'The archaeology of Irish tenant right'. In *U.J.A.*, 1st ser., vi
(1858).

W.G. Hoskins, 'The reclaimation of waste in Devon'. In *Econ. Hist. Rev.*
1st ser., xiii (1943).

––––––   *Provincial England*.   London, 1963.

––––––   'Harvest fluctuations and English economic history, 1480-1619'.
In *Ag. Hist. Rev.*, xii (1964).

––––––   'Harvest fluctuations and English economic history, 1620-1759'.
In *Ag. Hist. Rev.*, xvi (1968).

––––––   'An Elizabethan provincial town: Leicester'.   In Plumb.

R.J. Hunter.   A seventeenth century mill at Tyrhugh. In *Donegal Annual*,
ix (1970).

––––––   'The settler population of an Ulster plantation county'.   In
Donegal Annual, x (1971-3).

––––––   'English undertakers in the plantation of Ulster'.   In *Breifne*, x
(1978).

––––––   'Ulster plantation towns, 1609-41'.   In Harkness and O'Dowd.

––––––   'Sir Ralph Bingley, c.1580-1627: Ulster planter'.   In Roebuck,
Plantation.

G.P. Insch.   *Scottish colonial schemes*.   Glasgow, 1922.

M.E. James.   'The first earl of Cumberland and the decline of northern
feudalism'.   In *Northern History*, i (1966).

––––––   *Family, lineage and civil society*.   Oxford, 1974.

M.D. Jephson.   *An Anglo-Irish miscellany: some records of the Jephsons
of Mallow*.   Dublin, 1964.

E.S. Jones.   *The Trevors of Trevalyn and their descendants*.   Privately
printed, 1955.

W.J. Jones.   *The Elizabethan court of chancery*.   Oxford, 1967.

E.M. Jope.   'Scottish influence in the north of Ireland; castles with Scottish
features'. In *U.J.A.*, 3rd ser., xiv (1951)

H. Kamen.   *The iron century*.   London, 1976.

D.J. Kennedy.   'The presidency of Munster under Elizabeth and James
I.'   M.A., U.C.C., 1973.

E. Kerridge.   'The movement of rent, 1540-1640'.   In *Econ. Hist. Rev.*,
2nd ser., vi (1953).

––––––   *The agricultural revolution*.   New York, 1968.

––––––   *The agrarian problem in the sixteenth century and after*.
London, 1969.

A. Knox.   *A history of County Down*.   Dublin, 1875.

C.F. Kolbert, N.A.M. McKay.   *A history of Scottish and English land
law*.   London, 1977.

D. Konig. 'Community, custom and the common law: social change and the development of land boundaries in seventeenth century Massachusetts'. In *Am. jn. legal hist.*, xviii (1976).

J. Kraus. 'The medieval household: large or small'. In *Econ. Hist. Rev.*, 2nd ser., ix (1956-7).

P. Laslett. 'The gentry of Kent in 1640'. In *Camb. Hist. Jn.*, ix (1948).

———— (ed.). *Household and family in past time.* Cambridge, 1972.

W.T. Latimer. 'The old session books of Templepatrick'. In *R.S.A.I. Jn.*, xxv (1895), xxxi (1901).

H.G. Leask. *Irish castles.* Dundalk, 1973.

A.T. Lee. 'Notes on bawnes'. In *U.J.A.*, 1st ser., vi (1858).

J.T. Lemon. 'Early Americans and the social environment.' In *Jnl. Historical Geog.*, vi (1980).

H.H. Leonard. 'Distraint of knighthood: the last phase'. In *History*, lxiii (1978).

J.B. Leslie, H.B. Swanzy. *Biographical succession lists of the clergy of the diocese of Down.* Enniskillen, 1936.

S.M. Lipsett, N. Smelser (eds). *Social structure and mobility in economic development.* London, 1966.

K. Lockridge. *A New England town: the first hundred years.* New York, 1970.

———— *Settlement and unsettlement in early America.* Cambridge, 1981.

J. Lodge. *The peerage of Ireland.* 4 vols. Dublin, 1789.

R. Loeber. 'Sculptured monuments to the dead in early seventeenth century Ireland'. In *R.I.A. Proc.*, lxxxi, (1981), sect. C.

A.T. Lucas. 'Irish ploughing practices'. In *Tools and Tillage*, ii (1974-6).

S.G.E. Lythe. *The economy of Scotland in its European setting.* London, 1960.

W.T. McCaffrey. *Exeter, 1540-1640.* Harvard, 1975.

H.F. McClintock. *Handbook on the traditional old Irish dress.* Dundalk, 1958.

E. McCracken. 'Charcoal burning ironworks in seventeenth and eighteenth century Ireland'. In *U.J.A.*, 3rd ser., xx (1957).

———— 'Supplementary list of Irish charcoal burning ironworks'. In *U.J.A.*, 3rd ser., xxviii (1965).

B. McCuarta. 'Newcomers in the Irish midlands, 1540-1640'. M.A., U.C.G., 1980.

J. McDonald. *Clan Donald.* Loanhead, 1978.

K.B. McFarlane. *The nobility of later medieval England.* Oxford, 1973.

L. McKeown. 'The abbey of Muckamore'. In *Down and Connor Hist. Soc. Jnl.*, x (1938).

P.M. McKerlie. *The history of lands and their owners in Galloway.* 5 vols. Edinburgh, 1877.

A. McKerrall. *Kintyre in the sixteenth century.* Edinburgh, 1948.

A. McNaughton. *The chiefs of Clan McNachtan and their descendants.* n.p., 1951.

T.E. McNeill. *Anglo-Norman Ulster.* Edinburgh, 1980.

G. MacNiocaill. 'A propos du vocabulaire social Irlandais du bas moyen âge'. In *Études Celtiques*, xii (1971).

_____ 'Land transfer in sixteenth century Thomond: the case of Domhnall Óg Ó Cearnaigh'. In *N. Munster Antiquarian Jnl.*, xvii (1975).

_____ *Irish population before Petty: problems and possibilities.* O'Donnell lecture, Dublin, 1981.

W. Macafee, V. Morgan. 'Population in Ulster, 1660-1760'. In Roebuck, *Plantation.*

W.A. Maguire. *The Downshire estates in Ireland.* Oxford, 1972.

D. Mathew. *Scotland under Charles I.* London, 1955.

H. Maxwell. *A history of Dumfries and Galloway.* Dumfries, 1896.

J. Meehan. 'List of high sheriffs of Leitrim, 1605-1800'. In *R.S.A.I. Jn.*, xxxviii (1908).

B.R.S. Megaw. 'The date of Pont's survey and its background'. In *Scottish Studies*, xiii (1969).

S. Millsop. 'The state of the church in the diocese of Down and Connor during the episcopate of Robert Echlin'. M.A., Q.U.B., 1979.

S. Miskimmen (ed. E. McCrum). *The history and antiquities of Carrickfergus.* Belfast, 1909.

H. Moller, 'Sex composition and correlated culture patterns in colonial America.' In *William and Mary Qtrly*, ii (1945).

T.W. Moody (ed.). *Nationality and the pursuit of national independence: Historical studies xi.* Belfast, 1978.

E.S. Morgan. *American slavery, American freedom.* New York, 1975.

K.W. Nicholls. *Land, law and society in sixteenth century Ireland.* O'Donnell lecture, Dublin, 1976.

W. Nimmo. *A history of Stirlingshire.* 2 vols. Glasgow, 1881.

S. O'Ceallaigh. *Gleanings from Ulster history.* Cork, 1951.

C. O'Danachair (ed.). *Folk and farm: essays in honour of A.T. Lucas.* Dublin, 1976.

M. O'Dowd. 'Landownership in Sligo, 1580-1641'. Ph.D., U.C.D., 1980.

_____ Land inheritance in early modern county Sligo'. In *Ir. Econ. and Social Hist.*, x (1983).

J. O'Laverty. *A historical account of the diocese of Down and Connor.* 5 vols. Belfast, 1878-95.

T.F. O'Rahilly. *Irish dialects past and present.* Dublin, 1976.

D. Palliser. *Tudor York.* Oxford, 1979.

R.C. Parkinson. *The city of Down.* Belfast, 1928.

_____ 'Downpatrick, the medieval city'. In *Belfast Natur. Hist. Soc. Proc.*, viii (1970).

J. Paterson. *A history of the county of Ayr.* 2 vols. Ayr, 1847.

_____ *A history of the counties of Ayr and Wigton.* 3 vols. Edinburgh 1863.

J.B. Paul. *The Scots peerage.* 9 vols. Edinburgh, 1904-14.

D. Pennington, K. Thomas (eds). *Puritans and revolutionaries.* Oxford, 1978.

P.B. Phair. 'Seventeenth century regal visitations'. In *Anal. Hib.*, xxviii (1978).

J.H. Plumb (ed.). *Studies in social history.* London, 1955.

J. Pound. *Poverty and vagrancy in Tudor England.* London, 1971.

E. Power, M.M. Postan. *Studies in English trade in the fifteenth century.* London, 1933.

L. Price. 'Armed forces of the Irish chiefs in the early sixteenth century'. In *R.S.A.I. Jn.,* lxii (1932).

____ 'The Byrnes country in county Wicklow in the sixteenth century'. In *R.S.A. Jn.*, lxvi (1936).

G.R. Quaife. *Wanton wenches and wayward wives.* London, 1979.

T.K. Rabb. *Enterprise and empire.* Harvard, 1967.

T.I. Rae. *The administration of the Scottish frontier.* Edinburgh, 1966.

E. Rich. 'The population of Elizabethan England'. In *Econ. Hist. Rev.*, 2nd ser., ii (1950).

J.C. Roberts. 'The parliamentary representatives of Devon and Cornwall, 1589-1601'. M.A., London, 1958.

G. Robertson. *A genealogical account of the principal families of Ayrshire.* 4 vols. Ayr, 1823-7.

P. Robinson. 'Irish settlement in Tyrone before the Ulster plantation'. In *Ulster Folklife*, xxii (1976).

_____ 'British settlement in County Tyrone, 1610-60'. In *Ir. Econ. and Social Hist.*, v (1978).

_____ 'Vernacular housing in Ulster in the seventeenth century'. *In Ulster Folklife*, xxv (1979).

_____ *The plantation of Ulster 1600-1670.* Dublin, 1984.

P. Roebuck. 'The making of an Ulster great estate: the Chichesters, barons of Belfast and viscounts of Carrickfergus', in *R.I.A. Proc.*, lxxix (1979), sect. C.

_____ 'Landlord indebtedness in Ulster in the seventeenth and eighteenth century'. In Clarkson and Goldstrom.

_____ (ed.). *Plantation to partition.* Belfast, 1981.

Royal Commission on Ancient Monuments (Wales). *An inventory of the ancient monuments in Caernarvonshire.* 2 vols., H.M.S.O., 1956.

M.H.B. Sanderson. 'Kilwinning at the time of the reformation'. In *Ayrshire Arch. and Nat. Hist. collections,* 2nd ser., x (1970-71).

_____ 'The social and economic implications of the feuing of ecclesiastical property in Scotland'. Ph.D., Edinburgh, 1972.

_____ 'Some aspects of the church and Scottish society in the era of the reformation'. In *Records of the Scottish Church Hist. Soc.,* xvii (1970-1).

_____ 'The feuars of kirklands'. In *S.H.R.,* lii (1973).

_____ *Scottish rural society in the sixteenth century.* Edinburgh, 1982.

_____ 'The Edinburgh merchant in society, 1570-1603: the evidence of their testaments.' In Cowan and Shaw.

G.F. Savage-Armstrong. A genealogical history of the Savage family in Ulster. London, 1906.

R.S. Schofield. 'The measurement of literacy in pre-industrial England'. In Goody.

W.R. Scott. *The constitution and finance of English, Scottish and Irish joint stock companies.* 3 vols. Cambridge, 1910.

J.A. Sharpe. 'Domestic homicide in early modern England'. In *Hist. Jnl.,* xxiv (1981).

F. Shaw. 'Landownership on the western isles in the seventeenth century'. In *S.H.R.,* lvi (1977).

K. Simms. 'Gaelic lordships in Ulster in the late middle ages'. Ph.D, T.C.D., 1976.

A.W.B. Simpson. *A history of land law.* Oxford, 1961.

_____ *A history of contract at common law.* Oxford, 1967.

W.D. Simpson. *Scottish castles.* London, 1969.

A.H. Smith. *County and court.* Oxford, 1974.

J.M. Smith (ed.). *Seventeenth century America: essays in colonial hisory.* Chapel Hill, 1959.

M. Smith. 'Pre-industrial stratification systems'. In Lipsett and Smelser.

W.S. Smith. *Historical gleanings in Antrim and neighbourhood.* Belfast, 1886.

T.C. Smout. *A history of the Scottish people.* London, 1969.

W.J. Smyth. 'The western isle of Ireland and the eastern seaboard of America'. In *Ir. Geog.,* xi (1978).

M. Spufford. *Contrasting communities: English villagers in the sixteenth and seventeenth centuries.* Cambridge, 1974.

D. Stevenson. *The Scottish revolution, 1637-44.* Newtown Abbot, 1973.

_____ *Scottish covenanters and Irish confederates.* Belfast, 1981.

L. Stone. 'The educational revolution'. In *Past and Present,* xxviii (1964).

_____ *The crisis of the aristocracy.* Oxford, 1965.

_____ *Family, sex and marriage in England.* London, 1977.

R.M. Strain. *Belfast and its charitable society.* Oxford, 1961.

J.S. Strawhorne. 'Ayrshire's population'. In *Ayrshire Arch. and Nat. Hist. Collections*, 2nd ser., viii (1967-9).

J. Strype. *The life of the learned Thomas Smyth.* London, 1689.

B.E. Supple. *Commercial crisis and change in England, 1600-41.* Cambridge, 1959.

J. Thirsk (ed.). *The agrarian history of England and Wales*, iv. Cambridge, 1967.

_____ 'Younger sons in the seventeenth century'. In *History*, liv (1969).

_____ *Economic policy and projects.* Oxford, 1978.

K. Thomas. 'Age and authority in early modern England'. In *Brit. Acad. Proc.,* lxii (1976).

_____ 'The puritans and adultery'. In Pennington and Thomas. *Man and the natural world* (London, 1983).

R. Thompson. *Women in Stuart England and America.* London, 1974.

V. Treadwell. 'The Irish customs administration in the sixteenth century'. In *I.H.S.*, xx (1976-7).

_____ 'The establishment of the farm of the Irish customs'. In *E.H.R.*, xciii (1978).

B. Turner. 'An observation on settler names in Fermanagh'. In *Clogher Record*, viii (1973-5).

_____ 'Distributional aspects of family name surveys illustrated in the glens of Antrim', Ph.D., Q.U.B., 1974.

D. Underdown. *Pride's Purge.* Oxford, 1971.

A. Vicars. *Index to the perogative wills of Ireland.* Dublin, 1879.

Victoria County History, *Warwickshire.* 8 vols, London, 1904-69.

J. Walter, K. Wrightson. 'Dearth and social order in early modern England.' In *Past and Present*, lxxi (1976).

D.M. Waterman. 'A vanished Ulster house: Echlinville, County Down'. In *U.J.A.* 3rd ser., xxiii (1960).

D. Westropp, M. Boydell (ed.). *Irish glass.* Dublin, 1970.

I.D. Whyte. 'Written leases and their impact on Scottish agriculture. In *Ag. Hist. Rev.*, xxvii (1979).

_____ *Agriculture and society in seventeenth century Scotland.* Edinburgh, 1979.

H. Wood. 'The public records of Ireland before and after 1922'. In *R. Hist. Soc. Trans.*, 4th ser., xiii (1930).

K. Wrightson. 'Aspects of social differentiation in rural England, 1580-1660'. In *Jnl. of Peasant Studies*, v (1977).

E.A. Wrigley. 'Family limitation in pre-industrial England'. In *Econ. Hist. Rev.,* 2nd ser., xix (1966).

_____, R.S. Schofield. *The population history of England.* London, 1981.

INDEX